THE LOST HISTORY OF LIBERALISM

# The Lost History
# of Liberalism

## FROM ANCIENT ROME TO THE
## TWENTY-FIRST CENTURY

{~~~~~W~~~~}

## *Helena Rosenblatt*

PRINCETON UNIVERSITY PRESS

PRINCETON & OXFORD

Copyright © 2018 by Princeton University Press

Published by Princeton University Press
41 William Street, Princeton, New Jersey 08540
6 Oxford Street, Woodstock, Oxfordshire OX20 1TR

press.princeton.edu

All Rights Reserved

Library of Congress Control Number: 2018937066
ISBN 978-0-691-17070-1

British Library Cataloging-in-Publication Data is available

Editorial: Brigitta van Rheinberg and Amanda Peery
Production Editorial: Jenny Wolkowicki
Jacket image: Engraving of the icon of Liberalism, from *Iconologia, or Moral Emblems*, 1709
Production: Jacqueline Poirier
Publicity: James Schneider
Copyeditor: Joseph Dahm

This book has been composed in Miller

Printed on acid-free paper. ∞

Printed in the United States of America

10 9 8 7 6 5 4 3 2 1

To Marvin

# CONTENTS

## ACKNOWLEDGMENTS

I HAVE BEEN READING and thinking about liberalism for so long it would be impossible to list and thank all the scholars whose work has informed and shaped mine. I do, however, want to thank a few individuals in particular. Melvin Richter introduced me to conceptual history many years ago and shared his encyclopedic knowledge with me over many enjoyable lunches in the Hunter College area. My sincere thanks go also to Michael Freeden, Jörn Leonhard, and Javier Fernández Sebastián all, pathbreaking practitioners of conceptual history, whose work has been an invaluable source of inspiration.

I am especially indebted to those who read my manuscript in part or in full and who offered criticism and encouragement: David Bell, Aurelian Craiutu, Michael Freeden, Alan Kahan, James Mill, Samuel Moyn, Javier Fernandez Sebastián, Jerrold Seigel, Daniel Steinmetz-Jenkins, Jesse Prinz and K. Steven Vincent. I am grateful for the invitations to share early drafts of my work with participants in Philip Pettit and Melissa Lane's seminar at Princeton University, the 7th Concepta Research Training Seminar at the University of Malaga, and the New York French History Group, led by Jeff Horn and David Troyansky. Each of these occasions helped me clarify and hone my thoughts.

For the past nine years, while writing this book, it has been my privilege to direct the Graduate Center's PhD Program in History. I could never have managed to do both simultaneously without the help and collaboration of Marilyn Weber. Words cannot express my gratitude to her. I thank also the former and current presidents of the Graduate Center, William

Kelly and Chase Robinson, and Donald Robotham, director of its Advanced Research Collaborative, for their generous support. I have deeply appreciated the friendship of my colleagues in the History Program, especially Joshua Freeman, Dagmar Herzog, Thomas Kessner, and David Nasaw. A number of talented graduate students helped me with translations: Davide Colasanto, Nicole Farman, and Nicholas Levis at the Graduate Center and Mathieu Narindal at the University of Lausanne. Stefano DeLuca kindly led me to several pertinent Italian sources. Finally, I thank the extraordinary staff of the Graduate Center's library, whose professionalism and efficiency have been exemplary.

It was very lucky for me that Brigitta van Rheinberg of Princeton University Press took an early interest in my project. I can't thank her enough for the brilliant way in which she guided me through the entire project, gently but firmly pressing me to find my voice and express it more forcefully. I am profoundly grateful for her sensitivity, patience, and perseverance. I am indebted also to her assistant, Amanda Peery, for her courtesy and professionalism, and to Jenny Wolkowicki for hers. I thank Joseph Dahm for his copyediting.

Finally, I would like to express my deep gratitude to Jim Miller for his help, support, and friendship. At a critical moment, Jim offered crucial advice and moral support. Without his and Brigitta's guidance, I surely would have produced a less engaging book.

On a more personal note, I would like to thank my husband for his many inspirational ideas and belief in this project, and my children for their loving support. While I was working on this book, two gorgeous granddaughters, Natalie and Caroline, were born. They are an endless source of joy.

# THE LOST HISTORY OF LIBERALISM

# Introduction

*It is never a waste of time to study the history of a word.*
—LUCIEN FEBVRE, 1930

"LIBERALISM" IS A BASIC and ubiquitous word in our vo-cabulary.[1] But liberalism is also a highly contentious concept, one that triggers heated debate. Some see it as Western civili-zation's gift to mankind, others as the reason for its decline. A never-ending stream of books attacks or defends it, and hardly anyone can remain neutral. Critics accuse it of a long list of sins. They say that it destroys religion, the family, the commu-nity. It's morally lax and hedonistic, if not racist, sexist, and imperialist. Defenders are just as emphatic. They say that lib-eralism is responsible for all that is best about us—our ideas of fairness, social justice, freedom, and equality.

The truth is, however, that we are muddled about what we mean by liberalism. People use the term in all sorts of differ-ent ways, often unwittingly, sometimes intentionally. They talk past each other, precluding any possibility of reasonable de-bate. It would be good to know what we are speaking about when we speak about liberalism.

On that score, available histories of liberalism are seldom helpful. First, they are often contradictory. According to one recent account, for example, liberalism originates *in* Christianity.[2] However, according to another, liberalism originates in a battle *against* Christianity.[3] Second, genealogies of liberalism ascribe its origins and development to a canon of great thinkers, but the cast often fluctuates. John Locke is frequently conscripted as a founding father.[4] But some speak of Hobbes or Machiavelli instead; still others of Plato or even Jesus Christ. Some include Adam Smith and a list of economists; others do not. None of these early thinkers, it should be known, considered themselves liberals or espoused anything called liberalism, since neither that word nor concept were available to them. And it goes without saying that our notions of liberalism will vary according to our choice of key thinkers and how we read them. Someone who begins with Machiavelli or Hobbes is likely to be a critic of liberalism, one who begins with Jesus Christ a defender.

In this book I aim not to attack or defend liberalism, but to ascertain its meaning and trace its transformation over time. I clarify what the terms "liberal" and "liberalism" meant to the people who used them. I illuminate how liberals defined themselves and what they meant when they spoke about liberalism. This is a story that has never been told.

Most scholars admit that there is a problem defining liberalism. They begin their work with an acknowledgment that it's a slippery or elusive term. What's strange, however, is that most of them then proceed to stipulate a personal definition and construct a history that supports it. This, I contend, is to argue backward, and in this book I untangle our thoughts and set the story straight. Unless otherwise indicated, all translations are my own.

There are additional puzzles and curiosities. In colloquial parlance in France and other parts of the world today, being liberal means favoring "small government," while in America it signifies favoring "big government." American libertarians today claim that they are the true liberals. Somehow these people are all supposed to be part of the same liberal tradition. How and why did this happen? I offer an explanation.

What I propose, then, is, fundamentally, a *word history* of liberalism.[5] I feel certain that if we don't pay attention to the actual use of the word, the histories we tell will inevitably be different and even conflicting. They will also be constructed with little grounding in historical fact and marred by historical anachronism.

My approach leads to some surprising discoveries. One is the centrality of France to the history of liberalism. We cannot speak of the concept's history without considering France and its successive revolutions. Nor can we ignore the fact that some the most profound and influential thinkers in the history of liberalism were French. Another discovery is the importance of Germany, whose contributions to the history of liberalism are usually underplayed, if not completely ignored. The truth is that France invented liberalism in the early years of the nineteenth century and Germany reconfigured it half a century later. America took possession of liberalism only in the early twentieth century, and only then did it become an American political tradition.

We will see that many individuals who are relatively unknown today made significant contributions to liberalism. The German theologian Johann Salomo Semler invented religious liberalism. The French nobleman Charles de Montalembert may have invented the term "liberal democracy." Yet other key players contributed to the American journal the *New Republic* and thus imported and disseminated the concept in America.

Liberals who are usually regarded as canonical, such as John Locke and John Stuart Mill, do play important roles in my story, but, as we shall see, they were deeply immersed in the debates of their times. They conversed with and were inspired by French and German thinkers. They spoke directly to their contemporaries, not to us; they addressed the problems of their times, not ours. In addition, I highlight figures who *unintentionally* contributed to the history of liberalism, such as the two Napoleons, the Austrian chancellor Clemens von Metternich, and many counterrevolutionary figures, who forced liberals to hone and develop their beliefs.

Finally, I elucidate what I think is a crucial fact that has been lost from history. At heart, most liberals were moralists. Their liberalism had nothing to do with the atomistic individualism we hear of today. They never spoke about rights without stressing duties. Most liberals believed that people had rights *because* they had duties, and most were deeply interested in questions of social justice. They always rejected the idea that a viable community could be constructed on the basis of self-interestedness alone. Ad infinitum they warned of the dangers of selfishness. Liberals ceaselessly advocated generosity, moral probity, and civic values. This, of course, should not be taken to mean that they always practiced what they preached or lived up to their values.

As I also endeavor to show, the idea that liberalism is an Anglo-American tradition concerned primarily with the protection of individual rights and interests is a very recent development in the history of liberalism. It is the product of the wars of the twentieth century and especially the fear of totalitarianism during the Cold War. For centuries before this, being liberal meant something very different. It meant being a giving and a civic-minded citizen; it meant understanding one's connectedness to other citizens and acting in ways conducive to the common good.

From the very beginning, liberals were virtually obsessed with the need for moral reform. They saw their project as an ethical one. This concern for moral reform helps to explain their constant concern with religion, and another aim of this book is to recalibrate our discussions to make room for this important fact. I show that religious ideas and controversies drove debates about liberalism from the very beginning and that they polarized people into hostile camps. One of the earliest attacks on liberalism called it a "religio-political heresy," setting the tone for the centuries to come. To this day, liberalism is obliged to defend itself against unrelenting charges of irreligion and immorality.

The fact that liberals saw themselves as moral reformers does not mean that they were without sin. Much recent work has uncovered a dark side of liberalism. Scholars have exposed the elitism, sexism, racism, and imperialism of many liberals. How could an ideology dedicated to equal rights, they ask, have supported such heinous practices? I certainly do not deny the uglier sides of liberalism, but by placing liberal ideas in the context of their time, I tell a more nuanced and complex story.

My treatment cannot pretend to be exhaustive. Although I reference liberalism in other parts of the world, I focus on France, Germany, Britain, and the United States. This choice may seem arbitrary or overly restrictive to some. Of course, other countries contributed to the history of liberalism. But I do believe that liberalism was born in Europe and spread outward from there. More specifically, liberalism owes its origins to the French Revolution, and wherever it migrated thereafter, it remained closely linked to and affected by political developments in France.

I begin with a chapter on the prehistory of liberalism. Starting with the Roman statesman Cicero and ending with

the French nobleman the Marquis de Lafayette, in chapter 1
I explain what it meant to be liberal when its corresponding
noun was "liberality" and the word "liberalism" did not yet
exist. This deep history of the word "liberal" is good to know,
because self-titled liberals over the course of the following
centuries continued to identify with this ancient *and moral*
ideal, and dictionaries continued to define "liberal" in this
traditional way. In the mid-twentieth century, the American
philosopher John Dewey still insisted that liberalism stood for
"liberality and generosity, especially of mind and character." It
had nothing to do, he said, with the "gospel of individualism."
The first chapter tells the story of how a word initially used to
designate the ideal qualities of a Roman citizen was Christianized, democratized, socialized, and politicized, such that by the
late eighteenth century it could be employed to describe the
American Constitution.

The main part of the book then focuses on four key events
in the intertwined histories of France and liberalism, namely
the revolutions of 1789, 1830, 1848, and 1870, and the transatlantic debates that these revolutions engendered. The story of
liberalism effectively begins in chapter 2, which recounts the
coining of the word and the controversies that surrounded it.
Some of the topics discussed in this chapter are liberalism's relationship with republicanism, colonialism, laissez-faire, and
feminism, all of which are themes that are developed further
in the rest of the book. Perhaps the most important issue of all
is liberalism's fraught relationship with religion, whose origins
in the radical politics of the French Revolution are discussed
here as well. Chapter 3 tells the story of liberalism's evolution
from 1830 to the eve of the Revolutions of 1848, paying close
attention to the emergence of new political ideologies like socialism, on the one hand, and conservatism, on the other, and
to how they inflected liberalism, as France careened toward yet

another revolution. Chapter 4 deals with the perceived failure of liberalism in the upheavals of 1848, and how liberals sought to address this failure. They focused overwhelmingly on institutions like the family, religion, and Freemasonry in what they saw as an essentially moralizing and educational project. Chapter 5 turns to the topic of liberal governance and, with a focus on Napoleon III, Abraham Lincoln, William Gladstone, and Otto von Bismarck, recounts how their leadership engendered new ideas about the relationship between morals, liberalism, and democracy. The idea of a "liberal democracy" was born. Chapter 6 considers France's fourth revolution in 1870 and its repercussions. It describes the battles of the French Third Republic against the Catholic Church in the effort to create what republicans called the most liberal educational system in the world. Chapter 7 recounts how a new liberalism, friendly to socialist ideas, was conceived toward the end of the nineteenth century and how a "classical" or "orthodox" liberalism was conjured as a response. A great battle took place over which of these—the new or the old—was the "true" liberalism. Finally, chapter 8 recounts how liberalism entered the American political vocabulary in the early twentieth century and came to be seen as a uniquely American intellectual tradition, wrapped up also in the notion of American world hegemony. Policy makers now debated what exactly American liberalism meant in terms of foreign and domestic affairs. In the epilogue I offer some suggestions as to why we have come to believe that liberalism is so fundamentally centered on private rights and individual choices. I discuss how the mid-twentieth-century Americanization of liberalism came to eclipse the history recounted in this book to the point that many of us today don't remember it at all.

# CHAPTER ONE

# What It Meant to Be Liberal from Cicero to Lafayette

*Liberal:* 1. *Not mean, not low in birth,* 2. *Becoming a gentleman,* 3. *Munificent, generous, bountiful.*
—A DICTIONARY OF THE ENGLISH LANGUAGE, 1768

ASK ANYONE TODAY what liberalism means and you'll get a variety of responses. It's a tradition of thought, a form of government, a value system, an attitude, or a frame of mind. Invariably, however, people will agree that liberalism is centrally concerned with the protection of individual rights and interests and that governments are there to protect these. Individuals should have the maximum amount of freedom to make their own life choices and do as they wish.

The truth is, however, that this focus on the individual and his or her interests is very recent. The word "liberalism" did not even exist until the early nineteenth century, and for hundreds of years prior to its birth, being liberal meant something very different. For almost two thousand years, it meant demonstrating the virtues of a citizen, showing devotion to the common good, and respecting the importance of mutual connectedness.

## Republican Beginnings: A Moral and Civic Ideal

We could begin with the Roman statesman and author Marcus Tullius Cicero (106–43 BC). One of the most widely read and cited authors in the history of Western thought, Cicero wrote eloquently about the importance of being liberal. The word stems from the Latin terms *liber*, meaning both "free" and "generous," and *liberalis*, "befitting a free-born person." The noun form corresponding to these two words was *liberalitas*, or "liberality."

First and foremost, being free in ancient Rome meant being a citizen and not a slave. It meant being free of the arbitrary will of a master or the domination of any man. The Romans thought that such a state of freedom was possible only under the rule of law and a republican constitution. Legal and political arrangements were necessary to ensure that the government focused on the common good, the *res publica*. Only under such conditions could an individual hope to be free.

But to the ancient Romans, being free required more than a republican constitution; it also required citizens who practiced *liberalitas*, which referred to a noble and generous way of thinking and acting toward one's fellow citizens. Its opposite was selfishness, or what the Romans called "slavishness"—a way of thinking or acting that regarded only oneself, one's profits, and one's pleasures. In its broadest sense, *liberalitas* signified the moral and magnanimous attitude that the ancients believed was essential to the cohesion and smooth functioning of a free society. The English translation of the word is "liberality."

In *On Duties* (44 BC), Cicero described *liberalitas* in a way that would resonate over the centuries. *Liberalitas*, Cicero wrote, was the very "bond of human society." Selfishness was not only morally repugnant, but socially destructive. "Mutual helpfulness" was the key to civilization. It was the moral duty of free men to behave in a liberal way toward each other. And being liberal meant "giving and receiving" in a way that contributed to the common good.

Men are not born for themselves alone, Cicero asserted; they are brought into being for the sake of others:

> Since we are not born for ourselves alone; since . . . men were brought into being for the sake of men, that they might do good to one another, we ought to contribute our part to the common good, and by the interchange of kind offices, both in giving and receiving, alike by skill, by labor and by the resources at our command, strengthen the social union of men among men.[1]

A century after Cicero, another famous and influential Roman philosopher, Lucius Annaeus Seneca (ca. 4 BC–AD 65), elaborated on the principle of *liberalitas* in his book-length treatise *On Benefits* (AD 63). Seneca took pains to explain how to give, receive, and return gifts, favors, and services in a way that was moral and thus constitutive of the social bond. Like Cicero, he believed that for a system based on exchange to work properly, a liberal attitude was needed in both givers and receivers, in other words, a selfless, generous, and grateful disposition. Borrowing from the Greek stoic Chryssippus (ca. 280–207 BC), Seneca offered an allegory for the virtue of liberality: the circular dance of the Three Graces, giving, receiving, and returning benefits. To ancient thinkers like Cicero and Seneca, liberality quite literally made the world go around—and held it together.

Being liberal was not easy. Cicero and Seneca expounded at length upon the principles that should inform giving and receiving. Like freedom itself, liberality required correct reasoning and moral fortitude, self-discipline and command. It was clearly also an aristocratic ethos. It was designed by and for the free, wealthy, and well-connected men who were in a position to give and receive benefits in ancient Rome. It was regarded as a particularly praiseworthy quality in the patrician class and among rulers, as is shown by many ancient inscriptions, official dedications, and texts.

If *liberalitas* was a virtue appropriate to aristocrats and rulers, so was the liberal arts education that trained them for it and required considerable wealth and leisure time with which to study. Its primary purpose was not to teach students how to acquire wealth or to prepare them for a vocation but to ready them for active and virtuous membership in society. It was meant to teach society's future leaders how to think properly and speak clearly in public, thus enabling them to participate effectively in civic life. Citizens were made, not born. Cicero often asserted that the liberal arts should teach *humanitas*, a humane attitude toward fellow citizens. The Greek historian and Roman citizen Plutarch (AD 46–120) wrote that a liberal education gave sustenance to a noble mind and led to moral improvement, disinterestedness, and public spirit in rulers.[2] It was essential, in other words, to the inculcation of liberality.

## *Medieval Rearticulations: Liberality Christianized*

As antiquity gave way to the Middle Ages, this ancient view of liberality was not entirely lost but Christianized and further disseminated by early Church fathers like Saint Ambrose.[3] Saint Ambrose, who wrote a treatise modeled expressly on Cicero's *On Duties*, rearticulated Cicero's main ideas and principles. Any true community rested upon justice and goodwill, wrote Ambrose, and liberality and kindness were what held society together.[4]

Liberality during the Middle Ages was thus overlaid with Christian values such as love, compassion, and especially charity, values regarded as necessary not only in republics, but in monarchies as well. God, Christians were told, was liberal in his mercy, just as Jesus was with his love. Christians should imitate God by loving and giving in return. Dictionaries from the Middle Ages on, whether French, German, or English, defined "liberal" as the quality of someone "who likes to give," and "liberality" as "the quality of giving or spending freely." Great medieval theologians such as Thomas Aquinas spread such notions in their writings.[5]

The medieval Church continued to regard the liberal arts as the ideal educational program for society's leaders. Frequently contrasted with the "servile" or "mechanical arts" that ministered to the baser needs of humankind, such as, for example, tailoring, weaving, and blacksmithing, the liberal arts were seen to develop intellectual and moral excellence. They prepared young men for active roles in the public sector and for service to the state. As in the ancient world, a liberal arts education was also a marker of status, setting the elite apart from the rest. Every Christian, rich or poor, was urged to be liberal, but liberality continued to be regarded as especially important in persons "of a superior social station."

## Renaissance Liberal Arts

Liberality during the Renaissance continued to be an aristocratic, or "princely," virtue. As one of many Renaissance texts explained, avarice was the "sure sign of an ignoble and villainous spirit," while liberality was the proper virtue of the aristocrat.[6] The scope of a liberal arts education was now broadened and its prestige grew. The Italian humanist Pietro Paolo Vergerio (1370–1445), an admirer of Cicero, rearticulated many classical ideas about education in his treatise "On the Noble Character and Liberal Studies of Youth." First published in 1402, it passed through forty editions before 1600, becoming the most frequently copied and reprinted Renaissance pedagogical treatise. A liberal arts education, Vergerio explained, elevated those who received it above the "unthinking crowd."[7] It prepared them for positions of leadership and legitimized their claim to such positions. In the company of books, there was no greed; young boys learned virtue and wisdom, the duties of citizenship.

The focus on *men* in Vergerio's essay was certainly not accidental, since from its inception a liberal education was conceived with young men and not women in mind. Its association with independence, public speaking, and leadership made it very hard to imagine its relevance and value to women. According to Spanish humanist Juan Luis Vives (1493–1540), who wrote *the* major Renaissance work on female education, *The Education of a Christian Woman* (1524), a book that was translated into English, Dutch, French, German, Spanish, and Italian, the learning of women should focus on their domestic functions and, most importantly, on keeping them chaste. While it was reasonable for a man to "be equipped with the knowledge of many and varied subjects which will be of profit to himself and to the state," a woman was sufficiently instructed when she had been taught "chastity, silence and obedience."[8] For this purpose, religious texts were deemed especially effective.

This, however, does not mean that no Renaissance women received a liberal arts education. Evidence shows that some aristocratic women became highly educated.[9] Several even wrote treatises defending the liberal arts. But the prejudice against liberal women helps to explain why, in those rare instances when it was granted, a woman's education was normally said to reflect her *father's* liberality rather than her own. It conferred honor and prestige on a Renaissance *paterfamilias* because it showed that he could afford such a luxury and need not worry about marrying off an overeducated daughter. The educated woman herself, however, was often ridiculed and vilified. That an advanced education rendered a woman masculine was a common refrain. That it made her a sexual predator was another. Even the word "liberal" was problematic when used to describe a woman because it often took on a sexual connotation. A liberal woman became sexually promiscuous. Reflecting long-held prejudices about women's supposed deviousness, sinfulness, and lasciviousness, a ballad from around 1500 warns that women are often "liberall . . . in secret."[10]

Regarding Renaissance boys, however, and especially those destined for positions of power and influence, both liberality and the liberal arts education that prepared them for it were held to be essential. The Dutch humanist, priest, and theologian Erasmus of Rotterdam (1466–1536) referred to such well-educated boys as the "seed-beds from which will appear senators, magistrates, doctors, abbots, bishops, popes, and emperors."[11] His two treatises on education, *The Education of a Christian Prince* (1516) and *The Education of Children* (1529),[12] recommended the liberal arts as second in importance only to Christian piety in the formation of (wealthy and male) individuals. "Liberality," he made sure to clarify, meant more than just "handing out gifts"; it meant "using [your] power for good."[13] Among Renaissance artists, liberality continued to be symbolized by the ancient allegory of the Three Graces. The humanist polymath Leon Battista Alberti (1404–72) referenced Seneca when he explained that "one of the sisters gives, another receives, and the third returns the favor, all of which degrees should be present in every act of perfect liberality."[14] For Alberti, as for so many other Renaissance thinkers, the virtue of liberality was essential to any free and generous society.[15]

## The Politics of Giving

Renaissance texts frequently exhorted elites to give careful thought to how they acquired and dispensed their wealth. Conduct books explained that liberality was a moral virtue that moderated men's "desire and greed for money." Liberality was also about spending money "usefully and not excessively."[16] A liberal man used his wealth to support his household, friends, and relatives; he also helped those who had, due to no fault of their own, fallen into poverty. He did not spend money to show off.[17] Indeed, knowing how to spend was proof of a person's value.[18]

Such a regard for appropriate spending was considered as an especially important quality in rulers. Baldassare Castiglione's *Book of the Courtier* (1528), the period's principal handbook of aristocratic values, stated that "the good and wise prince . . . ought to be full of liberality," and that God would reward him for this.[19] But rulers were also advised not to be prodigal. Erasmus advised princes to practice moderation and discernment in their spending and, especially, never to take from the deserving to give to the unworthy.[20] With that particular blend of realism and idealism for which he became famous, Niccolò Machiavelli (1469–1527) warned that a liberal prince should not spend beyond his means because that would only drain his resources and force him to raise taxes, which would oppress his people and provoke their hatred.[21] Similarly, the French writer Michel Montaigne (1533–92), often regarded as the founder of modern skepticism, cautioned rulers that they should use justice and deliberation in their liberality lest they "pour the seed out of the bag."[22]

Well into the seventeenth and eighteenth centuries, elites and rulers were exhorted to be liberal but not indiscriminate in their giving. The French statesman and author Nicolas Faret (1596–1646) made sure to differentiate liberality from promiscuous giving. A prince's generosity should always be guided by reason, prudence, and moderation. It should be extended in an orderly way to "decent people" and with due consideration to rank, birth, age, means, and reputation. Most importantly, a prince should never be "perniciously liberal"; that is, he should never give in a way that might exhaust his own funds.[23] Other manuals show a similar concern to differentiate the lavish spending of the newly rich from the long-recognized virtue of liberality. The first edition of the *Dictionary of the Académie française* (1694) defined "liberal" as "he who likes to give . . . to people of merit"; by its fourth edition it had added "there is a big difference between a prodigal man and a liberal man."

## Protestant Developments

The Protestant Reformation altered the Catholic meaning of liberality, but subtly, at least initially. Protestant Bibles helped spread the notion that liberality was not just a princely or aristocratic value, but a universal Christian imperative. Where earlier translations of the Bible rendered the word "generous" as "noble" or "worthy to a prince," the new English and Puritan versions dropped the association with high status and substituted the word "liberal." In the King James version (1604–11), the word appears several times, each time referring to generous giving, especially to the poor.[24] Moreover, Proverbs 11:25 suggests that God rewards liberal behavior: "The liberal soul shall be made fat; and he that watereth shall be watered also himself."

A sermon delivered before the English King Charles I at Whitehall on April 15, 1628, suggests a subtle change of emphasis. John Donne (1572–1631), a poet, lawyer, and cleric, began by reiterating the well-known principle that liberality was essential to kings, princes, and "great persons." But then he added that even the population at large, that is, the people, should be liberal. Reminding his congregation that "Christ is a liberal God," Donne declared that it was important for *all* Christians to give freely. And being liberal, Donne added, was not only about sharing one's wealth. It was important to continuously find "new ways to be liberal." Following Isaiah 32, "But the liberal deviseth liberal things, and by liberal things he shall stand," they should "believe liberal purposes," "accept liberal propositions," and "apply them liberally." Donne exhorted his congregation to show their liberality by divesting themselves of all ill feelings toward others. Being liberal was about sharing not simply one's gold, but also one's knowledge and wisdom. These, Donne urged, should be communicated to others, even to the general public. And yet Donne offered an important caveat: it was important to be liberal only to Christians or one would be guilty of "spiritual prodigality," a transgression.[25]

The purpose behind the much-vaunted liberality, endlessly encouraged in moral treatises and sermons, was certainly not to redistribute property in any significant way or to disturb the religiopolitical order. Most Christian preachers, whether Catholic or Protestant, taught that one should give according to one's rank in society and not in ways that might endanger it. Matthew 26:11 states that "ye have the poor always with you," and this was generally interpreted to mean that poverty was an unavoidable part of the social and political order. As one typical English courtesy book explained, "God, in his wisdom, discerning that Equality of Conditions would breed Confusion in the World, has ordered several states, design'd some to Poverty, others to Riches." But liberality spread a sense of goodwill, benevolence, and Christian brotherhood; it sustained society and held it together.[26]

In some important ways, then, liberality in early modern Europe was meant to preserve the existing sociopolitical and religious order. As Cicero, Seneca, and their many disciples knew, gift giving was a kind of social cement. Society functioned and cohered through the giving and receiving of "benefits," in Seneca's terminology, that is, favors, honors, privileges, and services of various kinds. Christian charity and almsgiving also spread a sense of community and goodwill. Finally, the display of liberality enhanced a person's dignity and standing in society.

## American Exceptionalism
## and the Liberal Tradition

And yet Christian liberality, especially in its Puritan manifestations, could and did lead to potentially disruptive positions. This can be seen in the famous "City upon a Hill" sermon delivered by Puritan preacher John Winthrop (1587–1649) upon his arrival at the Massachusetts Bay Colony in 1630. Still on board the ship *Arabella*, Winthrop declared that the very unusual times through which his Puritan community was living demanded "extraordinary liberality" from them. Under the very difficult circumstances they were facing, there was no such thing, he made a point of saying, as being "*over* liberall." *Extraordinary* liberality was their only recipe for survival. Liberality was now demanded of the *whole community* toward each other. They must think of the public good before themselves. In the years to come, this sermon would often be invoked to support the idea of American exceptionalism, whose liberal founding principles were a beacon to the world. The colonists should "bear one another's burdens" and view themselves as a "company of Christ, bound together by love."[27]

Winthrop's advocacy of extraordinary liberality was certainly unusual in the seventeenth century. More common were exhortations to a moderate, discriminating, and aristocratic liberality less threatening to the aristocratic and monarchical status quo. Humans were, in the words of the Dutch natural law theorist Hugo Grotius (1583–1645), sociable and reasonable creatures by nature. They were both able and morally obligated to act in a liberal way toward one another. Cicero's *On Duties* was published in fourteen English and many more Latin editions between 1534 and 1699. It was a basic text at schools like Westminster and Eton and at various Cambridge and Oxford colleges. Between 1678 and 1700, a shortened version of Seneca's *On Benefits* was also edited.[28] Young boys in elite institutions across Europe were taught that society depended on their liberality—that is, on their generosity, moral probity, and civic values.

Thus, by the mid-seventeenth century Europeans had been calling liberality a necessary virtue for more than two thousand years. If ever there was a liberal tradition this was it.

## Thomas Hobbes and John Locke on Liberality

Today, Thomas Hobbes (1588–1679) and John Locke (1632–1704) are often regarded as founding fathers of liberalism. This is curious, however, because they never used the word and had radically different perspectives on liberality.

Hobbes rejected the liberal tradition described above root and branch. Men, he declared, were naturally violent and selfish. "Poore," "nasty," and "brutish," they were driven by mutual fear. War was their natural condition. Human beings, Hobbes claimed, were unable to govern themselves or live peacefully together without a powerful leader "to keep them all in awe, and to direct their actions to the common benefit." A "perpetuall war, of every man against his neighbor" could be avoided only by a strong and undivided government in the hands of an absolute monarch.[29] Liberality played no discernible role in Hobbes' narrative.

Natural law philosophers, moralists, and religious thinkers across Europe reacted in horror to Hobbes' propositions, accusing him of atheism and immorality. Tract after tract presented a more optimistic view of man and reaffirmed the reality and central importance to society of liberality, often calling on the authority of Cicero to do so. Men were both capable and duty bound to practice liberality. Human beings had been endowed by God to express goodness toward others. Despite Hobbes' animadversions, the belief in the power of liberality survived and even prospered.

In France, however, an influential group of Catholic moralists heavily influenced by Jansenism developed views very similar to those of Hobbes.[30] Blaise Pascal, François de la Rochefoucauld, Pierre Nicole, and Jacques Esprit all subscribed to a very pessimistic view of human nature. Man was, in the words of Pascal, a vile and abject creature, whose overriding drive was always self-love.[31] Pierre Nicole, another eminent French moralist in the Jansenist tradition, asserted that man loved himself "without limits or measure," and that this rendered him violent, unjust, and cruel. Without an absolute monarchy to contain them, men would be in a perpetual state of war with each other. Fear and cupidity were what held society together.[32] For the French Jansenists as for Hobbes, when men traded services and civilities with one another, it was not due to any innate capacity to practice liberality, but always out of self-interest.

Curiously, however, the Jansenists did not deny the importance of liberality. What they did instead was to describe liberality as a false but nevertheless necessary virtue. In their minds, it was something akin to politeness, a way that men hid their natural sinfulness. In his *Falsity of Human Virtues* of 1678, Jacques Esprit summed up the Jansenists' way of thinking when he said that the most human beings could ever do was to "*pass themselves off* as liberal."[33] It is noteworthy, however, that several of these Jansenist thinkers, and Nicole in particular, came to the conclusion that even such hypocrisy was necessary for human society to function. Liberality need not be sincere for society to cohere.

Other philosophers, theologians, and writers either ignored or rejected this pessimism about human nature and its obsession with sinful motives and hypocrisy. One such philosopher was John Locke. Locke translated some of Nicole's essays and, in the process, accentuated the positive: "love and respect are the bonds of society," he wrote, "and necessary to its preservation." Society depended on "the traffic of kindness." Without it, society could "hardly hold together."[34]

The idea that human beings were naturally capable and duty bound to behave liberally toward each other was reiterated in almost everything Locke wrote. In his most influential *Essay Concerning Human Understanding* (1689), he argued against orthodox notions of original sin and reigning epistemological theories by claiming that moral ideas were learned, not inborn; therefore, all human beings could and should be taught the moral principles by which to lead their lives. In *The Reasonableness of Christianity* (1695), Locke stressed the importance for Christians to engage in good works. Jesus commanded, "Loving our enemies, doing good to those that hate us, blessing those that curse us, praying for those that despitefully use us; patience and meekness under injuries, forgiveness, liberality, compassion."[35]

Such ideas about the capacity and duty of human beings to be liberal also form the substratum to Locke's *Two Treatises of Government* (1690), in which he again recognized that men had obligations toward their fellows, including, in particular, the duty to contribute to the preservation of mankind. In clear opposition to Hobbes, Locke argued that it was in large part because men could behave ethically that they did not need an absolute monarch to rule them. Men in a state of nature were capable of knowing and following a moral law. In other words, it was precisely because men were capable of liberality that they could live under a limited, constitutional monarchy characterized by a significant amount of self-government.

Locke contributed in other ways to the liberal tradition we are recounting here. He wrote, for example, about the importance of teaching children liberality. In *Some Thoughts Concerning Education* (1693) he enumerated a few of the most fundamental moral principles that he believed children must learn. They should be taught to be "kind, liberal and civil" to others. Selfishness should be "weeded out, and the contrary Quality [. . . implanted]." Children should learn to "part with what they have easily, and freely to their friends."[36] Such an education, said Locke's disciple and friend, the Third Earl of Shaftesbury (1671–1731), formed a "generous Temper and Disposition, well-regulated Appetites, and worthy Inclinations."[37]

The Scottish theologian George Turnbull (1698–1748) elaborated further on these principles in his widely read *Observations on Liberal Education in All Its Branches* (1742). The purpose of a liberal education, he explained, was to train young boys to become worthy members of society. For this it was necessary to teach them "self-mastership" and what Turnbull called "inward liberty," by which he meant the overcoming of selfishness and vice. Young men had to be trained to love the right things: justice, truth, and the greater good of mankind. This is what it meant to "humanize the mind" and "wake the generous affections."[38]

## Enlightenment Liberality

Today some say that liberalism owes its origins to the Enlightenment, but once again it is important to know that no one spoke of liberalism during the eighteenth century. The word and concept had not yet been conceived. However, liberality continued to be championed and, thanks to new forms of communication, disseminated like never before.

Enlightenment liberality remained a virtue mainly associated with noble birth and aristocratic elites. Dr. Johnson's *Dictionary of the English Language* defined the word "liberal" as "not mean; not low in birth" and "becoming a gentleman." As before, it was widely assumed that only a select few would have access to the education that would form the "generous, kindly temper"[39] of such a liberal man. John Locke wrote his educational treatise with the sons of gentlemen in mind and the moral ethos he promoted was aristocratic. He delivered lectures on morality for the sons of gentlemen, organized a social club for gentlemen, and signed his works "John Locke, Gent."[40] According to Shaftesbury, an appropriate education for gentlemen should form a "genteel and liberal Character," suitable to the natural leaders of society, but not the "vulgar."[41] Turnbull addressed his widely read *Observations* to the young sons of the "nobility and gentry." The purpose of a liberal education was to instill in the minds of young boys of "good breeding" "a truly liberal and manly temper."[42]

References to gentlemen and manliness are common in eighteenth-century texts on the virtues of a liberal education. Hardly anyone at the time thought it a good idea to enlarge the minds of girls. François Fénelon's *On the Education of Girls* (1687) succinctly summarized the reigning consensus. Written at the invitation of the Duke and Duchess de Beauvilliers, who had nine daughters, it was quickly translated into English and German and was frequently reissued during the eighteenth and nineteenth centuries, making it one of the most popular education manuals of the time. The learning of girls, Fénelon wrote, should be kept within narrow bounds. It was important to "restrain their minds as much as possible," keeping them focused on their domestic duties, that is, "managing a household, making a husband happy and raising children." Humanistic study should explicitly be withheld from women because it might "turn [their] head[s]."[43]

One hundred years later, an enlightened reformer like Adam Smith (1723–90) still thought it commendable that the girls of his time were taught only what was *useful* for them to know, and "nothing else." Every element of their education should prepare them for their predestined domestic roles: "either to improve the natural attractions of their person, or to form their mind to reserve, to modesty, to chastity, and to economy; to render them both likely to become the mistresses of a family, and to behave properly when they have become such."[44] By Smith's time, biomedical theories about women's "nature" were reinforcing traditional notions about what constituted a suitable education for women by suggesting that sustained intellectual labor was harmful to their health.[45]

Meanwhile, however, the shaping of liberal male minds was ever more prized during the Enlightenment. Smith himself benefited from a liberal arts education, which prepared him well for university studies and eventually his position as professor of moral philosophy at the University of Glasgow. There Smith studied moral philosophy under Francis Hutcheson (1694–1746), whose teachings stressed the importance of liberality, that is, of engaging in "acts of kindness to others."[46] Hutcheson's inaugural lecture at Glasgow was on "The Natural Fellowship of Mankind." Explicitly refuting the egoistic philosophy of Hobbes, Hutcheson asserted that human beings were endowed with a moral sense, which made them capable of seeing the virtue of compassionate, generous, and benevolent affections and encouraged them to behave accordingly. The "culture of our minds," he taught, "principally consists in forming just opinions about our duty" and constantly keeping in mind the common interest was one of the most important duties of all.[47] To learn about these duties, Hutcheson recommended that students read Cicero, Locke, and Shaftesbury.

A liberal disposition was often comingled with condescension, if not outright disdain, for the poor. Certainly this was the case in France, where well into the eighteenth century liberality remained closely identified with noble status. As the Catholic bishop and preacher Jean-Baptiste Massillon (1663–1742) explained in one of his famous sermons, the lower classes were less capable of liberality, while generosity, elevated sentiments, and sensitivity to the unfortunate were marks of nobility.[48] John Locke made similar observations. A liberal arts education, he said, was not intended for "the greatest part of Mankind, who are given up to Labour, and enslaved to the necessity of their mean condition." He wrote that poor children from the age of three could be sent out to work.[49] As an agent of English colonialism, Locke also helped author texts that supported slavery.[50] Magazines, treatises, and dictionaries well into the nineteenth century disseminated such ideas. They described a liberal arts education as "fit for Gentlemen and Scholars," while an education in the "Mechanick Trades and Handicrafts" was appropriate for "meaner People" destined for "servile" occupations.[51]

In America, too, the more established gentry tended to regard the common people as naturally narrow-minded and bigoted. To Nathanael Greene (1742–86), one of George Washington's generals, "the great body of the People" was always "contracted, selfish and illiberal." They should never be confused with gentlemen, who had more noble natures.[52] Washington himself is known to have spoken of "the grazing multitude," and John Adams of "the common Herd of Mankind." "Common Persons," he wrote, "have no Idea [of] Learning, Eloquence and Genius." Their "vulgar, rustic Imaginations" were easily led astray.

## Enlightenment Transformations

Although the Enlightenment carried forward the importance of liberality, it also introduced new uses of the term. Its scope was expanded and, in some senses, democratized. It now became possible to speak not only of liberal individuals but of liberal *sentiments*, *ideas*, and *ways of thinking*. Such sentiments, ideas, and ways of thinking could manifest themselves in larger circles of people: writers and scholars, preachers and officials, the educated public, and even an entire generation.

While a liberal arts education was still regarded as an important way to inculcate liberality in boys of the elite, Enlightenment philosophes began thinking that one could learn to be liberal in other settings too. A person might acquire liberality in any number of social venues, such as gentlemen's clubs, Masonic lodges, salons, and art exhibitions, all of which were proliferating at the time.[53] Thus, an eighteenth-century gentlemen's club in London described its purpose as being the "mutual improvement by liberal conversation and rational enquiry." The club saw itself as disseminating throughout the country a "liberality of spirit" that its members believed was conducive to progress.[54] Apparently, one could now become liberal by thinking and speaking freely to others. And such liberality would lead to the improvement of all of society.

The Scottish historian William Robertson (1721–93) took obvious pleasure in reporting the diffusion of liberality. Over the course of history, he wrote, liberal sentiments were growing and being disseminated throughout Europe. They were causing the manners of Europeans to become more gentle, refined, and civilized.[55] Liberal tenets, an eighteenth-century German thinker proffered, were principles in sync with the reasonable, moral, and progressive forces in history.[56] Many others agreed. George Washington celebrated the "growing liberality of sentiment" of his age, certain that it was having a "meliorating influence on mankind."[57]

One of the most important ways that liberality was improving mankind was by fostering religious toleration. This was something new. Christian arguments going back at least as far as Saint Augustine (354–430) held that the punishment of heretics was an act of charity since it helped to save them in the eyes of God and prevented society from descending into chaos. While the French court preacher Jacques-Bénigne Bossuet (1627–1704) urged his king to be liberal and "think great thoughts" for the "good of mankind,"[58] he saw no contradiction in also commending the king for his escalating persecution of French Protestants, which included the forcible conversion, imprisonment, and exile of hundreds of thousands of French men and women. There is no evidence that he—nor anyone else at the time—made a connection between the virtue of liberality and the idea of religious toleration.

John Locke appears to have been the first to make that connection. Alarmed by Louis XIV's mounting persecution of Protestants in France, and worried also about continuing dissensions among Protestants at home, Locke drew the concepts of liberality and toleration together in his *Letter Concerning Toleration* (1685). Toleration, Locke proposed, was not only "agreeable to the Gospel of Jesus Christ," but the "chief identifying mark of the True Church." In this way, Locke made religious toleration a Christian duty. But merely tolerating one another was not good enough, he said. Christians were enjoined to *be liberal* to each other. "Nay," Locke said, "we must not content our selves with the narrow Measures of bare Justice. . . . Charity, Bounty, *and Liberality* must be added to it. This the Gospel enjoyns; this Reason directs; and this that natural Fellowship we are born into requires of us."[59] Locke extended the injunction to be liberal very broadly, at least for his time. It applied to all Protestant sects, and even pagans, Muslims, and Jews. But liberality for Locke still had limits; he did not include most Catholics or atheists.[60] Others after him would extend it more broadly.

Indeed, over the course of the eighteenth century, religious toleration became a core liberal value. Protestant Dissenters—Protestants who did not belong to the established Church of England—were especially important in its dissemination. Subject to a number of legal disabilities, they campaigned for the repeal of these restrictive laws under the banner of liberality. For example, in a sermon on "liberal things," the Dissenting minister Samuel Wright (1683–1746) declared that being liberal meant standing up to bigots. Liberality enjoined all Christians to support "Principles of Liberty both in civil and religious Matters."[61] In this way, liberality became linked not only with religious toleration, but also with the demand for political and legal reform.

Richard Price (1723–91) was a leader of the Dissenting community and a friend of both Benjamin Franklin and Thomas Jefferson. Price asserted the following about "liberal sentiments": "They extirpate the wretched prejudices which make us shy of one another; and enable us to regard, with equal satisfaction and pleasure, our neighbours, friends, and acquaintances, be their modes of worship or their systems of faith what they will."[62] The *Oxford English Dictionary* records that by 1772 the word "liberal" had come to mean "free from bias, prejudice, or bigotry; open-minded, tolerant." And by the very end of the century, a growing number of liberal-minded gentlemen advocated increasingly expansive notions of religious toleration, calling it the most "just and liberal" policy for governments to adopt.[63]

One such gentleman was George Washington, who, as president of the United States, advocated what he called a liberal religious policy. By this he meant a generous and tolerant policy that accorded freedom of worship not just to the various Protestant sects but also to Catholics and Jews. In a now famous "Letter to the Roman Catholics in the United States of America," Washington wrote on March 15, 1790, "As mankind become more liberal they will be more apt to allow that all those who conduct themselves as worthy members of the community are equally entitled to the protection of civil government. I hope ever to see America among the foremost nations in example of justice and liberality."[64] To the Hebrew Congregation in Newport (1790), he wrote a few months later: "The citizens of the USA have a right to applaud themselves for having given mankind examples of an enlarged and liberal policy—a policy worthy of imitation. All possess alike liberty of conscience and immunities of citizenship."[65] Soon America would become famous for its liberal laws regarding religion and the separation of church and state seen as a quintessentially American principle.

## Liberal Theology and Liberal Christianity

The Enlightenment made another critical contribution to the history of liberality: it invented the notions "liberal theology" and "liberal Christianity," which would have a much-neglected influence on the history of liberalism. "Liberal theology" was coined by German and Protestant scholars like Johann Salomo Semler (1725–91), who first used it in 1774.[66] By this term Semler meant a religious perspective and way of reading the Bible that was enlightened and scholarly, and therefore suited to liberal men of an enlightened century.[67] It was a theology free from dogmatic constraints and open to critical inquiry. Semler's "liberal" approach to the Bible led him to conclude that the essence of Christianity was not dogmatic, but moral.

Semler's ideas inaugurated a long and heated debate about religious liberalism's relationship to orthodoxy. His liberal theology quickly gained ground in Germany, becoming the dominant theological current by the end of the century. Its influence spread even beyond Germany. In 1812, the American Unitarian journal *General Repository and Review* praised Semler effusively, calling him "the most learned [and] most enlightened" theologian because he "opened a free range for liberal minds" and advocated "bold and liberal notions."[68]

The term "liberal Christianity" (as opposed to "liberal theology") may have been invented in America, where it was advanced by a small but vocal group of Protestant clergymen clustered in the Boston area. Called "liberal Christians," and sometimes the "liberal party," they eventually adopted the label "Unitarian." Their most famous proponent was William Ellery

Channing (1780–1842),[69] whose writings were translated and disseminated broadly beyond the United States. Both liberal Christianity and liberal theology sparked a heated and enduring controversy that would greatly impact the history of liberalism and tarnish it in the eyes of many.

Liberal Christians tended to be well-to-do and educated gentlemen. Their religion, they said, was appropriate for the polite and learned, men of liberal education and good taste. Such men abhorred the "deplorable illiberality" of the uneducated,[70] those who were susceptible to "enthusiasm" and prone to bigotry. A liberal gentleman's religion was "a calm and rational thing, the result of thought and consideration."[71] It was the very antithesis of the "religious Phrenzy," "bitter Shriekings and Screamings; Convulsion-like Tremblings and Agitations" that characterized various forms of popular revivalism.[72]

To its advocates, liberal Christianity was an updated and much-needed version of Christianity, more compatible with the enlightened values of the age in which they lived. It did not dwell on gloomy doctrines about man's sinfulness, nor stress dogmas and the supernatural. Instead it emphasized the importance of moral comportment and belief in man's ability to improve himself. Liberal Christians prided themselves on their toleration of other Protestant sects and on being sociable and reasonable. They subscribed to a religion that cultivated what one of Locke's favorite preachers called the "free and liberal dispositions."[73]

## Liberality Politicized

Not all Enlightenment thinkers were convinced that society was improving under the influence of liberality. As economies grew, changed, and generated unprecedented wealth, some began to worry about the growing inequality, vanity, and selfishness that seemed to be accompanying it. In an essay that caused a sensation at midcentury, the Genevan philosopher Jean-Jacques Rousseau (1712–88) rejected the idea that the liberal arts were ameliorating society. Sounding much like the Jansenists who came before him, he claimed that they were just masking a deeply corrupt society.[74] Men were becoming more learned and polite but were also losing their civic values, their devotion to the public good. Modern men did not measure up to the ancient Roman ideal of citizenship, described, among others, by Cicero.

Scottish thinkers were particularly troubled by the effects of economic change. Adam Ferguson (1723–1816), a close reader of both Cicero and Rousseau, deplored the mercenary values that he felt were spreading. Selfishness was threatening the very bonds of society, turning Scotland into a "servile nation of helots."[75] The obsession with commerce and wealth was leading to the abandonment of civic duties, creating what his more famous compatriot Adam Smith (1723–90) would call a society of strangers.

Rousseau, Ferguson, and Smith were joined by many other Enlightenment thinkers who thought deeply about how to teach citizens to concern themselves more with the general welfare. It seemed to these philosophers that the liberal arts, as they were being taught, were not working. Even a scientist like Joseph Priestley (1733–1804) complained that the liberal arts education of his time had become too technical—there was nothing truly liberal about it. A useful liberal arts education should pay more attention to civics, he said. Students should learn patriotism, wrote one Scottish reformer, while another argued that young boys should learn the love of liberty and public spirit and even zeal for the constitution. Liberality, Adam Ferguson reminded people, was not a synonym for mere refinement or cosmopolitan sociability but meant "that habit of the soul by which we consider ourselves as but a part of some beloved community . . . whose general welfare is to us the supreme object of zeal and the great rule of our conduct." Truly liberal sentiments concerned themselves with the maintenance of a free constitution.[76] They encouraged civic engagement.

## From Liberal Charters to Liberal Constitutions

Since medieval times, kings and emperors had granted charters conferring rights or privileges to towns, companies, or individuals. The sovereigns granting them, or the charters themselves, were called liberal when the rights they conferred were regarded as robust and, for example, involved generous economic concessions and considerable self-government.[77] When Englishmen left their homeland for the New World, they brought with them what they often called liberal charters establishing the colonies,[78] and when tensions arose between England and America in the mid-eighteenth century, much discussion revolved around whether the British government had the right to change the terms of these charters and impose new regulations and taxes on the colonies. Americans insisted that such impositions violated the charters as well as the protections accorded to them by the British constitution. They were no longer generous, not based on the principle of reciprocity; they were no longer liberal.

It was in this highly politicized environment that Adam Smith published his famous book, *An Inquiry into the Nature and Causes of the Wealth of Nations* (1776). Today regarded as a foundational text of classical liberalism, it spoke directly to American concerns. Smith himself called it a "very violent attack . . . upon the whole commercial system of Great Britain."[79] Not only did he denounce English trade policies and advocate instead what he called a "liberal system of free exportation and free importation," but he used the economy of North America to highlight the flaws of that of England. America illustrated the advantages of a system of natural liberty, in which the un-impeded investment in agriculture was causing rapid progress toward wealth and greatness.[80] By contrast, Britain's compli-cated and corrupt system of tariffs, bounties, monopolies, and other legal devices was just enriching the already wealthy while leaving the rest of the country impoverished.

Smith's use of the word "liberal" in his *Wealth of Nations* conjured up a centuries-old meaning with which we are now familiar. It was a word whose moral meaning every educated gentleman of his time would have understood. In book IV, chap-ter 9, Smith favored "allowing every man to pursue his own in-terest his own way *upon the liberal plan of equality, liberty and justice.*" Smith's "liberal plan," his readers would immediately have recognized, was about not only freedom but also generosity and reciprocity.

It is often forgotten that Smith's first major and possibly most influential work was on ethics. In his *Theory of Moral Sentiments* (1749), Smith wrote that "he is not a citizen who does not wish to promote, by every means in his power, the welfare of the whole society of his fellow-citizens." "The wise and virtuous man," he continued, "is at all times willing that his own private interest should be sacrificed to the public in-terest of his own particular order or society. He is at all times willing, too, that the interest of this order or society should be sacrificed to the greater interest of the state or sovereignty of which it is only a subordinate part."[81] Moreover, Smith en-dorsed "liberality" as one of the cardinal virtues and the trea-tise contains a long discussion of gratitude and benevolence.[82]

The liberal principles Smith advocated in the *Wealth of Na-tions* were "in the interest of the public," while mercantile ones

favored the "mean rapacity" of British merchants and manufacturers who, in league with the landowning aristocracy, con-
spired against the public good.[83] Smith defended free trade on
the grounds that it would increase the welfare of "the lowest
ranks of the people" and work "for the benefit of the poor and
the indigent."[84]

Unsurprisingly, Americans read the *Wealth of Nations*
as a vindication of their policy of separation from England.
Within a few months of its publication, the Continental Congress opened American ports to all foreign vessels and American calls for free trade grew louder. The new country's very
survival depended on it. Through the negotiation of new and
liberal trade agreements with the nations of the world, Americans hoped for the advent of a new era of prosperity and peace.
And on July 4, 1776, the Continental Congress adopted the
Declaration of Independence by which the United States announced its secession from the British Empire and its reasons
for doing so.

Governments, the Americans argued, derived their authority from the consent of the governed. They were instituted to
secure the unalienable rights of men. Whenever a government
became destructive toward those ends, it was the right of the
people to resist and even overthrow it. Men, moreover, were
created equal and possessed the rights to life, liberty, and the
pursuit of happiness. All thirteen new states soon provided
themselves with written constitutions establishing virtually
the same principle: it was to secure the unalienable rights of
men that governments were instituted.

Of course, the concern for rights and their protections was
not new in 1776. The British government itself recognized
that it had granted charters conferring rights and privileges
to the colonies. A major difference in the Declaration of Independence was that rights were now seen as natural, equal,

and binding. They were no longer understood to be privileges granted by a liberal sovereign and thus subject to revocation by him.

This inflection in the concept of rights involved a corresponding change in the use of the word "liberal." While it had previously been employed to designate the generous and freedom-loving concessions of a sovereign to his subjects, or the magnanimous and tolerant behavior of an aristocratic elite, it was now used to describe the generous and free constitution of a people who legislated themselves.

## America, the Most Liberal Country in the World

In the years that followed, and as Europeans heard about America's constitutions, a debate took take place about which was the more liberal form of government, the British or the American. Americans often boasted that their own constitutions were the most liberal in the world. Patriotic sermons spread the message. American pastors combined Christian, republican, and liberal language to make this point. In a sermon commemorating the constitution of Massachusetts delivered in 1780, Samuel Cooper (1725–83), a Harvard-trained congregational minister in Boston, expressed certainty that America's "most liberal governments [and] wise political institutions" would attract immigrants from far and wide.[85] Ezra Stiles (1727–95), a Yale-trained Congregationalist minister who served as president of Yale College, similarly hailed America's republican system as the "most equitable, liberal, and perfect" imaginable.[86] Reverend Joseph Lathrop (1731–1820) noted that the British constitution had at one point been "more liberal . . . than most other forms of government in Europe"; but now the American Constitution was "still more liberal."[87] Such references could be multiplied indefinitely. David Ramsay's *History of the American Revolution* (1789) laid down the fundamental reason why America's Constitution was more liberal than European ones: "The freedom of modern European governments," he wrote, was "for the most part, obtained by the concessions, or the liberality of monarchs or military leaders. In America alone, reason and liberty concurred in the formation of constitutions."[88]

In Europe, too, people discussed which form of government was more liberal. Richard Price concluded that it was the American. His "Observations on the Importance of the American Revolution" was published in 1784 and quickly translated into French. America, he wrote, now possessed governments "more liberal than any that the world has yet known."[89] Many Europeans agreed.[90] America's constitutions made it the land of liberty, the most liberal country in the world.

A liberal country was not a democratic one. By any measure, the United States was not a democracy in the eighteenth century. And, in any case, to most people at the time, "democracy" was synonymous with anarchy or mob rule. But neither did the United States recognize hereditary privilege. And thus it demanded that *each citizen* display a "truly noble liberality of sentiment and affection," a civic commitment by each individual "to embrace the good of all."[91]

Their admiration for the US Constitution does not mean that Europeans approved of every aspect. Many deplored the institution of slavery and denounced it in their writings. In 1778, Scottish professor of law John Millar (1735–1801), a student of Adam Smith, had already written the following: "It affords a curious spectacle to observe, that the same people who talk in a high strain of political liberty, and who consider the privilege of imposing their own taxes as one of the inalienable rights of mankind, should make no scruple of reducing a great proportion of their fellow-creatures into circumstances by which they are not only deprived of property, but almost of every species of right. Fortune perhaps never produced a situation more calculated to ridicule a liberal hypothesis, or to show how little the conduct of men is at the bottom directed by any philosophical principles."[92]

In the former colonies, too, it became ever harder to reconcile "liberal sentiments" with the support for slavery.[93] Signing himself "A Liberal"—perhaps the first ever use of the word as a noun—the author of an article in the *Pennsylvania Packet* of March 25, 1780, came out for the abolition of slavery.[94] Another writer, under the name "Liberalis," wrote to the *Pennsylvania Journal* in 1781: "A good whig should consider how inconsistent to the people of Europe the citizens of these states must appear, who, tho'enlightened to their own rights, are still blind to the case of the poor Africans." Naturally, he declared, "all men [are] alike free and equal."[95] And yet, as is well known, the federal constitution did not abolish slavery, but protected it.

Moreover, anti-abolitionists argued that slavery was not at all inconsistent with liberal principles. The nation's liberal and founding principles, wrote one, were not antagonistic to the institution of slavery. The British statesman Edmund Burke (1729–97), today regarded as a founder of conservatism, also did not think slavery impaired the "spirit of freedom" in the South. On the contrary, he proffered that it was precisely in the South that freedom was "more noble and liberal."[96]

Some suggested that liberal principles should apply to women. While John Adams was attending the Continental Congress in Philadelphia, his wife, Abigail, famously wrote to him, "In the new code of laws which I suppose it will be necessary for you to make, I desire you would remember the ladies and be more generous and favorable to them than your ancestors. Do not put such unlimited power into the hands of the husbands. Remember, all men would be tyrants if they could."[97] When she was brushed off by her husband, Abigail Adams (1744–1818) wrote to the political writer Mercy Otis Warren (1728–1814) voicing frustration that there had not yet been established "some laws in our favor upon just and Liberal principals" so that "the Arbitrary and tyranick" would be unable to "injure us with impunity."[98]

The establishment of a liberal system of government in America did indeed prompt a renewed thinking about the purposes of a liberal education and to whom it should be granted. Noah Webster (1758–1843), famous for his dictionary, spellers, and readers, wanted America to distinguish itself from Europe by means of a new system of public education. Citing the French philosophe Montesquieu, he argued that a country's system of education should be "relative to its principles of government." In despotic governments, people should have little or no education; and in monarchies, education should be adapted to the rank of each class of citizens. But in republics, "where [government] is in the hands of the people," knowledge should be disseminated more broadly, even to "the poorer rank of people." And "when I speak of a diffusion of knowledge," he explained, "I do not mean merely a knowledge of spelling books, and the New Testament." Nor should education merely be about science. It was extremely important to Webster "that systems of education should . . . implant in the minds of the American youth the principles of virtue and of liberty and inspire them with just and liberal ideas of government."[99]

The years immediately following the American Revolution witnessed a considerable expansion of educational opportunities. Some even believed that women's education should be expanded. "Thoughts upon Female Education" (1787) by Benjamin Rush (1746–1813), army surgeon-general and signer of the Declaration of Independence, expressed regret that many men held such "illiberal" ideas about the education of women.

They worried that a liberal education would make their wives inattentive to their domestic duties and harder to govern. Rush thought all of this was wrongheaded. A better education would make American mothers better wives and companions, and better educators of their sons. America's republican form of government made it necessary for American women to be given a suitable education. In this way, they could better instruct their citizens in the principles of their government.

⊹⊱──⊰⊹

As we can see, by the eve of the French Revolution, and before the invention of "liberalism," there existed in Europe a centuries-old tradition of exhorting men to be liberal. A term originally used to designate the ideal qualities of a Roman citizen, his love of freedom, generosity, and civic-mindedness, it had been Christianized, democratized, and politicized, such that by the eighteenth century it could be used to describe the American Constitution. A liberal constitution, it was said, required liberal citizens—in other words, men who were freedom-loving, generous, and civic-minded, and who understood their connectedness to others and their duties to the common good. To learn such values required a liberal arts education. Some also believed that it required a liberal form of Christianity, tolerant, reasonable, and open to free inquiry and science.

# CHAPTER TWO

# The French Revolution and the Origins of Liberalism, 1789–1830

*Disputes about words are always disputes about things.*

—MADAME DE STAËL, 1810

ON AUGUST 3, 1787, the Marquis de Lafayette wrote to his friend George Washington with some excellent news: "The spirit of liberty is spreading in this country at a great rate," he said, "liberal ideas are cantering about from one end of the kingdom to the other."[1] Lafayette had served under Washington in the American Revolutionary War and was a great admirer of the American Constitution. He was happy to report that the French, who had lived for centuries under an oppressive absolute monarchy, were ready for a liberal system of government similar to America's.

When Lafayette wrote this letter, he was serving on the Assembly of Notables, a council called by the French king,

Louis XVI, to advise him on resolving a crisis—his treasury was bankrupt and his people were demanding reform. Of course, Lafayette had no way of knowing that a revolution was about to erupt, and that it would give rise to the cluster of ideas people would call "liberalism."

Those of us accustomed to hearing that liberalism is an Anglo-American tradition might be surprised to know that it actually owes its birth to the French Revolution. The word itself was coined only around 1811, and it was men and women like the Marquis de Lafayette and his friends, Madame de Staël and Benjamin Constant, who first formulated the ideas to which it referred.

⟨ ⤙⤚ ⟩

For hundreds of years, "liberal" was a word used to describe the laudable attributes of a member of a ruling elite. In Roman times it was a citizen of the republic, in eighteenth-century France a nobleman. A Parisian dictionary of 1771 stated what was then still a commonplace: liberality was a quality "essential to the nobility."[2] On the eve of the French Revolution, the word "liberal" still described the magnanimous and patriotic ideals identified with a ruling class. Being liberal was a kind of *noblesse oblige* and, as such, buttressed a hierarchical sociopolitical order based on hereditary privilege. Many French nobles would undoubtedly have liked to think of themselves as liberal in this traditional sense.

Thanks to people like Lafayette and his circle of friends, however, a new and competing meaning of the term was beginning to spread. Some individuals were beginning to use the word to describe laudable *ideas, sentiments*, and even *constitutions*. Lafayette often praised what he referred to as America's "free and liberal" constitution or its "liberal system,"[3] and this was one way that the political meaning of the word "liberal" spread.

America's Constitution became especially relevant in the years leading up to the revolution, when the French were debating their own need for political reform. Copies of the US federal Constitution reached France in November 1787 and engendered lively debates between so-called *anglomanes* and *américanistes* over which constitution was better, the British or the American. These debates only intensified when the revolution broke out in 1789 and a National Assembly began implementing reforms. Lafayette served not only on the Assembly of Notables and the Estates General that followed, but on the National Assembly as well, and he was a vocal advocate of the American Constitution. His friend Thomas Jefferson, then the American ambassador in Paris, offered advice on these issues as well. In their circles, the idea of a liberal constitution spread.

The most important of the National Assembly's early reforms was undoubtedly the Declaration of the Rights of Man and of the Citizen, a document that Lafayette and Jefferson helped to write. In language reminiscent of the American Declaration of Independence, its first two articles stated that men were born and remained free and equal in rights, and that the purpose of government was to preserve these rights. Other articles decreed that all sovereignty resided in the nation, and that the government's powers were instituted for the advantage of all. Still another article promised every French citizen the right to participate, whether in person or through his representatives, in the making of laws. By such simple words, the Old Regime was abolished. France seemed to be heading toward the sort of liberal system that Lafayette and others hoped for.

This early and relatively peaceful phase of the revolution was met with great enthusiasm almost everywhere in the

Atlantic world. In England, the Whig leader Charles James Fox famously described the revolution as "the greatest event that has happened in the history of the world." Many liberal-minded Britons agreed. France seemed to be abandoning absolutism and adopting a liberal constitution like their own. Some sent messages to the French National Assembly praising the deputies' "liberal principles" and the "liberal legislation" they were passing, now beginning to use these relatively new and political terms with increasing frequency. The American public was also largely enthusiastic, while many Germans, Spaniards, and Italians welcomed the revolution, hoping that liberal reforms would come to them as well.

Of course, not everyone was pleased. Soon a fierce dispute broke out over whether the reforms being passed were in fact liberal or not. The argument produced one of the great texts of political theory, Edmund Burke's *Reflections on the Revolution in France*, a pamphlet now regarded as a founding text of conservatism.

From the perspective adopted here, one of the most interesting things about Burke's text is his refusal to concede the term "liberal" to the French revolutionaries. He insisted on calling them "illiberal" instead. Such wars of words might seem trivial to us today, but their ferocity and longevity over the course of the nineteenth century are indications of the stakes involved. As Madame de Staël explained, "Disputes about words are always disputes about things."[4] The battle over the word "liberal" concerned more than semantics.

The contest began in Britain on November 4, 1789, when the clergyman and philosopher Richard Price delivered a sermon that ignited a firestorm of controversy. Price, as we know, was a religious Dissenter and a fierce campaigner for the abolition of the legal disabilities suffered by his coreligionists. He was also a friend of Benjamin Franklin and had distinguished himself for his support of the American Revolution. Now, at a meeting to celebrate the anniversary of England's revolution of 1688–89, he used the occasion to propose that Britons take inspiration from the American and French revolutions and "liberalize" their own founding principles, most likely coining the term "liberalize" in the process.[5]

Addressing himself directly to the British people, Price declared that like the French they too had the right to choose their leaders, dismiss them for misconduct, and even change their form of government if they so wished. Soon after Price's speech, the London Revolution Society, to which he belonged, sent a message of friendship to the French deputies of the National Assembly expressing its members' support for their "liberal and enlightened sentiments."[6] Like Price, they hoped that their own constitution would be liberalized as well.

Price's sermon, published and disseminated widely, triggered a heated debate. Edmund Burke, a prominent Whig and member of Parliament, was horrified. Burke was a staunch supporter of constitutional limits on the monarchy, opposed the persecution of Catholics, and, like Price, had been a supporter of the American Revolution. He would certainly have thought of himself as liberal in the traditional sense of the word. What was happening in France, however, was altogether different in his estimation. By Burke's reasoning, the Americans had fought for historically existing rights, while the French were inventing new ones. He was also deeply worried that French ideas of popular sovereignty and natural rights would cross the English Channel to Britain. His *Reflections* fiercely defended the legitimacy of aristocratic rule. Berating the French legislators' "presumptuous ignorance" and "savage manner," he insisted that they were "*not* liberal." France's destiny had fallen into the hands of a "swinish multitude."[7] Burke's pamphlet became an instant best seller: thirteen thousand copies were purchased within the first five weeks, it went through eleven editions in the first year, and the text was translated and disseminated across Europe.

What exactly was happening in France that distressed Burke so? In the intervening months since Price's sermon, the French deputies had passed a series of reforms that had shaken the foundations of the country's traditional aristocratic and religious order. On June 19, 1790, they had declared hereditary nobility forever abolished. They had eliminated primogeniture, put an end to all seigneurial dues and tithes, and declared monastic vows no longer legally binding.

Impending fiscal disaster had then moved the deputies to take additional steps of momentous consequence. In November 1789, they confiscated virtually all Church property with the intention of selling it to pay off the national debt. They promised to pay clergy state salaries instead. Deputies then followed up with perhaps the most drastic and controversial measure of all: the so-called Civil Constitution of the Clergy. The measure, passed in July 1790 without prior consultation with the pope or French Church leadership, rationalized the structure of the Church and placed it under state control. The law redrew the boundaries of existing dioceses and eliminated more than a third of existing bishoprics. Most astonishingly, it decreed that voters would elect their own parish priests and bishops. When the deputies encountered resistance to these reforms, they responded by requiring all clergy to sign an oath of loyalty to the Constitution or they would be forced to resign. In the end, about half of the French clergy refused to take the oath and many Catholic faithful, sympathetic to their local priests, became hostile to the revolution.

Burke's *Reflections* condemned all these measures unequivocally, calling the deputies fanatical atheists out to destroy religion. His very language betrayed his aristocratic outlook.

He accused the deputies of vulgarity. They were behaving like "sordid barbarians." They clearly knew nothing of what it meant to be gentlemen and, prima facie, could not be liberal. In other words, Burke held on to the old, aristocratic meaning of the word and used it to assail the French deputies. They were nothing but savages and traitors bent on wreaking havoc for personal gain.[8] He predicted disaster for France.

British readers of the *Reflections* sympathetic to the French Revolution rebuked Burke for his insults and allegations. His reference to the swinish multitude triggered violent reactions.[9] The historian Catherine Macaulay scolded him for lacking the very qualities he was supposed to be defending; he wasn't liberal himself.[10] Mary Wollstonecraft, soon to become known as an advocate of women's rights, denounced Burke's aristocratic bias and refusal to embrace liberal values, using the term in the new way.[11] But the political philosopher and activist Thomas Paine truly struck at the heart of the matter when, in the first part of his hugely popular *Rights of Man*, he argued that Burke's aristocratic leanings rendered him completely insensitive to the all-important distinction between "persons" and "principles."[12] The critical issue, Paine realized, was no longer whether an individual or group of individuals were liberal, but whether the founding principles of a nation were.

By the time the second part of Paine's pamphlet appeared in 1792, France's National Assembly had passed additional reforms. A constitution had been approved in 1791. It created a limited monarchy with a unicameral assembly and gave the vote to all adult white males over twenty-five years of age who paid the equivalent of three days' wages in direct taxes. Although women were not granted the vote, new laws legalized divorce, broadened women's rights of inheritance, and made it possible for them to obtain financial support for illegitimate children. The Assembly also overhauled the tax system and passed laws to end feudal obstructions to the economy. It abolished guilds and dismantled internal tariffs and trading monopolies. It reduced restrictions on imports. After a major revolt in Saint-Domingue, it abolished slavery in the colonies. Looking back at this early stage of the revolution, Swiss writer Madame de Staël praised the deputies for having given France the "liberal institutions" necessary to ensure civil liberty to all.[13] In so doing, she memorialized and placed her own seal of approval not only on the reforms but also on the new meaning and use of the word "liberal."

But liberal institutions had powerful enemies, and none were more powerful than the Catholic Church and Bourbon monarchy. In the spring of 1791, Pope Pius VI made a momentous decision, resolving to denounce the revolution wholesale. In his papal brief *Quod aliquantum* he took aim directly at the Declaration of the Rights of Man and the Civil Constitution of the Clergy and condemned both as vicious attempts to destroy the Church and wreak havoc. Three months later, in a related decision of far-reaching consequence, Louis XVI tried to flee his country to join émigré nobles in Austria who were plotting counterrevolution. He left behind a note denouncing all the recent reforms. Caught just as he was about to cross the border, the king was arrested, brought back to Paris, and imprisoned. His attempted flight provoked charges of treason that ultimately led to his execution in 1793.

Today historians speak of what happened next as a derailment of the revolution: a relatively moderate and peaceful first phase gave way to a second, more radical, and more violent one. The causes of the derailment are debated, but what is beyond dispute is that the escalation of violence—and the repeated pressure upon events brought by angry crowds— greatly discredited the revolution. In a matter of months, France's ancient monarchy was overthrown and replaced by a republic. The king and queen were tried and executed for trea-son. An all-consuming war resulted in hundreds of thousands of deaths. In the West, a royalist uprising turned into a bloody civil war that produced countless atrocities and casualties on both sides. The Terror against "enemies of the people" killed thousands more by guillotine. To critics, this phase was not a derailment of the revolution but its logical outcome. "Liberal principles" had led to nothing but mayhem. Burke's fears and predictions seemed to be coming true.

Convinced, not incorrectly, that the Catholic Church was their most powerful enemy, radicals launched a brutal dechris-tianization campaign. Thousands of priests were forced to resign their posts, imprisoned, killed, or driven into hiding or exile. Public worship was forbidden and visible signs of Christianity removed. Churches and religious monuments and images were vandalized and destroyed. Towns, streets, and public squares were renamed to erase any mention of saints, kings, queens, and nobles. The Gregorian calendar was replaced by a republican one instituting a ten-day week with no Christian Sabbath and marking the beginning of time with the founding of the French Republic rather than the birth of Christ. Concerted attempts were made to replace Christian ceremonies with civil ones. In Paris, the cathedral of Notre-Dame was renamed the Temple of Reason. Recognizing no difference between liberal and radical phases of the revolution, counterrevolutionary theorist Joseph de Maistre denounced it in a way that would resonate for over a century. It was, quite simply, "satanic."[14]

## *The Liberal Principles of Benjamin Constant and Madame de Staël*

The Reign of Terror came to an end in the summer of 1794 when its most prominent advocate, Maximilien Robespierre, was deposed and executed. A year later, the Swiss couple Benjamin Constant and Madame de Staël arrived in Paris, and soon established themselves as the formidable partnership they would remain for seventeen years. Reacting to the pressing circumstances brought about by the revolution, they formulated the cluster of ideas that collectively came to be known as "liberalism."

Madame de Staël was born Anne-Louise-Germaine Necker, the daughter of Jacques Necker, a famous Swiss banker from Geneva who served as minister of finance to Louis XVI during the final years of the French monarchy. A precocious and gifted young girl, she had been exposed to Enlightenment ideas in her mother's salon in Paris, which attracted the city's intellectual and political elite. When Madame de Staël met Constant in 1794, she was married to the Swedish ambassador to France, Eric Magnus de Staël-Holstein, and was running her own Parisian salon for the city's intellectual and political elite, including Lafayette, whom she knew from childhood, and Thomas Jefferson. Already a published author and celebrity, she was thoroughly immersed in the political debates of the day and determined to play a part in them.

Benjamin Constant, on the other hand, was a virtual unknown. Born in Lausanne to a Swiss army captain in the service of the United Provinces, he had showed early signs of intellectual promise and had been sent to study first at the University of Erlangen in Bavaria and then the University of Edinburgh. At Edinburgh he had imbibed the philosophy of the Scottish Enlightenment and acquired a deep interest in the study of religion. When the revolution broke out, he was serving as chamberlain at the court of the Duke of Brunswick-Wolfenbüttel, where he watched the unfolding events from afar. Later, Constant remembered that during these early and exciting days he had called himself a democrat and had even defended Robespierre; but that would soon change. In any event, like de Staël, Constant was eager to play a part in the dramatic events unfolding in Paris.

Upon meeting de Staël in the fall of 1794, Constant fell head over heels in love and courted her so intensely that she eventually surrendered, and the two began what was to be a long and stormy love affair. Despite their turbulent romantic life, they maintained a lasting intellectual and political partnership for nearly two decades. So close were they that it is sometimes impossible to differentiate who wrote what.

Smitten by Madame de Staël and ambitious for fame, Constant accompanied her to Paris in the spring of 1795, arriving in the city just two months after the fall of Robespierre. The political atmosphere in the city was tense and polarized, the government besieged by extremism right and left. On the left were irreconcilable neo-Jacobins disappointed by the end of the Terror. These were joined by Babouvists calling for the abolition of private property. On the right were die-hard royalists and angry émigrés plotting the overthrow of the regime. In a set of brilliant pamphlets that launched his career, Constant defended what he and de Staël regarded as the essential achievements of the revolution and what he was among the first in France to call "liberal principles."[15]

At this early stage in his career, Constant did not specify exactly which political ideas and institutions he meant by liberal principles. Nor did either he or Madame de Staël ever use the word "liberalism," a term that had not yet been coined. Only gradually would they discover the set of precepts we now recognize as "liberalism". A few things are clear, however. Both wanted to consolidate and protect the main achievements of the revolution by preventing both a counterrevolution and a return of the Terror. Most pressingly, it was critical to restore peace and calm to France. Thus began the thinking that would lead to the invention of liberalism.

Liberalism was forged in an effort to safeguard the achievements of the French Revolution and to protect them from the forces of extremism, whether from the right or the left, above or below. In 1795, when Constant and Madame de Staël arrived in Paris, "liberal principles" meant defending the republican government in place from counterrevolution. They meant supporting the rule of law and civil equality, constitutional and representative government, and a number of rights, primary among which were freedom of the press and freedom of religion. Beyond that, what liberal principles meant was somewhat vague and debatable.

Another thing is clear: being liberal was not the same thing as being a democrat. Today we are so used to speaking of "liberal democracy" that it is easy to conflate the two terms. During this early period, however, when liberalism was just being born, liberal and democratic principles were often opposed to each other. Certainly, neither Constant nor de Staël was a democrat in our sense of the word. The Terror only confirmed their view that the majority of Frenchmen (not to mention women) were utterly unprepared for political rights. Politicized crowds had repeatedly shown themselves to be irrational, undisciplined, and prone to violence. Like the Constitution of 1791, the Constitution of 1795 that Constant and Madame de Staël defended included stiff property requirements for both office holding and voting. According to Madame de Staël, they stood for "the government of the best," which should not be confused with democracy.[16]

Nor did being liberal concern constitutional arrangements alone. The primary meaning of the word still referred to a cluster of moral and civic values, such as magnanimity and generosity, openness and toleration, values that had virtually disappeared during the revolution's radical phase. At the outset, some revolutionaries had naïvely believed that the overthrow of the Old Regime would somehow spontaneously trigger moral regeneration.[17] Once the shackles of the monarchy, aristocracy, and Catholic Church were thrown off, they reasoned, humanity would be restored to its natural goodness. To their dismay, however, the opposite seemed to have come true. The revolution had unleashed terrible passions such that public morality appeared to be worse, not better.

The politicized poor were not the only problem. All Madame de Staël could see around her, she lamented, was the corruption and selfishness of the upper classes.[18] "What we need is a lever against egoism," she wrote; "all the moral force of each man is focused on his self-interest."[19] While cold winters and rising food prices were causing the poor unimaginable suffering, those accruing fortunes supplying the revolutionary armies or speculating on the sale of Church land were engaging in conspicuous consumption and flagrant displays. During the winter of 1795, mothers unable to feed their children committed suicide by jumping into the Seine, while the newly rich flaunted their wealth at lavish dinner parties. To de Staël, having liberal principles meant showing kindness, generosity, and compassion, without which France would be ruined forever.

Her novels were intended to cultivate and spread these necessary virtues. As Constant later explained, Madame de Staël's books were meant to foster "gentle, noble, [and] generous sentiments."[20] As far away as America, the transcendentalist Margaret Fuller spoke of their positive moralizing effects.

Fostering morals involved religion; this everyone knew. But here the "friends of liberty" encountered a serious problem. Traditionally, the Catholic Church had taught morality in France. For liberals like Madame de Staël and Benjamin Constant, however, its centuries-long support for absolute monarchy and an oppressive system based on hierarchy and privilege disqualified it from this role. The Church simply could not be trusted to promote the moral regeneration of the republic. This also partly explains why the dechristianization campaign continued during the Directory and why lively debates took place about what might supplant Catholicism in the job of moralizing France.

Madame de Staël and Benjamin Constant took part in these spirited discussions. Both had Enlightened Protestant backgrounds. Constant had even studied liberal theology in Germany and, under its influence, had just begun a major work on religion.[21] Both believed that Catholicism was an obsolete religion and an impediment to their political principles. Its superstitious dogmas and stress on human sinfulness could never foster moral improvement; instead it encouraged what Constant called "moral shrinking" and "stupefication."[22] It made the French superstitious, passive, and weak. Without a change of religion, the republic could not survive, wrote de Staël in 1798.[23]

Not surprisingly, such ideas drew angry responses. That Constant and de Staël could defend the revolution, support the Directory, and call their principles liberal struck their monarchist adversaries as an outrage. They were taking a term traditionally associated with Christian and aristocratic values and using it against them. The revolution they were defending had tried and executed a lawful king, stripped the nobility of its age-old privileges, and expropriated the Catholic Church. Moreover, the government they were supporting was continuing to pursue a brutal dechristianization campaign and was using military force to put down peaceful royalist demonstrations.[24] In the minds of counterrevolutionaries and conservatives, such actions could hardly be called liberal.

And the truth is that not all Catholics thought their religion incompatible with liberal political principles. A few Catholic leaders, including Abbé Henri Grégoire, came forward and insisted the contrary.[25] A committed republican from the region

of Lorraine, Grégoire had sworn the oath to the Civil Constitution of the Clergy, been elected bishop, and then labored
tirelessly to build a new and constitutional Catholic Church
friendly to revolutionary principles. Elected to the National
Convention convened in 1792, he had somehow even survived
the Terror and, under the Directory, served on its Council of
Five Hundred. In his newspaper, *Annales de la religion*, Grégoire celebrated the political system born of the revolution and
argued that Catholicism was in "perfect harmony with liberal
principles."[26]

Facts on the ground seemed to prove otherwise, however.
Grégoire's constitutional church attracted few adherents, while
an underground, counterrevolutionary church grew dramati-
cally. But Grégoire inaugurated what would be a very long and
heated debate about Catholicism's relationship to liberal principles. Was it possible, people would ask, to be both Catholic
and liberal? What *was* the relationship between religion and
liberalism?

## Enter Napoleon

Despite all their best efforts, the hopes of de Staël and Constant did not come to pass. The Directory was unable to sta-
bilize France. In 1799, its efforts were halted by Napoleon
Bonaparte's coup d'état. Fear of counterrevolution and civil
war now led many people, including de Staël and Constant,
to support Napoleon, hoping that he would consolidate and
protect liberal principles and bring the revolution to a peaceful
conclusion.

At first, things looked good. The day after his coup, in his
now famous proclamation of the 19th Brumaire, Bonaparte
promised to act in defense of "conservative, protective [and]
liberal ideas."[27] Many took this to mean that he would work to

restore peace, safeguard the achievements of the revolution, and protect against counterrevolution. Royalists understood his words this way, the newspaper *L'Ami des Lois* observing that "from the mouth of Bonaparte, liberal ideas have another meaning than from the mouth of aristocrats."[28]

In throwing their support behind Napoleon, liberals like de Staël and Constant did not think that they were betraying their own principles. At this moment, Madame de Staël even called Napoleon "the best republican in France [. . . and] the most liberal of Frenchmen."[29] But they were soon disappointed. As early as 1801, a dejected Lafayette wrote to Thomas Jefferson to say that the situation in France had changed radically for the worse. The "liberal Seeds" sown early in the revolution were being trampled upon.[30] Benjamin Constant, who had been granted a seat on Napoleon's Tribunate in 1799, used his position to denounce Napoleon's measures and was summarily dismissed. Madame de Staël now made it her mission to expose his rule as a "monstrous system of despotism,"[31] and was forced into exile. Constant accompanied her abroad.

Napoleon trampled on liberal principles in a number of ways. He revised the French Constitution, placing all real authority in his own hands, and further centralized France's administration with a system of prefects responsible directly to himself. Almost immediately upon assuming power, he announced that Catholicism was essential to "strengthen the foundations of good government"[32] and began negotiations with the pope for a restoration of the Church. These discussions led to the Concordat of 1801, by which he turned the Church into an effective ally and supporter of his increasingly authoritarian regime.

The new constitution gave all men the vote, but elections were carefully managed and manipulated. Napoleon shut down sixty-nine out of seventy-three Parisian newspapers and turned the remaining ones into government organs. He closed political clubs and used spies and informants to cow any opposition. He ordered secret agents to follow Constant and de Staël. In 1802, he restored slavery in the colonies and, in 1803–4, amended the divorce law making it particularly restrictive for women. And, of course, he pursued wars of conquest and pillage.

Napoleonic propaganda tried to spread the notion that he was the "hero of liberal ideas" and, because of this, the term was disseminated wherever his armies went. Italian newspapers at first reported that "liberal men" greeted the French soldiers enthusiastically, hoping that they would help free Italy from political and clerical subjugation. However, as Napoleon's armies began looting "liberated" areas in Europe, and as the leaders he installed there became increasingly oppressive, people began changing their minds. Debates took place across Europe about what constituted a true liberal man as opposed to a false one. Could one be liberal and "Napoleonist" at the same time? An Italian dictionary reminded people that being liberal meant displaying generosity, benevolence, and the love of freedom. In politics, it meant being a supporter of constitutional government. According to this definition, Bonaparte and his soldiers were "not liberal."[33]

Napoleon's betrayals continued. In 1804, he had himself crowned emperor in the presence of the pope and France's assembled bishops. A few years later, he established an Imperial University under centralized state control. Henceforth instruction would promote loyalty to the emperor and his dynasty, which, according to the university's founding documents, alone safeguarded "the liberal ideas proclaimed in the constitution."[34]

In truth, Napoleon created a new kind of authoritarian regime that made a mockery of everything Constant and de Staël had fought for and believed in. Recognizing that there was something unprecedented about the dictatorship that he was creating, Napoleon's critics invented new words for it. Constant called it "usurpation."[35] Others would call it "bonapartism,"[36] and eventually "caesarism."[37] It was obvious to them that it wasn't liberal, and this prodded Constant to clarify what a liberal regime really was and what values it should stand for.

Many saw the emperor's economic policies as another violation of liberal principles. Word soon spread that he was contemplating the reinstatement of monopolies and prohibitions, and the raising of tariffs and taxes. The situation led Jean-Baptiste Say, Adam Smith's most prominent French disciple, to write the *Treatise on Political Economy*. He used Adam Smith's ideas to attack Napoleon's policies, sharply criticizing tariffs and prohibitions and advocating what he called liberal principles of trade, stressing the advantages of treating all nations as friends.[38] Like Smith, moreover, he expressed strong disapproval of a colonial system based not only on prohibitions and tariffs, but on slavery, which he called a "violent method of exploitation."[39] It was a morally abhorrent system, he wrote, one that corrupted both master and slave. It conferred few real economic advantages on anyone, while it constituted an unjust tax on the people. Published in 1803, the *Treatise on Political Economy* was a great publishing success. It was quickly translated into English and studied in England and the United States, thus spreading the early ideas of liberal political economy.

Unsurprisingly, Say's book infuriated Napoleon, who demanded that he revise it or be censored. When Say refused, he was dismissed from the Tribunate, to which he had been appointed along with Constant in 1799. Say was also prevented from publishing during the remainder of Napoleon's reign. To counter his ideas, the emperor encouraged the publication of books favorable to tariffs and the colonial system, such as

François Ferrier's *On Government Considered in Its Relations with Commerce* of 1805. Ferrier subsequently became Napoleon's director of customs. His book openly mocked Smith's and Say's ideas, dismissing them as nothing but naïve fantasies.[40] Ferrier took the opportunity to denounce the revolution as a terrible catastrophe.[41] The French, he told a friend, were like spoiled children. They should be ruled with a tight rein.[42] The book was reissued several times, only cementing in people's minds the close connection between tariffs, the colonial system, and authoritarian rule. It became clear to them that liberal trade policy and liberal politics went together.

Napoleon further betrayed liberal politics by the way he manipulated and seduced the masses. Liberals saw his manufactured popularity as further evidence of the masses' immaturity, irrationality, and gullibility. It was proof of France's moral degradation, by which the emperor profited and which he, in turn, aggravated. Napoleon "destroy[ed] morality," wrote Constant. He bribed people with honors, privileges, and material rewards, while he distracted them with military victories. Under despotic regimes like Napoleon's, men "plunge into selfishness." They turn inward, focusing on their private interests and pleasures. Moral and political apathy was the result; generous ideas "dr[y] up."[43]

The way Napoleon used religion to prop himself up was especially distressing. Almost every French bishop had attended Napoleon's coronation and supported his regime. The alliance between the Catholic Church and the Napoleonic state culminated in the Imperial Catechism of 1806. It stated that the emperor was "the Lord's Anointed" and that resisting a political order "established by God Himself" would make a person "worthy of eternal damnation."[44]

Liberals did not give up on their hope that Catholicism might be replaced. In some ways their aspirations only grew.

Since the revolution had greatly weakened the French Church, some sensed an opportunity. What France needed, they said, was not Catholicism but an enlightened religion that fostered the qualities of mind and character necessary for good citizenship. But which one? Constant and Madame de Staël favored a liberal form of Protestantism, and they were not alone. In 1803, the prestigious Institut de France ran an essay competition in which contenders were asked to evaluate the long-term effects of the Protestant Reformation. Coming so soon after Napoleon's conclusion of the Concordat, it was an opportunity for participants to evaluate that agreement. It was not an accident that the first prize was awarded to an essay that advocated a liberal form of Protestantism and warned against the baneful effects of Catholicism.

The author of the essay was Charles de Villers, a friend of Madame de Staël's. Born in France and raised a Catholic, Villers had immigrated to Germany during the revolution. At Göttingen University, a renowned center for biblical scholarship, he had been won over to some of the most advanced German ideas on religion, which he now transmitted to his French audience. Some of these ideas can be traced back to Johann Salomo Semler, who, as we noted in the previous chapter, coined the term "liberal theology" in 1774.

Villers's essay asked a fundamental question: Could liberal political principles survive without the support of liberal religious principles? His answer was no. He warned of the dangers that Catholicism, allied with the state, posed. What France needed, he wrote, was not a retrograde religion that fostered superstition, intellectual apathy, and a slavish respect for authority but the "liberal ideas of Protestantism." Only Protestantism encouraged the critical thinking and love of freedom necessary for citizenship. Liberal Protestantism, Villers argued, encouraged values conducive to, and supportive of, liberal moral and political principles.[45] Published in 1804, Villers's essay was reissued three times. James Mill, the father of John Stuart, admired it so much that in 1805 he published an English version, for which he wrote a laudatory preface.

It is unclear how many people believed that France could be converted to liberal Protestantism; in any case, it didn't happen. The idea of making it France's state religion was proposed to the emperor, but he rejected it. Instead, and to the great distress of many, a Catholic revival took place, encouraged by counterrevolutionary propagandists like Louis de Bonald and Joseph de Maistre. These prolific men led a concerted defamation and vilification campaign against advocates of liberal principles while they preached obedience to the established order. Catholics like Abbé Grégoire found themselves in a very difficult position. It only confirmed in many people's minds that Catholicism and liberal principles of government were incompatible.

## Liberal Parties and the Birth of Liberalism

While Napoleon's illiberal domestic policies caused French liberals to develop and hone their ideas, his wars gave rise to the first liberal parties.[46] In 1805, the Swedish King Gustav IV Adolph, a confirmed absolute monarchist and a staunch enemy of the French Revolution, led his country into war with France. Although Sweden won the battle, wars with France's allies, Russia and Denmark, followed, and Sweden lost a large amount of territory. Dissatisfied with the leadership of their king, a circle of high government officials staged a palace coup and deposed him in 1809. It was around this time that a group calling itself "the liberal party" came into existence. Not much is known about its members except that they were influenced by French revolutionary ideas and advocated principles such as equality before the law, constitutional and representative government, and freedom of the press, conscience, and trade. They were also known as "the liberal side," or just "the liberals."

The Spanish liberal party emerged soon after Napoleon's armies invaded Spain in 1808, deposed the Spanish King Ferdinand, and replaced him with Napoleon's brother, Joseph. The Spaniards promptly rebelled and established a government in Cádiz. In 1810, a group of delegates to the parliament there, called the Cortes, took the name Liberales and labeled their opponents Serviles, from the Latin *servi*, meaning slave. The Spanish Liberales, like the Swedish liberals, advocated principles such as equality before the law and constitutional, representative government. A "liberal impulse," wrote Madame de Staël joyfully, was sweeping Western Europe.[47]

The new Spanish Constitution triggered myriad commentaries not only in Europe but in the Spanish Americas, where it encouraged independence movements based on local understandings of what liberal principles should mean in practice.[48] Debates over the Spanish Constitution took place as far away as India and the Philippines.[49] It was, in some ways, very radical for its time. It granted the vote "to all men, except those of African descent, without need for studies or property," establishing a more democratic system than existed in Britain, the United States, or France.[50] Interestingly, however, and unlike liberals elsewhere, the Spanish liberals did not advocate freedom of religion. Article 12 of their constitution stated explicitly that "the religion of the Spanish Nation is and forever will be the one, true, Roman, apostolic, Catholic religion. The Nation protects it with wise and just laws and forbids the exercise of any other."

The hopes of the Spanish liberals were soon shattered when, after negotiations with Napoleon, their king was allowed to return to power. Encouraged by conservatives and the Catholic Church hierarchy, he declared the deliberations of the Cortes illegal and its legislation null and void. Claiming that sovereignty resided entirely in his own person, he restored absolute rule and, along with it, the Inquisition. As many as twelve thousand liberals were sent to prison or forced into exile.[51] A vilification campaign was launched against liberals, and it was around this time that the word "liberalism" came into use.

The first manifestations of the word suggest that it was invented as a term of abuse. The early part of the nineteenth century generated an unusual number of such "isms." These new words were most often used to accuse people of heresies, like Anabaptism, Lutheranism, or Calvinism.[52] And, indeed, one of the very first instances of the word "liberalism" found in print is in a Spanish newspaper published very soon after the appearance of the liberal party, in 1813. The paper asked, "What does liberalism mean?" and went on to explain that liberalism is a system "founded upon ignorant, absurd, anti-social, anti-monarchic, anti-Catholic [ideas]."[53] It listed a number of heretical sects, including Jansenism, Lutheranism, and Calvinism, before concluding that liberalism was just another heresy. Central among its heretical principles was its promotion of civil equality and constitutional government responsible to the people, not to a king, aristocracy, or church.

After what had just happened in Spain, it is no wonder that French liberals looked with suspicion upon their own Bourbon king, Louis XVIII, when he returned from exile after the defeat of Napoleon in 1814 and promised to give them what he called "a liberal constitution."[54] The constitution that he and his advisors designed soon became the subject of heated debate. Also called the Charter, it established a representative system of government and recognized key liberal principles such as equality before the law and freedoms of the press and religion. Its vaguely worded articles, however, left many issues unresolved. The precise limits of the king's powers were unclear, as were the role of the representative assembly and the extent of individual liberty guaranteed by the constitution. The Charter also contained a number of contradictions. It recognized freedom of religion, but declared Catholicism the national religion. It proclaimed freedom of the press, but stated that laws could be made to curtail it. And while liberals argued that the new constitution should be regarded as a social contract between the king and the French nation, the constitution was instead said to be "granted" by the king as a gift to his people. This, of course, suggested that the Charter could legitimately be revoked. These factors stimulated, broadened, and deepened debates about what a "liberal constitution" really meant, debates that attracted commentators from far and wide.

Debates about liberal constitutions only intensified with Napoleon's return from exile during the so-called Hundred Days (March 29–July 8, 1815). Escaping from his captivity on the island of Elba on February 26, 1815, the former emperor landed near Cannes in the South of France with nearly a thousand soldiers and made his way to Paris. As he marched, he recited powerful anticlerical rhetoric: "I have come to save Frenchmen from the slavery in which priests and nobles wish to plunge them. . . . Let them take guard. I will string them up from the lamp posts!" In response, he was greeted with cries of "Down with the priests! Down with the aristocrats! Hang the Bourbons! Long live liberty!" More soldiers joined him, and when he neared Paris he was accompanied by what looked like an entire army. Louis XVIII fled and Napoleon returned to power.

Napoleon's dramatic return was followed by another surprise. He now promised to govern constitutionally and invited none other than Benjamin Constant, one of his staunchest and most vocal critics, to help draft a new constitution. Although Constant had attacked Napoleon viciously only a few days before, he agreed to collaborate with him. The resulting document was called the Additional Act to the Constitutions of the Empire and nicknamed the Benjamine in honor of its author. Constant's flip-flop in the matter of Napoleon earned him the epithet "the Inconstant Constant," which dogged him for the rest of his life.

## Liberalism Theorized

But Constant had not abandoned his liberal principles. The Benjamine promised a more democratic franchise, expanded liberties, and, crucially, no longer decreed Catholicism the religion of state. Describing the new constitution to his friend, the Marquis de Lafayette, Constant boasted that "there has never been one that is more liberal."[55] He also produced a book that was meant to serve as a companion piece to the constitution: The *Principles of Politics Applicable to All Governments*, now rightly celebrated as a founding text of liberalism.

The *Principles* shows how much Constant's views had evolved and crystallized since his time in Brunswick, when he had admired Robespierre and called himself a democrat. Constant had learned the lessons of the Terror and Napoleon's authoritarian rule. He had seen how easily popular sovereignty could ally itself with dictatorship. One of his main goals, therefore, was to prevent a dictatorship based on popular sovereignty from masquerading as a liberal regime.

The first sentence of the *Principles* states clearly that the new constitution formally recognizes the principle of popular sovereignty. Very soon thereafter, however, Constant argues for the need to limit this sovereignty. Unbounded power, he writes, whether exercised in the name of a people, a king, or an assembly, is a very perilous thing. This is because when sovereignty is unlimited "there is no means of sheltering individuals from governments." He lists a number of necessary intermediary institutions and guarantees that should curtail the authority of government, no matter whose hands it is in. Primary among these were what came to be regarded as essential liberal freedoms: freedom of thought, freedom of the press, and freedom of religion.

It was less the *form* of government that mattered, Constant wrote, than the *amount*. Monarchies and republics could be equally oppressive. It was not *to whom* you granted political authority that counted, but *how much* authority you granted. Political power is dangerous and corrupting: "Entrust [unlimited authority] to one man, to several, to all," "you will still find that it is equally an evil." "All the ills of the French revolution," he said, stemmed from the revolutionaries' ignorance of this fundamental truth.[56] These are the ideas that have accorded Constant a prominent place in the canon of liberal thinkers. One might even call him the first theorist of liberalism.

As always, moral apprehensions pervaded Constant's thinking, and his ideas were "liberal" in that sense too. The *Principles* testifies to his persistent worries about selfishness, vanity, and the love of luxury. He spoke of the need for courage, generous ideas, and devotion to the public good. Self-sacrifice, he never tired of saying, was necessary to sustain a liberal regime.

Constant also spoke eloquently about religion. He articulated a point that he would emphasize throughout his career: a liberal government could not survive without religion. Religion, he said, was an essential moralizing force. It inspired selflessness, high-minded principles, and moral values, all crucial in a liberal society. But it mattered *which* religion, and it mattered what its relationship was to the state. In the end, the problem was not so much religion, he explained, but its association with power. In the hands of authorities, political or religious, it became an oppressive political tool. This fatal problem led Constant to pronounce what was to become a founding principle of liberalism: the separation of church and state. Religion and the state are two distinct things, he said. A liberal constitution should guarantee freedom of religion to all.

## Liberalism Confronts Reaction

Before Constant's constitution could be implemented, the Prussian general Marshal Blücher and the British Duke of Wellington defeated Napoleon at the Battle of Waterloo. Allied armies entered Paris on July 7, 1815, and Louis XVIII returned to the throne, under the old Charter, which, among other things, meant that Catholicism was reestablished as France's state religion. A wave of reprisals punished those who had served Napoleon during the Hundred Days. Constant fled to England and returned only after being assured that he would not face punishment.

Three months after the return of the king, the so-called Holy Alliance of Russia, Austria, and Prussia was signed, inaugurating a period of reaction disastrous for liberal principles. In France, ultra-royalists worked in alliance with the Catholic Church to reduce the Charter's importance and narrow its purview.[57] Liberals tried to safeguard its importance and broaden its applications. Running for election as a member of what he now referred to as the "liberal party,"[58] Constant promised to fight for the extension of the Charter to "its fullest scope."[59]

The ostensible purpose of the Holy Alliance was to instill Christian values in European political life. The monarchs of Orthodox Russia, Catholic Austria, and Protestant Prussia promised to act together to further "justice, love and peace" in both domestic and international affairs. In practice, however, the Austrian foreign minister, Clemens von Metternich, turned the alliance into a weapon in the battle against liberal reforms of any kind. For this purpose, he encouraged collaboration with traditional religious authorities.

Royalists across Europe received critical support from the Catholic Church for their battle against liberals. In France, Catholic missions disseminated a combined religious and political message: having sinned during the Enlightenment, and having been punished by the revolution, Christians were now being offered a chance of redemption if they promised obedience to their Church and king. Between 1815 and 1830, more than fifteen hundred missions were undertaken in France alone. Mission priests erected giant crosses, offered mass instruction in Catholic doctrine, and attacked the revolution relentlessly. Hellfire sermons promised eternal torment for those who resisted. Often the meetings involved throwing the works of famous philosophes onto giant bonfires. In 1816, a reinstituted Spanish Inquisition condemned Constant's *Principles of Politics* for containing "perverse doctrines" subversive to the state and religion,[60] in the process only proving that Constant had been right about the collusion of church and state.

A torrent of reactionary articles and pamphlets spewed forth, lambasting anyone who spread liberal ideas. Liberals everywhere were accused of trying to destroy religion, monarchy, and the family. They were not just misguided but wicked and sinful. Peddlers of heresy, they had no belief in duty, no respect for tradition or community. In the writings of counterrevolutionaries, liberalism became a virtual symbol for atheism, violence, and anarchy.

Pamphlets and articles with titles like "On the Abuse of Words" appeared. They endlessly repeated the charge that liberals were twisting the meaning of the word "liberal" to deceive people. In the old days, wrote the counterrevolutionary theorist Louis de Bonald, "liberal" described a person who made noble use of his fortune. Now, however, evil people were misusing the word to play a trick on the country.[61] *La Quotidienne*, one of the first reactionary newspapers of the Restoration, accused liberals of misleading people with high-sounding words: "For some time there has been a lot of talk of liberal ideas. What is understood by that word? The Academy has not approved it in its *Dictionary*; It is evident that the word is very modern and that it was born during the revolution. The era of it is origin must make it suspect."[62]

Such accusations forced liberals to defend themselves, and in so doing, they honed their principles and disseminated them to an ever growing public. Liberals, they insisted, were fighting for the good of everyone. They stood for equality before the law, and constitutional and representative government. Their adversaries, on the other hand, favored despotism. Priests, in cahoots with absolute monarchs, peddled superstitions to keep the people docile. Claiming the high ground, liberals repeatedly reminded people of the Latin origins of the word and its principled, moral, and communitarian meaning. One typical pamphlet stated that a political idea was liberal when it was "directed toward the advantage of all, toward the public good and not toward the particular good of an individual or a class; when it favor[ed] generous, elevated, patriotic sentiments and not vanity, cupidity and weakness."[63]

Germans, who are so often left out of histories of liberalism, participated energetically in these verbal battles. Many of Germany's intellectual elite had welcomed the early stages of the French Revolution hoping that reforms would come to them as well. However, many if not most lost their initial enthusiasm during the Terror, the revolutionary wars, and Napoleon's domination of Germany. Edmund Burke's *Reflections*, which appeared in German translation in 1793, also played a role.

The French defeat of Prussia in 1806 led to some important reforms that resembled in many ways those made in France between 1789 and 1791, especially in the economic realm.[64] Guilds and corporations were disbanded, and peasants emancipated. Some internal tariffs and tolls were abolished and a more uniform tax burden imposed. Prussia's administrative structure was streamlined and a limited amount of municipal self-government was granted. But in contrast with what happened in France, these reforms were imposed from above. That fact gave hope to reform-minded Germans that they could work with their governments to make further reforms while avoiding revolution and violence. After the defeat of Napoleon and the granting of the Constitutional Charter in France, there were Germans who hoped that they might be granted what they called "liberal constitutions" as well.[65]

After Napoleon's second defeat, however, and the establishment of the Holy Alliance, what happened in the rest of Europe happened in Germany as well: political reaction set in. While Germany had been for years the incubator and exporter of liberal theology, rulers now began to lend their support to a movement of neo-orthodoxy in an obvious attempt to shore up their own power. In part itself a reaction to the French Revolution, this movement stressed man's sinful nature and his religious duty to subordinate himself to the God-given order. Its leaders promised to fight with all their might what they called the "liberal Zeitgeist." The writings of French reactionaries Maistre and Bonald were translated and disseminated.

In response, German liberals defended their principles, always with one eye trained on France. Like their French counterparts, they faced a very hostile climate. German liberals were especially vulnerable because such large numbers of them were government employees and thus depended on the state for their livelihoods. Placed in this difficult situation, they worked within the system to effect gradual change. They insisted that they wanted not revolution but peaceful reform and progress. They stood for principles such as equality before the law, constitutional government, and freedom of thought and religion. Like French liberals, moreover, they often described what they stood for rather vaguely: a liberal tenet, one German liberal explained, protected "the rights of the citizen against illegal caprice"; it ensured "public liberty" and "encourage[d] the best for everyone."[66]

As elsewhere, German liberals were accused of encouraging license, sin, and upheaval. They were charged with employing a kind of "abracadabra" to distract and blind people from their trickery.[67] Again and again, and from wherever they came, liberals were charged with preaching heresy. They promoted license, sin, and upheaval. They hated God.

In Britain, conservatives tried to vilify liberal ideas as foreign and dangerous. In a speech delivered in the House of Commons in early 1816, the Tory foreign secretary, Viscount Castlereagh, condemned the "Spanish *Liberales*" as "a French party of the very worst description." They were, he said, a "Jacobinical party," because they insisted on the principle of popular sovereignty.[68] An 1816 article in the Tory *Quarterly Review* tried to denigrate their adversaries, the reforming Whigs, by calling them "British *Liberales*."[69]

And yet liberal ideas coming from France also had British defenders. Around 1817, the *Edinburgh Review*, the *Quarterly Review*'s principal rival, informed its readers of the emergence of a French liberal party in a favorable way.[70] Founded in 1802 by a group of young Scottish intellectuals, the periodical aimed to defend "liberal, enlightened and patriotic policy" and spoke particularly well of Benjamin Constant, a man knowledgeable enough, the *Review* said, to convey instruction even to the British.[71]

We can see, then, that liberal political ideas were everywhere regarded as quintessentially French. In America, too, the word "liberal" in its political meaning most often appeared in newspapers in conjunction with reports on French events. Here, as in Britain, an "e" was frequently added to the end of the word, "liberale," or it was italicized to indicate the word's novelty and foreignness. Sometimes papers spoke of the "so-called liberals." But generally, they also expressed support for them and their ideas. Around 1817, American newspapers began reporting that their great hero, the Marquis de Lafayette, and a man called Benjamin Constant were "the leaders of the Liberals." The two men were engaged in a noble battle against the forces of reaction.[72]

## *Liberal Insurrectionism*

A series of politically motivated assassination attempts soon gave conservative forces in Europe a pretext for reaction. On March 23, 1819, in Mannheim, Germany, a student activist murdered the conservative poet and journalist August von Kotzebue. A few weeks later, an attempt was made on the life of Nassau president Karl von Ibell. Conservatives now intensified their defamation campaign, accusing liberals of instigating assassinations as a prelude to revolution. "Liberalism is progressing," Metternich fumed, "it's raining murderers."[73] On September 20, 1819, he issued the Carlsbad Decrees requiring the thirty-eight German member states to root out the subversive ideas circulating in their universities and newspapers. The decrees banned student associations, removed liberal university professors from their positions, and expanded censorship. They also established a permanent committee with spies and informers to investigate and punish any liberal organization.

A few months later, a mentally disturbed man named Pierre Louvel assassinated the presumptive heir to the French throne, the ultra-royalist Duc de Berry. Liberals were blamed and a fierce reaction followed. One ultra-royalist declared, "I have seen Louvel's dagger; it was a liberal idea."[74]

The stakes were raised when a revolution erupted in Spain in 1820, forcing King Ferdinand VII to restore the Constitution of 1812 and reconvene the Cortes. This revolution then inspired liberals in neighboring countries to demand constitutions as well. A military revolt broke out in Naples against King Ferdinand, who was forced to promise a constitutional monarchy on the Spanish model. A similar uprising obliged Vittorino Emmanuele I of Piedmont to abdicate. Prince Carlo Alberto, who was appointed regent, accepted the demand of the revolutionaries for the Spanish Constitution of 1812 and the Inquisition was once again abolished. The same year, Sardinia obtained a constitutional monarchy thanks to revolutionary action. Comparable insurrectionary movements took place in Portugal, Sicily, Greece, and Russia. "These events," wrote one panicked commentator, "have all served to keep up the hopes and spirits of the great confederation of European Liberals."[75] But the events didn't just affect Europe. In the Spanish Americas, local liberals combined calls for constitutional government with demands for self-determination and autonomy. Similar movements touched Goa and Calcutta in India and other places in Asia such as the Philippines. "Liberalism," in other words, went global.[76]

The liberal revolutions triggered a new avalanche of books, pamphlets, and newspapers that discussed the closely entwined political and religious questions involved. The Spanish Constitution gained popularity across the globe and ignited debates, not just between liberals and absolutists, but among liberals themselves.[77] Benjamin Constant's multivolume *Course in Constitutional Politics*,[78] which included his *Principles of Politics*, was also translated and disseminated. Liberal newspapers employing Spanish, Italian, and English writers and funded by political refugees further spread liberal ideas. In response, liberalism was denounced as an international conspiracy against legitimate sovereigns everywhere.

Although anxious rulers and their supporters often exaggerated the liberals' ability to coordinate their activities across borders, they did, in fact, constitute an international network that engaged in both legal and illegal activities.[79] Secret societies like the Freemasons and their offshoot, the Carbonari, were instrumental in organizing the rebellions of 1820–21. The Carbonari established covert cells throughout Western Europe that plotted the overthrow of repressive regimes. The prominent Spanish liberal Evaristo San Miguel later recalled that Masonic lodges became "liberal and conspiratorial juntas."[80] Lumped together with philosophes, Jacobins, Freemasons, and Carbonari, *all* liberals were denounced as dangerous subversives and atheists conspiring to provoke revolution and anarchy.[81] In fact all liberals were *not* plotting insurrection, though some were.

Paris was one of the main centers of the liberal network, and one of its most important leaders was the Marquis de Lafayette. Himself a supporter of the secret society of Carbonari, Lafayette boasted that the uprisings were part of a vast and spreading liberal movement that had begun with the American Revolution and whose leadership had now passed to France. It was in this context that he wrote joyfully to Thomas Jefferson: "France Holds the Honor to be a kind of political Head Quarters for liberalism. Much attention is paid to Her debates as if there was an instinctive universal Sentiment that on Her Emancipation depends the solidity of Every other Success in the Cause of Europe."[82]

The international liberal movement did not last long, despite the liberals' best efforts. Russia, Austria, and Prussia signed a protocol in November 1820 that proclaimed their right to intervene militarily in other states with the purpose of suppressing revolution. Austrian troops soon crushed the revolutions in Naples and Piedmont and drove more Italians into exile. Two years later, and over the loud protestations of liberal deputies in the Chamber, the ultra-royalist French government sent an army into Spain to restore Ferdinand VII to absolute rule.[83] Ferdinand once again abolished the Cortes, annulled its acts, imprisoned many liberals, and reinstated the Inquisition. Upon the news of the French invasion of Spain, a coup in Lisbon reestablished the Portuguese absolute monarchy.

But the counterrevolutionaries were unable to quash the liberal movement entirely. England became a favorite destination of many political refugees and another center of the European-wide liberal network. Most prominent Spanish liberals fled there in 1823 after their movement was crushed. With this influx of political refugees, English conservatives grew ever more fearful that revolution might spread across the channel. A writer in the *Morning Chronicle* had already in 1822 denounced the "influenza of liberalism" afflicting Europe, calling it a "moral plague."[84] An *Essay on Liberalism* condemned what it called the "universal Liberalism" that was spreading confusion and chaos everywhere. France, it noted, was the "fountain head of liberalism." Its revolution had created the vile and dangerous ideas that were now spreading to the rest of Europe. Thanks to France, the word "liberal" no longer meant "a man of generous sentiments, of enlarged, expansive mind . . . [but] a person [professing] political principles averse to most of the existing governments of Europe."[85]

English conservatives continued to use the French spelling (*liberale*) to suggest that liberal ideas were foreign and revolutionary. They derided the new term as continental jargon and accused liberals of using high-sounding words to deceive people.[86] By this duplicity, they had "produced such a Babel of confusion" that people could no longer distinguish right from wrong. The truth, they said, was that liberals were neither noble nor generous; they were proud, selfish, and licentious. They were interested primarily in the "unbounded gratification of their passions," and refused restraints of any kind. Liberalism, one British writer noted, was the very opposite of liberality.[87] It was simply another word for Jacobinism and deliberately intended to sow confusion and disorder. Liberalism, another writer declared, "is the very principle of Satan."[88]

Such vitriol occluded the fact that liberals in fact favored a broad spectrum of political, economic, and religious ideas. They argued over many issues, such as how broad a franchise should be, whether they favored a constitutional monarchy or a republic, and whether to plot insurrections or not. Critics spoke derisively of a "liberal cocktail" of people.[89] John Stuart Mill, who was just beginning to make a name for himself during the 1820s, observed that "the *libéraux* comprise every shade of political opinion" from moderate to radical.[90]

Much of Benjamin Constant's work can be seen as an effort to unite and educate European liberals as to peaceful, constitutional principles. He campaigned tirelessly to disseminate liberal ideas and to elect liberals to office. He published books, pamphlets, and articles, and gave countless speeches within and outside the Chamber of Deputies. The subtitle of one of his most substantial publications, published in 1818–20, speaks for itself: *A Kind of Course in Constitutional Politics*.

The book was quickly translated into both Spanish and Italian, and several editions followed. It was read as far away as Mexico and Argentina.[91] Constant also worked hard to develop the networks necessary to ensure liberal electoral success.[92] Because of this, he was under police surveillance for most of his career as a member of Parliament. The counterrevolutionary propagandist Louis de Bonald called Constant the "choir leader" of the liberal party.[93] But Constant's campaign to unite liberals behind certain agreed-upon principles and legal tactics was never quite successful. At the end of his life, he complained bitterly that his fellow liberals were not listening to him and that he was tired of repeating himself. United in their abhorrence for the Old Regime, liberals disagreed on many issues. Early liberalism was neither monolithic nor unchanging.

By 1824, and with the defeat of liberal revolutions, liberals everywhere in Europe were on the defensive. In France, the right possessed a majority in the legislature since 1820, and when new elections were held in February 1824, they won all but 19 seats in the 430-seat Chamber. Some prominent liberals were now forced to shut down their journals and go into exile. A number went underground to join secret societies. Lafayette joined such a group; Benjamin Constant did not.

Eventually Lafayette embarked on a trip to America, hoping that the publicity generated would help the liberal cause in France. His voyage triggered a spurt of publications that described him as "the hero of two worlds" and America as the land of "really great and liberal institutions."[94] But his enemies just repeated the same mantra: liberals were atheist anarchists who would wreak havoc everywhere. Such accusations were supported by the papal bull *Ecclesiam a Jesu Christo*, which denounced the "multitude of wicked men . . . united against God and Christ."

German liberals did not see Catholicism as the only problem; Orthodox Protestantism was an obstacle as well. After the revolutions of the 1820s, reactionary political forces stepped up their collaboration with Protestant churches, calling themselves orthodox, to combat the spread of liberal principles, whether religious or political. An example is Ernst Wilhelm Hengstenberg, professor of theology at the University of Berlin and editor of the neo-orthodox *Evangelische Kirchen-Zeitung*.

Hengstenberg became a grand strategist of a reinvigorated Prussian Throne and Altar alliance. His aim was to purge the Protestant Church of liberal theology and to root out all possible opposition to the will of the king. "Our politics," he wrote, "consists in unconditional obedience . . . to the God-given order." In his newspaper, as in other German venues, liberalism was endlessly denounced as a foreign import, which, if allowed to spread, would result in atheism and anarchy. Obedience to God meant obedience to one's "worldly masters." Alarmed and frustrated, German liberals struck back. They denounced the "shameless use of religion by the 'sons of darkness.'"[95]

It was this highly polarized situation that gave rise to what appears to have been the first ever history of liberalism, by the Prussian professor of philosophy Wilhelm Traugott Krug in 1823. Born in Radis, Prussia, Krug had succeeded Immanuel Kant in the chair of logic and metaphysics at the University of Königsberg, before moving to Leipzig where he taught philosophy and became a well-known publicist.

Krug's *Historical Depiction of Liberalism* confronted the reactionaries head-on by giving liberalism unimpeachable Christian and German credentials. God himself had created liberalism, Krug claimed, and he had done so by implanting the desire for freedom in all human beings. The desire for freedom had been given to man, Krug added, in order to encourage his progressive self-improvement and the related gradual reform of institutions like the Christian Church.

According to Krug, the most important freedom was freedom of thought. His history recounted how the love of this particular freedom passed from God to the ancient Greeks and on to the early Church fathers, all of whom were "liberal" in their general orientation. But because they engaged in critical thinking, they encountered fierce resistance from established authorities.

Germany played an essential role in Krug's history. It was none other than the German Protestant reformer Martin Luther who had invented "religious liberalism." And religious liberalism, he wrote, was essential to the improvement of the human institutions wanted by God. Protestantism liberated Christians from the serfdom of "blind faith" and encouraged the critical thinking essential to progress. Unfortunately, however, the Reformation led to battles between liberal and illiberal principles. Some continued to cling to outmoded religious dogmas.

Political liberalism, Krug went on to explain, emerged among the Whigs of England. While Tories believed in the divine right of kings, Whigs derived sovereignty from the people. From England, liberalism traveled to the North American colonies, where it found fertile soil, and then on to France, where it was radicalized. There was now a terrible battle taking place across Europe between liberalism and antiliberalism. But the progress of liberalism, Krug concluded, was unstoppable. It was wanted by God.

Krug's history of liberalism was quite obviously a rejoinder to the pretensions of the so-called Holy Alliance. It was liberalism, and not reaction, that was holy. But Krug also warned liberals not to be seduced by radicalism and provoke revolution. Only "a few idiots," he said, espoused "ultraliberalism" and engaged in "exaggerations." There was no need for that. The future belonged to the gradual and "thoughtful" kind of liberalism.[96]

## *Liberal Economic Principles*

The ultra-royalists who dominated the French Chamber during the mid-1820s also pushed through regressive economic policies. Large landowners, manufacturers, and colonial planters joined together to form a powerful protectionist lobby. They clamored for a return to tariffs, especially on wheat and sugar. They also demanded the restitution of France's colonies and the official restoration of the slave trade. Despite having agreed to its ban in 1815, the Bourbon kings in fact encouraged the trade surreptitiously and repressed abolitionist publications. The protectionist lobby also fought for the restoration of primogeniture and entail.

The government had already imposed a tariff on imported grain in 1819. Two years later, a new ultra-royalist majority followed up by imposing an outright prohibition on the importation of grain below a certain price. The following year, it pushed through another law that steeply increased tariffs on foreign sugar, iron, and cattle. The writings of François Ferrier and Jean-Baptiste Say now became more relevant than ever. Ferrier's treatise mocking liberal principles of trade was republished in 1821 and 1822. Say's *Treatise on Political Economy*, which, as we have seen, denounced tariffs, protections, the colonial system, and slavery, was reprinted as well. Benjamin Constant denounced the new laws from the floor of the Chamber, calling them cruel, unjust, and self-serving. He denounced the rich for using the government to enrich themselves further, at the expense of the laboring poor, not to mention slaves. A giant publicity campaign was organized to disseminate liberal ideas of political economy and to put pressure on legislators. Constant published a text trying to rally liberals around a policy of "laissez-faire, laissez-passer." But he did not succeed in convincing everyone. Liberals were never of one mind on the issue of tariffs.

Constant also made speeches denouncing the slave trade and demanded that the government enforce the ban. The right wing of the Chamber regularly heckled him for this.[97] He joined other liberals in showcasing the success of Haiti, the first black independent nation in the Americas. He praised the constitution its black citizens had produced.[98] According to his friend Jean-Charles-Léonard Sismondi, "the sons of Africa" had proved that they deserved to be free and that all Africans had the potential to become "civilized."[99]

Constant was, of course, aware that, due to electoral laws of the Restoration, legislative power in France lay in the hands of large landowners and wealthy merchants, the same combination of men that Adam Smith had warned against in the *Wealth of Nations*. Wealthy businessmen, with the support of aristocratic landowners, were "an order of men, whose interest is never exactly the same with that of the public, who have generally an interest to deceive and even to oppress the public, and who accordingly have, upon many occasions, both deceived and oppressed it."[100] Constant was also well aware that customs agents composed 20 percent of the total of state agents employed by the Restoration government, and that they included the secret police as well as a network of informants and spies. He himself was under police surveillance for much of the 1820s. Customs agents, it should be known, were charged with inspecting all imported books to make sure that "they contained nothing contrary to the government or the interest of the state."[101] In April 1816, an ultra-royalist majority of the Chamber had adopted a number of measures ostensibly against smuggling, blaming it on the immorality supposedly spread by the "disastrous Revolution." These measures increased the powers of the customs administration to search travelers, merchants, and private homes in an area that was extended to twenty-five kilometers inland from France's borders. The laws also augmented penalties for smuggling. When liberals like Constant advocated laissez-faire, laissez-passer, they had such measures in mind too.

Their shared commitment to the free circulation of goods, ideas, and persons did not mean that laissez-faire liberals opposed *all* government intervention in the economy. Contrary to what is often said today about nineteenth-century liberalism, early liberals were not doctrinaire about laissez-faire. They did not stress property rights or celebrate the virtues of unbounded self-interest. What today is called "classical" or "orthodox" liberalism did not exist.

Constant believed that private property was not a natural right but merely a social convention and therefore under the jurisdiction of society. Say recognized explicitly that governments had the right to regulate any type of industry and believed that regulation was useful and proper in many circumstances. It was entirely appropriate, for example, for governments to intervene to help workers made redundant by introduction of machinery in industry. Governments could legitimately restrict the use of new machines and find work for the unemployed. "Without a doubt," Say wrote, a government "must protect the interests of workers."[102] It was the duty of every government, Say declared, "to aim at the constant amelioration of its subjects' condition."

But, as always, liberals did not always agree. Charles Comte and Charles Dunoyer, who were the editors of the liberal journal *Le Censeur européen*, endorsed laissez-faire to extremes not found in either Smith or Say. Dunoyer opposed government involvement in education, public works, and even mail delivery. Sismondi, however, advocated *more* government intervention, not less. In 1803 he published *On Commercial Wealth*, in which he argued for the absolute freedom of commerce and industry. But by 1819, with the publication of *New Principles of Political Economy*, he had changed his mind, explaining that he was obliged to modify and develop his earlier ideas because of the shocking facts that were emerging about the conditions of workers in industrializing economies— particularly England. Government, Sismondi now said, should intervene to protect the weak from the strong. Most liberals advocated freer international trade, and a freer domestic circulation of people and goods, but they could disagree on the legitimate and desirable bounds of government intervention in the economy. They could argue over what constituted "true liberalism," "liberalism" being a word in any case used rarely by liberals, most likely because it had negative connotations.

Evidence from outside France confirms that liberals as a rule did not endorse a strict version of laissez-faire. In Germany, Spain, Italy, Spanish America, and India, self-identified liberals endorsed a spectrum of views on the economy that depended on local circumstances. In the period so often referred to as the heyday of laissez-faire, there was no united position on the question, and the term "economic liberalism" was not used. Though Krug spoke favorably of "religious liberalism" and "political liberalism," he did not mention anything called "economic liberalism." In America, where the term "liberalism" was anyway extremely rare, it did not designate an economic policy.

## Liberal Exclusions

As we know, early liberals were not democrats. Endorsing popular sovereignty did not mean endorsing universal suffrage. Their reticence on this issue owed much to their experience with the Terror and the Napoleonic regime. Universal suffrage was introduced in France in 1792 for the election of a National Convention, the same Convention that launched the Reign of Terror. Napoleon's dictatorship was approved by plebiscite. Universal suffrage was associated on one hand with mob rule, violence, and disorder and on the other with gullibility, poor judgment, and submissiveness. For Constant—as for most liberals at the time—the right to vote was a trust and not a right. They thought that property ownership was necessary to give people the independence and leisure time to acquire the knowledge and character they needed to make informed political decisions.

This helps to explain why not one of the liberals mentioned in this chapter, with the notable exception of Mary Wollstonecraft, advocated voting rights for women. Women were, after all, legally dependent persons, with little access to the property and education deemed necessary to exercise the vote. Only a handful of texts published between 1789 and 1793 even mentioned political rights for women.

Those who did advocate such rights often used recognizably liberal language to support their cause. They compared women to slaves and marriage to a form of despotism. An October 1789 petition addressed to male legislators exclaimed: "You have broken the scepter of despotism; you have pronounced the beautiful axiom [that] the French are a free people. Yet still you allow thirteen million slaves shamefully to wear the irons of thirteen million despots!" They accused legislators of being selfish, that is, illiberal, for ignoring them.

Wollstonecraft was a fervent supporter of the liberal principles of the revolution, as we know from her *Vindication of the Rights of Men* (1790) and her critique of Edmund Burke. Two years later, she followed up with the *Vindication of the Rights of Woman*, in which she urged French legislators to correct their constitution by giving voting rights to women. This text reads like one long refutation of the notion that the French deputies could call themselves liberal when they ignored half of the human race. Instead, they were selfish and protective of hierarchy. Mary Hays, Wollstonecraft's disciple, derided them for sitting on a "self-erected throne" from which they kept women in chains. "How long," she asked, "will man refuse the liberty he claims; how long will he cherish, with narrow policy and superstitious veneration, the maxims of tyranny, and the institutions of barbarism?"[103] In denying women the vote, liberals were contradicting their own principles.

Lawmakers generally ignored such pleas, and in October 1793 a decree prohibited women from even attending clubs where politics was discussed. Its language focused on women's domestic duties. Speaking on behalf of the Committee of General Security, deputy Jean-Baptiste Amar declared that women should not be allowed to meet in clubs because "nature" dictated that they tend to their families and homes. They should stick to "the private functions to which women are destined by nature itself."

This is a somewhat curious and misleading line of argument, since few if any advocates of women's rights challenged the idea that women had domestic duties, or that their natures were different from men's. Wollstonecraft herself never questioned this. Most advocates of reforms for women did not even request political rights. They asked for things like increased access to education, better jobs, and control of their own property. They requested the right to divorce and for laws to make marriage more egalitarian. A greater degree of equality within marriage, they argued, would allow for friendship and collaboration in the carrying out of a couple's "duties to humanity."[104] A more companionate marriage would help regenerate the nation, improve morals, and encourage the citizenly virtues.

Although Madame de Staël never advocated voting rights for women, her novels celebrated female courage and intellectual capacity. Women, she wrote, could help heal and regenerate France because they "are the ones who animate everything relating to humanity, generosity, delicacy."[105] De Staël's own novels were intended to do just that, in other words, to foster feelings of compassion and kindness in her readers, moral values that she thought were essential to modern and liberal regimes. *Delphine*, published in 1802, centered on a beautiful and brilliant woman who was victimized by society's antiquated principles. It praised both divorce and Protestantism.

Counterrevolutionaries opposed the right to divorce for the same reason that Madame de Staël and other liberals supported it. The stability of a state, they said, depended on the superior authority of the husband and the indissolubility of marriage. In his pamphlet *On Divorce*, originally published in 1801, Louis de Bonald rejected its legalization as something that would create "democracy in the family" (clearly an abominable thing)—and thus would provoke a second revolution.[106] Joseph de Maistre also held that the stability and strength of the state depended on women's subordination to their husbands.[107] With the return of the monarchy in 1816, such ideas provided the rationale for abolishing the right to divorce over the vehement objections of liberals in the Chamber.

On September 16, 1824, Louis XVIII died and his brother, Charles X, ascended the throne. A devout Catholic and staunch counterrevolutionary, Charles promptly asserted his intentions to restore the authoritarian and Catholic monarchy. With the help of ultra-royalists in the Chambers, he passed a series of laws that horrified liberals.

One of the most controversial of these measures compensated former émigrés for property lost during the revolution.

Charles also tightened the Throne and Altar alliance and intensified efforts to re-Catholicize the country. He passed two religious bills, one legalizing religious orders that had been banned during the revolution and another criminalizing religious "sacrileges," very vaguely defined.

Liberals protested loudly, more than ever convinced that the Catholic Church was their most formidable enemy. They counterattacked with a well-organized propaganda offensive, flooding the country with political pamphlets, cartoons, songs, and cheap editions of anticlerical texts. It has been estimated that over the span of seven years, 2.7 million anticlerical books were published, including Constant's *De la religion*.

By 1827, the political pendulum had swung back in their favor. Increasingly panicky ultra-royalists feared that liberalism was winning the battle.[108] They accused liberals of being "republican, anarchist and seditious gazeteers who, for more than twelve years, have relentlessly attacked all that is true and good . . . [and who] long ardently for a new revolution, more complete than the first."[109]

Faced with the growing popularity of the liberal opposition, Charles's government became increasingly desperate and turned to colonial ventures to regain popular support. Using a minor diplomatic dispute with Algeria as a pretext, the king sent an expedition to seize the capital city of Algiers. After a quick military victory, he then moved against liberals at home with the July Ordinances, suspending freedom of the press, dissolving the Chamber, and raising property qualifications for voting. These actions triggered the three-day insurrection that overthrew him.

# CHAPTER THREE

# Liberalism, Democracy, and the Emergence of the Social Question, 1830–48

*The whole problem of modern society will be worked out, as I have long thought it would, in France and nowhere else.*

—JOHN STUART MILL, 1849

LED BY LIBERAL journalists and politicians, the people of Paris rose up in late July 1830 and overthrew their government. What came to be called the July Revolution took only three days and was relatively bloodless. The reactionary King Charles X abdicated and his more liberal cousin, Louis Philippe, Duke of Orléans, replaced him on the throne.

These Three Glorious Days marked a clear victory for liberalism. Expressions of joy flowed in from around the world. John Stuart Mill rushed to Paris to observe events firsthand. The American ambassador sent home a favorable report and both President Jackson and Secretary of State Van Buren offered congratulatory messages. German liberals called it a victory for all of Europe, if not the world. As far away as India, newspapers reported on what was transpiring in France. The Bengali reformer Rammohan Roy celebrated the ascension of the French citizen-king, Louis Philippe.[1] As one foreign observer remarked, "the whole world is influenced by all that is done in Paris."[2]

François Guizot, who became a leading spirit of the new government, issued a jubilant proclamation. The heroic population of Paris had won the battle against absolute monarchy. According to Adolphe Thiers, another leading light of the period, liberals had finally "arrived" and constitutional monarchy was now safe.[3] From the floor of the Chamber, Benjamin Constant expressed special pride over the role of workers in the uprising.

Very soon, however, these very same liberals would confront a formidable new adversary, known by the term "socialism."

## The Liberal Government Turns Conservative

Early excitement over the July Revolution quickly gave way to disappointment. Sharp disagreements arose among French liberals over what policies they should pursue now that they were in power. They stood for constitutional government, but what else? They favored popular representation, but how much? How should they deal with growing worker unrest? These issues divided and weakened liberals and exposed them to new attacks this time from not just the right, but also the left.

The first fissure arose over the question of the franchise. King Louis Philippe and François Guizot, saw the July Revolution as a defensive movement meant to protect the Charter. They opposed those who saw it as an opportunity to undertake further reforms and, in particular, a meaningful expansion of the electorate. The liberal deputy Odilon Barrot's *Memoirs* recount that "men of movement" like himself pushed for progressive reforms, but that they were constantly thwarted by "men of resistance" like the king and Guizot.

Eventually, the resistance liberals won the battle. The new constitutional charter differed little from the one it replaced. Property qualifications for the suffrage were lowered only minimally, so that the right to vote and stand for office in national elections remained the privilege of a very small group of wealthy notables. The electorate under the Restoration came to 140,000 voters out of a total population of over 26 million; in the July Monarchy, the number rose to not more than 241,000. England, with a much smaller population, had a little over 400,000 voters after 1832. The French king defended this moderate expansion of the electorate by saying that it would wisely maintain a *"juste milieu* [just middle]" between the excesses of democracy and the abuses of royal power. Guizot described the *juste milieu* position as both "liberal and conservative," apparently seeing no contradiction in that.[4] Charles Rémusat famously declared: "We are the government of the bourgeoisie," at a safe distance from both aristocratic rule and democracy.[5]

Left-wing critics denounced it as just another type of aristocracy—this time one of money. Deputy Etienne Cabet voiced the sense of outrage felt by many former supporters. The new constitution was not liberal, he protested. It was "illiberal" since it placed power in the hands of a moneyed elite that was even more selfish and disdainful than the nobility it had replaced.[6] Accused of treason, Cabet was dismissed from his position as a civil servant in Corsica and fled to England.

Frustrated, some radicals began to advocate the overthrow of the monarchy and the establishment of a republic based on universal suffrage. Their supposedly liberal government responded with laws restricting freedom of the press and the right of association. Between July 1830 and February 1832 there were four hundred government prosecutions of newspapers. In April 1831, a strict new law against public demonstrations was passed. When, a year later, republican groups in Paris tried to turn the funeral of one of their leaders into an uprising, the liberal government imposed a state of siege on the capital. It became illegal to call oneself a republican.

Many former supporters now accused the liberals in power of betraying their own principles. In the Chambers, Benjamin Constant expressed his deep disappointment. Lafayette resigned in protest from the command of the National Guard. Charles Comte and Charles Dunoyer, who had taken jobs in the new government, gave up their posts. Alexis de Tocqueville, as yet relatively unknown, left for America. Having initially welcomed the new regime, he soon came to despise it.

The resistance liberals' conservative turn distressed the young John Stuart Mill. Ten years earlier, he had visited Paris and lived in the home of political economist Jean-Baptiste Say. He had been introduced to many leaders of the liberal party and, as he later recalled in his autobiography, had acquired a "strong and permanent interest in Continental Liberalism."[7]

Hearing the news of the outbreak of the July Revolution, Mill rushed to Paris. There he met and befriended the Marquis de Lafayette and other movement liberals, with whom he developed a close rapport. Letters home to his father show that Mill quickly grew disappointed with the direction that the revolution took. The new government showed little interest in real reform. France, he lamented, had become a "monied . . . [and] narrow Oligarchy."[8]

After returning to England, Mill continued to follow developments in France closely, producing a series of articles for the *Examiner*. He called France's new leaders a "stationary or stagnation party," and labeled them "*so-called* liberals" since they were mainly interested in maintaining the status quo.[9]

They showed an aversion to reform, especially to help the poorest classes. They cared only about their selfish interests. They were betraying the liberal cause.

Such disappointment was deep and widespread. As early as 1831, journalists in the United States lost their enthusiasm and reported that the liberal government in France had turned conservative. A rift had developed between those who wanted more reforms and those who did not; "trouble [was] brewing."[10] The *Encyclopedia Americana*, edited by German the émigré Francis Lieber, reported that a breach had occurred in the French liberal party between conservatives and progressives. A twenty-seven-page article on liberalism in the German *Staats-Lexikon* expressed regret and displeasure. Any liberal government should, by definition, be about *movement*, it said. Liberals were supposed to promote the common good and not the selfish interests of a party or privileged class.[11] By such criteria, the French liberals in power were no longer liberal.

## Liberals on Democracy

Such dissensions among liberals should not make us think that even "movement liberals" favored democracy in our modern sense of the term. Since the very beginning, liberals worried about the "incapacity" of the masses, whom they thought were irrational, prone to violent behavior, and unaware of their own best interests. Most liberals continued to favor strict property qualifications for both voting and office holding. Liberal reformers wanted a reduction in these qualifications, not necessarily their abolition. Representing the will of the people, they reasoned, was not the same as giving them the vote.

The *"true* majority," wrote one German liberal, should be distinguished from the "majority by head count."[12] A liberal government was not the same thing as government by plebiscite, said another. It was important to differentiate between equality before the law and universal suffrage.

Our understanding of liberalism's relationship with democracy is complicated by the fact that neither word had a fixed or agreed-upon meaning and both were used in ways unfamiliar to us today. The word "democracy" did not necessarily designate an electoral system based on universal suffrage. It could also mean a *type of society*—for example, a society that recognized civil equality and in which social mobility was feasible. In that sense, it was possible for many European liberals to accept and even celebrate democracy while simultaneously opposing universal suffrage.

Democracy in the sense of equality under the law was one of the proudest achievements of the Revolution of 1789. And it was in this sense that the liberal deputy Royer-Collard, in an 1822 speech delivered in the Chambers, asserted that democracy "is everywhere in France."[13] Today, that seems a rather strange thing to say about a country in which not more than 140,000 of 26 million had the vote. But it is perfectly intelligible when you realize that the word "democracy" did not necessarily mean an electoral system.

This fact also helps to explain some otherwise rather odd conflations. In 1825, Thomas Jefferson lumped liberals together with democrats as if there were little difference between them. Explaining the political divide that exists in every country, he reasoned that "some are whigs, liberals, democrats, call them what you please. Others are tories, serviles, aristocrats etc. The latter fear the people, and wish to transfer all power to the higher classes of society; the former consider the people as the safest depository of power in the last resort; they cherish them therefore, & wish to leave in them all the powers to the exercise of which they are competent."[14] Jefferson was here not necessarily suggesting that liberals and democrats advocated what we mean by democracy today. Whigs, liberals, and democrats, he says, wish to leave in the people as much power as *they are competent* to exercise. Exactly how much or what kind of power is left unclear.

It is also worth pausing a minute to consider the fact that Jefferson was here explaining European politics to an American interlocutor. The word "liberal", as a political term, was virtually unknown in America at the time. The entry "liberal" in the *Encyclopedia Americana* of 1831 states that the word's new and political meaning comes from France. In that country, the article explains, the word now stands for "equal rights" and "democratic principles."[15] What exactly "democratic principles" means is left unexplained. The encyclopedia contains no entry on "liberalism."

The liberal leader François Guizot, who was, in many ways, the very symbol of the July Monarchy, saw universal suffrage as completely incompatible with liberty. With the French Revolution of 1789 and Napoleon in mind, he was certain that it led inevitably to dictatorship. But Guizot was not an advocate of placing power in the hands of a hereditary aristocracy either. Instead, he favored the *juste milieu*—a system by which the propertied middle class ruled through representative institutions. Like many other liberals at the time, he believed that the franchise should be given only to men with the requisite degree of education, judgment, and leisure to be trusted with something as important as the vote. He could accept democracy as a type of society but not as a form of government.

These discussions about democracy provide the context for Alexis de Tocqueville's masterpiece, *Democracy in America*, the first volume of which appeared in 1835 to great acclaim. Born in 1805 to an old and aristocratic Catholic family, the young Tocqueville studied law and, at the age of twenty-two, earned a judgeship in the lower courts. He welcomed the July

Revolution at first, but soon became disenchanted. In 1831 he therefore requested an assignment to travel to America ostensibly to study its prison system. The request was granted, and he took the opportunity to travel widely and study other things besides. The result was *Democracy in America*.

Today regarded as one of the great classics of liberalism, *Democracy in America* was at its time meant to deliver some pointed lessons to Guizot's *juste milieu* government. As the book shows, Tocqueville shared the conservative liberals' concerns about democracy, whether social or political. He worried about the masses' lack of capacity. He was especially concerned about democracy's tendency to foster egoism or individualism, as he also called it. "Egoism blights the seeds of every virtue," he wrote. Like Constant and others, however, Tocqueville believed that the forward march of equality was unstoppable. Political democracy was therefore "a providential fact."[16] Under the circumstances, the best that could be done was to prepare France for the inevitable: the population had to acquire capacity.

Preparing France for democracy meant adopting some of the political institutions, practices, and values he had found in America. Among these were administrative decentralization, freedom of association, and church/state separation, some of the very reforms that the Guizot government was firmly resisting. Such liberal measures, Tocqueville suggested, could perform the necessary role of "educating democracy," in a sense neutralizing, or at least minimizing, its dangers. Liberals should work not to stop democracy but to instruct it and tame it, so that it did not threaten liberty and devolve into the new kind of despotism France had seen under Napoleon.

*Democracy in America* earned Tocqueville great celebrity and helped get him elected to the Chamber of Deputies in 1839. There, he joined the opposition to the government of

Louis Philippe and Guizot, who never followed his advice. As for Tocqueville himself, he became more and more pessimistic about democracy in the years to come.[17]

## Liberals and Insurrection, Again

Liberal worries about democracy were closely related to fears of popular violence. And yet evidence shows that some liberals continued to advocate popular insurrection to overthrow repressive regimes across Europe. The majority of liberals denounced such liberals as "ultraliberal," "exalted," or "extremist" and distanced themselves from them.

When the July Revolution of 1830 broke out, there were liberals in Italy, Poland, and Germany who hoped to receive help from the French government in support of their own revolutions. However, despite the intense lobbying of liberals like Lafayette, the new French government would do little to upset the European status quo. Except for in Belgium, where France helped establish a lasting constitutional monarchy, the *juste milieu* government refused to intervene, and the uprisings in Italy, Poland, and Germany were easily squashed.

Some liberals went underground from where they continued to plot insurrections. The Italian revolutionary Giuseppe Mazzini was one. Born in the Republic of Genoa in 1805, Mazzini joined the Freemason-like secret society, the Carbonari, as a young man. The Carbonari's main goal was to overthrow absolutist regimes throughout Europe and replace them with constitutional ones. In 1830, Mazzini and his Italian comrades hoped for French help in this endeavor. But none came. Instead, Mazzini was arrested, imprisoned, and forced into exile. He eventually made his way to London, where he continued to plot insurrections in coordination with counterparts across Europe. Today heralded as a pioneer of "liberal internationalism,"[18]

Mazzini was at his time a highly unusual type of liberal whose insurrectionary tactics and democratic ideas were rejected by most others.

Radical liberals such as Mazzini saw no contradiction between advocating liberal principles and encouraging insurrection. After all, liberalism owed its very origins to the French Revolution. Liberals of Mazzini's ilk regarded all liberals as part of a family fighting for the same thing and regularly appealed to established governments for help. In London, Mazzini made friends in the liberal community, where he was widely esteemed. John Stuart Mill, who first met Mazzini in 1837, expressed great admiration for him. He called him "one of the men I most respect" and "in every way a superior man among all the foreigners I have known."[19] In fact, admiration for Mazzini was widespread among British liberals and the population at large. Lord Morley, ministerial colleague and biographer of William Gladstone, called Mazzini "one of the most morally impressive men I ha[ve] ever known." When Morley was in Mazzini's presence, he could hardly resist "this feeling of greatness."[20]

But this admiration for Mazzini did not mean that liberals necessarily approved of his methods or all his ideas. Support for insurrection was exceedingly rare. Although Mill expressed respect for him, he also professed not to like "his mode of working."[21] Indeed, the majority of liberals rejected his "exaggerated" liberalism. More moderate liberals continued to believe that the best way forward was to cooperate with existing European governments and to press them for gradual reforms. In Italy, some of these moderates placed their hopes in rulers like Charles Albert of Piedmont or even Pope Pius IX, who was elected in 1846 and soon acquired the reputation of being a liberal pope.

Certainly, most German liberals wanted to distance themselves from those who were plotting insurrections. We have already seen that the liberal professor Wilhelm Krug, in his 1823 *Historical Depiction of Liberalism*, derided the "few idiots" who espoused what he called an exaggerated form of liberalism. The *Staats-Lexikon*, a veritable compendium of liberal beliefs, also took a firm stand against "ultra-liberals" and instead advocated a measured and gradual approach to reform.[22] The very purpose of the encyclopedia, its foreword stated, was to furnish "sane" political ideas with which all reasonable and mature liberals could agree. Its goal was certainly not to encourage either insurrection or political democracy. German liberals like Krug and the writers of the *Staats-Lexikon* were dedicated to fighting the extremism of both the right and the left, both absolutism and radicalism.

The long entry on liberalism in the *Staats-Lexikon* is revealing. Written by Paul Pfizer, a liberal politician, journalist, and philosopher from Württemberg, it responded forcefully to attacks coming from the right. Liberalism, it asserted, was being unjustly impugned. Liberals were being described as deranged, sick, and crazy. They were being accused of inciting violence and mob rule. But this, Pfizer insisted, was a gross misrepresentation of the facts. True liberals deplored radicalism, violence, and mob rule. What they wanted, the *Staats-Lexikon* declared, was simply movement in the direction of constitutional and representative government. They stood for piecemeal reform and progress and did not wish to proceed too quickly. Liberals strove for improvements appropriate to Germany's historical circumstances.

Like their counterparts in Italy, Germans labored under very difficult circumstances. They had no united nation. The leading German states had no parliaments, and where they existed, they had very limited power. The population was unschooled politically and many feudal, military, and bureaucratic privileges remained. The draconian Carlsbad Decrees had been renewed in 1832. King Frederick William IV of Prussia, who ascended the throne in 1840, condemned liberalism as a disease and vowed to make no concessions whatsoever to liberal demands, or what he referred to as "French" forms of government. He wished instead to revive medieval notions of divine monarchy.

While writers for the *Staats-Lexikon* were anxious to assuage their right-wing critics that German liberals did not want revolution, they also wished to unite liberals under a moderate banner. While it was true, Pfizer said, that there existed some "ultra-liberals" who were willing to perpetrate excesses, *real* liberals were not revolutionaries. And it was also true that revolutions were more often provoked by governments' foolish resistance to change. If rulers wanted to avoid revolution, they should embrace liberal reforms. Sounding quite like Tocqueville and Krug, the *Staats-Lexikon* asserted that liberalism was in any case unstoppable because it was willed by providence.

Most German liberals tried to distance themselves from the violence associated with the French Revolution. Many instead sought ways to identify their liberalism with England and its peaceful and gradual political evolution. They attempted to argue that Germany's political evolution could and should resemble England's. To that effect, they revived and utilized the Anglo-Saxon myth: the idea that England owed its liberal political institutions to German origins.

The idea that the English form of government was indebted to the "Old-Saxon" tribes, who migrated to England in the early Middle Ages, was an old legend, widely disseminated in the eighteenth and early nineteenth centuries. The influential French philosopher Montesquieu, who greatly admired England's constitution, traced it back to the forests of Germany, using Tacitus's *Germania* to support his views. In her *On Germany*, Madame de Staël expressed admiration for the traits of character and spirit of independence of the ancient Germans, to whom she also thought the English constitution was indebted. In England itself, it was a common belief that the country's political institutions stemmed from Saxon times and owed much to the early German tribes.

It was not peculiar, then, that nineteenth-century German liberals should express admiration for the English constitution and the way it supposedly incorporated the ancient institutions of the Old-Saxon tribes. "Large bands of Saxons," wrote F. C. Dahlmann, a liberal from Schleswig-Holstein, were "thoroughly imbued with legal concepts of freedom" and brought these concepts to Britain, where they made their way into the English constitution.[23] For German liberals to campaign for liberal principles of government was entirely natural, since these principles had deep roots in their own history. At least that is what German liberals wanted their fellow Germans to believe.

## Liberals Face the "Social Question"

Related to liberal fears of democracy and revolution were anxieties about the so-called "social question." Here again the French led the way. During the 1830s and 1840s, Paris became a gathering place of radicals and revolutionaries and the place where some of the most advanced socialist thinking in Europe took place. Not for nothing did Karl Marx make it his home in 1843 until he was expelled by the Guizot government in 1845. In Paris Marx immersed himself in some of the most radical thinking of the time.

The importance of the July Monarchy to the history of socialism was noted by the liberal professor Lorenz von Stein in his widely read book, *Socialism and Communism in Contemporary France*, published in 1842. Born in Schleswig-Holstein, von Stein rose to become one of the most influential scholars in the new field of sociology and has been credited with introducing the term "social movement" into scholarly debate. A resident of Paris from 1841 to 1842, he was clearly influenced by the political discussions going on in the city.

The 1830 Revolution, von Stein wrote, was a great watershed in the history of mankind. It destroyed forever the idea of the divine right of kings. This, in itself, was a great step forward. The problem was, however, that the selfishness and shortsightedness of the liberals brought to power by the revolution were giving rise to a self-conscious, politicized and angry working class. If liberals did not implement serious reforms, they should expect another revolution.

France's government did not heed such warnings. It did very little to alleviate the distress of French workers, whose condition had only worsened since 1789. The revolution had destroyed the guilds that traditionally protected them and forbidden any new forms of worker organization that might enable them to bargain collectively with their employers. Napoleon's Penal Code of 1810 imposed heavy fines for violations of this rule and instituted a new system of passports—the *livrets*—which enabled authorities to monitor workers' movements. From roughly 1827 to 1832, a depression caused food prices to soar, while a cholera epidemic hit Paris. Urban population growth under these conditions contributed to a miserable situation for workers. Extreme poverty, unemployment, and disease were widespread.

During the years leading up to the July Revolution, the workers had identified with the liberal cause. They had built and manned the barricades during the Three Glorious Days. Having lent such crucial support, they expected assistance from liberals when the revolution was over. Soon after the new regime was installed, they began to hold peaceful demonstrations and sent delegates to the government. They asked for shorter workdays, higher wages, and a ban on the new machinery that was threatening their livelihoods.

Once in power, however, the liberals did little to answer the workers' needs. They exacerbated matters by speaking about them in condescending and even disdainful ways. Some liberal newspapers called workers "barbarians" and "savages" or accused them of behaving like children. They were lectured on the "laws of the economy." "In the ordinary course of events," Guizot explained, the relations between capital and labor "settle themselves." Any attempt to intervene with the freedom of industry would be ineffective or even harmful.[24]

Some liberals said that government programs to help the poor bred laziness. Raising wages or reforming conditions of work would not improve anything but just inhibit the development of the values and habits that workers needed to acquire. The problem, it was often said, was that workers were indolent and degenerate; they spent their money on alcohol and prostitutes rather than on their homes and families. Intervention by the state should therefore be avoided as much as possible. It would simply exacerbate the situation and might also encourage workers to think that they could demand aid as a right.

The truth, moreover, is that the liberals in power *did* intervene in the economy, but it did so selectively and in ways that favored themselves and their class. They supported employers against workers, repeatedly sending out troops to suppress strikes and demonstrations. They imposed censorship on their critics, and persecuted and exiled political adversaries. They imposed taxes that hit the poor disproportionately hard and maintained a high tariff regime that favored wealthy producers and landowners. The only nominally social law passed by the July Monarchy was an 1841 prohibition on the labor of children under eight years of age and the employment of children younger than thirteen for nighttime work. The law, however, was routinely flouted.

Despite their illegality, strikes took place frequently during the July Monarchy. One such strike was by the silk weavers of Lyons in 1831. Rendered desperate by a reduction in their wages, the weavers rose up in protest. They mixed economic demands with political ones and changed chanted republican slogans, provoking violent retaliation. The government sent in an army to restore order. In 1834, there was another strike in Lyons. This time the confrontation escalated. Close to three hundred persons were killed in two days of fighting. Hundreds of leaders were tried, condemned, and exiled.

Feeling insulted and betrayed by their liberal government, and forbidden by law to associate, workers began meeting in secret. They founded newspapers of their own. In the years 1839 and 1840, several socialist treatises also appeared, including Louis Blanc's *The Organization of Labor*, Pierre Leroux's *On Humanity*, Pierre-Joseph Proudhon's *What Is Property?*, and Etienne Cabet's *Voyage to Icaria*. These were some of the works that Karl Marx read while he was in Paris.

It was in this context that the word "socialist" was introduced and disseminated. Originally, the term described anyone who sympathized with the plight of the working poor. Marxism was still many years away, and at the time there was no necessary contradiction between being liberal and being socialist. The word seems to have come from England, where it was associated with the wealthy industrialist and reformer Robert Owen. As early as 1815, Owen was writing about a new "social system" that he hoped would replace the current system that was causing such hardship for the poor.

Owen was certain that his socialist ideas were "truly liberal" since they were generous, enlightened, and designed to advance the common good. He hoped to convince men of "enlarged, liberal habits of thought"[25] to embrace his socialist ideas. His followers similarly addressed themselves to "liberalminded persons of different classes and parties," and thought it completely natural and logical to be both liberal and socialist, in the sense of sympathizing with workers and wanting to help them.[26]

But the July Monarchy changed all that. Accusations came from all around that liberals were incorrigibly selfish. They cared only about their own class and not at all about the poor. They were good at making speeches about equal rights, freedom, and reform, but were really only playing "word games."

Liberals were devoid of any generosity, heart, or feeling.[27] The policies they pursued, wrote one critic, were liberal only in appearance, but "murderous" in reality.[28] A small number of rich people were growing richer, while for the rest, life was "a social Hell."[29] Liberals, some began to say, had served their purpose: they had toppled the Old Regime but offered no solutions to the problems now afflicting France.

Soon Friedrich Engels, the close friend and associate of Karl Marx, expanded on von Stein's critique of liberalism. In an essay for the *Deutsch-Französische Jahrbücher* published in 1844, Engels denounced the "sham philanthropy" and "sham humanity" of liberalism, calling it blatant hypocrisy.[30] In 1845, he published *The Condition of the Working Class in England*, based on his own research in Manchester. It was not only the French liberals who were an abomination, he asserted, but English liberals too. They were narrow-minded, shortsighted, and selfish. Thanks to them, workers were being treated as brutes and in some ways were even worse off than slaves. The liberal system of government justified a war of each against all, from which only liberals benefited.

What was happening in England and France, Engels predicted, would soon afflict Germany since their social systems were essentially the same. Three years later, Engels coauthored with Marx their famous *Communist Manifesto*, in which they warned of a coming revolution. Its opening lines denounced the French liberal minister François Guizot, who had by then become the very symbol of the liberalism Marx and Engels wished to overthrow. The *Manifesto* was published in London on the eve of the Revolutions of 1848.

## Laissez-Faire and Liberalism

From this socialist critique of liberalism, it would be wrong to conclude that all mid-nineteenth-century liberal thinkers believed in laissez-faire or that liberal governments pursued strictly laissez-faire policies. Liberals across Europe and the Atlantic world were divided on the best way to grow the economy and remedy "pauperism," a new word important from England at this time.[31] There simply was no unified liberal position on economics.

Some liberals believed that the best way to help workers was to lower the price of bread. In Britain, during the thirties and forties, such liberals campaigned for the abolition of the so-called Corn Laws, duties on grain imposed at the end of the Napoleonic Wars. The laws excluded foreign wheat until the price of domestic wheat reached a certain level. Like the French Corn Laws, passed around the same time, they were seen as benefiting primarily the aristocratic, landed elite while causing the poor to suffer.

French free traders were irritated when their new government made only meagre efforts to lower tariffs. They accused the "*so-called* liberal party" of acting in contradictory ways and tried hard to make it change its policies.[32] They founded the Political Economy Society in 1841 and launched the *Journal économique*, which relentlessly demanded "truly liberal legislation," particularly a more "liberal system of commerce."[33] The very fact that they argued over what "truly liberal legislation" meant is a clear indication of the sharp divisions that existed within the liberal camp.

The French free traders' most articulate spokesman was Frédéric Bastiat. Today Bastiat is a revered by American libertarians for his strong advocacy of what they call "classical liberalism." At the time, however, he represented a minority point of view and had little if any success convincing liberal governments to implement his ideas. And, of course, he did not see himself as the founder of, or even an advocate for, classical liberalism, which didn't exist.

Born in the South of France to a prominent business family, Bastiat became politically active after the 1830 Revolution. He made his public debut as an economist in 1844, when his first article was published in the *Journal économique*. Thereafter he became perhaps Europe's most famous and certainly most enthusiastic proponent of laissez-faire. Among his better known works is *Economic Sophisms*, published in 1846, which contains a satirical parable known as the "candle makers' petition": candle makers lobby their government to block out the sun to prevent its unfair competition with their products.

Bastiat became politicized when, in the early 1840s, he learned about the British Anti-Corn Law League. In 1838, a number of merchants in Manchester had joined together to form this group of free traders. It launched a vigorous publicity campaign to educate electors to the benefits of free trade. Many claimed to be disciples of Adam Smith. They advocated the establishment of "Smithian societies" throughout England and often cited sections of Smith's writings that supported their cause. Their societies, they hoped, would contribute "to the spread of liberal and just views of political science."[34] Thanks to their initiatives and propaganda, Adam Smith's message was disseminated broadly, but also truncated and distorted. He was turned into an extreme proponent of laissez-faire, as if he had said nothing else, which, as we know, is far from true.

Bastiat visited England and was well received by the Anti-Corn Law League. Upon his return to France, he published his first book, *Cobden and the League*, and became the nation's most energetic propagandist of liberal trade policies. More publications followed. In 1846 he formed the National Association for Free Markets, which had among its members Horace Say, the son of Jean-Baptiste, and Charles Dunoyer. Bastiat toured the country speaking about the benefits of laissez-faire.

Ultimately the free traders were unsuccessful. Liberal politicians refused to listen to the liberal political economists. They disagreed about what constituted a liberal economic policy. Adolphe Thiers, minister of commerce, derided Bastiat's "*so-called* liberal" ideas.[35] "Liberty of commerce," Thiers said, was "a theory that should stay in the books where it belongs; policy must be determined by reference to facts."[36] Whether one was a protectionist or not should depend on circumstances, he said, and not on abstract theories of little relevance in the real world. Many French liberals agreed. One of their arguments was that England had economic advantages that France could not duplicate. Allowing French manufacturing to compete with the English without the protection of tariffs would lead to the collapse of French industry and massive unemployment. The "*so-called* liberal" ideas of the free traders would hurt, not help, French workers.

Undeterred by such reasoning, French free traders became more doctrinaire. Dunoyer opposed government involvement in education, public works, mail delivery, and even the regulation of child labor. The only legitimate role of the state, he said, was to provide internal and external security. Bastiat was only slightly less extreme. Running for election, he explained what the word "liberal" meant to him: fighting to keep government within the most narrow limits of its functions.[37] The best policy was one of the strictest laissez-faire.

Critics increasingly calling themselves socialist now joined conservatives in denouncing liberals for their "liberalism," a term both sides used interchangeably with laissez-faire. The socialist Louis Blanc, for example, denounced the "narrow and anarchic doctrines of liberalism, the catechism of *laissez faire*."[38] Anticipating Marx, he called liberalism a mere reflection of the political power of the bourgeoisie.[39] It referred to the fatalistic economic policies that led to pauperism. The responsibility for pauperism was said to lie with Adam Smith's French disciples, for whom individual interests ruled the world.

On the eve of the Revolution of 1848, liberalism was thus being attacked from the left and right for some of the very same reasons: it was a selfish, immoral, and anarchical doctrine that was dissolving the social fabric only to line the pockets of a favored few. This may be the reason why liberals themselves used the word "liberalism" so sparingly. It had very bad connotations.

## The Many Necessary Functions of Government

When socialists attacked liberals for advocating laissez-faire and caring nothing for workers, they were neither accurate nor fair. European liberals were divided on the issue of laissez-faire. Few were doctrinaire on the issue. While socialist and reactionaries tended to lump them together and accuse them all of "liberalism," liberals themselves disagreed about what *true* liberalism entailed. Given the grave problems caused by industrialization and urbanization that were growing ever more visible during the July Monarchy, a growing number liberals began to say that the government needed to intervene. Indeed, there is abundant evidence that liberals in France, England, and Germany saw no contradiction in being liberal and favoring government intervention of one type or another. The idea that the nineteenth century was a heyday of laissez-faire is an oversimplification and distortion of history.

Take, for example, Tocqueville. He struggled with the question of government intervention and was not entirely consistent on the issue. His writings on political economy are somewhat vague and even contradictory. Shortly after starting work on *Democracy in America*, he visited England, where he had occasion to observe the working-class neighborhoods of Manchester. Appalled by the large numbers of impoverished people, he wrote a *Memoir on Pauperism*. Like many other liberals, Tocqueville worried that the unintended consequences of such programs such as the Poor Laws would be to erode the motive to work and encourage idleness, which in turn would breed crime and immorality. He condemned what he called "legal charity," that is, state-sponsored public assistance programs. But he also accepted the idea that some public assistance programs, for example, those for the aged, the insane, and the ill, were necessary.

A few years later, in the second volume of *Democracy in America* (1840), Tocqueville called for increased state intervention to help the poor. Private charity was not enough, he now declared; "public charity" was necessary. He worried about the emergence of an "industrial aristocracy." Factory owners were growing ever richer, more powerful, and more arrogant while the workers became increasingly demoralized and dehumanized. "This man resembles more and more the administrator of a vast empire," he wrote, "that man a brute." Because of the painful effects of industrialization and the division of labor, Tocqueville now concluded that workers required "the special consideration of the legislator." The government needed to address endemic problems such as "the helplessness of infancy, the decrepitude of old age, sickness, insanity," and it should furnish aid "in times of public calamities." "It is at once necessary and desirable," said Tocqueville, "that the central power that directs a democratic people be active and powerful. There is no question of rendering it weak or indolent, but only of preventing it from abusing its agility and force."[40]

In Britain, parliamentary reformers held a range of views on laissez-faire and government intervention. They could also be self-contradictory, arguing for one kind of intervention one day and another the next. And when certain circumstances arose—for example, when they became convinced that economic distress somewhere in the country had become too important to ignore and local government was unable or unwilling to remedy the situation—they frequently called on Parliament to intervene.

This helps to explain why scholars have a hard time categorizing Mill. Some call him a liberal, others a socialist. In fact, however, his thought on the matter of intervention was not all that different from that of contemporary liberals. He provides a perfect example of the pragmatic, nonideological, and nondoctrinaire liberalism that dominated in the nineteenth century. At midcentury it was possible for a liberal to be socialist.

By the time Mill published his *Principles of Political Economy*, he had acquired considerable renown as a philosopher. His *Logic* of 1843 had been recognized as a work of major importance. His *Principles* was equally influential, if not more so. The first edition was published in April 1848 and sold out within a year, leading to a second edition in 1849, and then five more when it became established as a text in American and British universities. There was also an inexpensive 1865 people's edition, which sold more than ten thousand copies.[41]

There were, in Mill's estimation, many necessary functions of government. Although he defended a "general practice" of laissez-faire, he also acknowledged that exceptions were often required "by some great good" and the "public interest." Government should play a role in the protection of the less able, for example. It should institute regulations for the conservation of forests and water, as well as "all other natural riches, above and below the surface." Government might also legitimately undertake functions such as the coining of money, the standardization of weights and measures, the making or improving of harbors, and the building of lighthouses. It should provide for obligatory public education. Examples of such necessary government functions, Mill noted, "might be indefinitely multiplied."[42]

The liberal *Edinburgh* and *Westminster Reviews* encouraged their readers to trust the market but also approved of new economic regulations, and became more accepting of them over time. John McCulloch, a leading political economist who wrote for the *Westminster Review*, advocated not only laws to protect child labor, but also statutory poor relief, government-sponsored land reform programs, and public education.[43] "Freedom is not," he wrote, "the end of government: the advancement of public prosperity and happiness is its end: and freedom is valuable in so far only as it contributes to bring it about."[44] The *Westminster Review* ran articles on police reform, factory legislation, mining conditions, school aid, and the regulation of asylums, in which it described government as an instrument of benevolence. As the *Times* explained, the legislature was not just empowered but *obliged* to interfere with the rights of individuals, when "the general advantage of the community requires it."[45] Such thinking persuaded many members of Parliament to vote for government action again and again. Just how and when the government should intervene was decided in an *ad hoc* and pragmatic fashion.

In America, the leading advocate of laissez-faire was the editorial writer William Leggett, whose faith in the unbridled market was certainly extreme. The interest of the community, he wrote, was always best served by trusting the "simple order of nature." The most effective policy for governments to pursue was to abide by the "*laissez-nous faire* maxim," in other words, allowing for free competition between individuals and restricting government intervention within the narrowest limits.[46]

As elsewhere, however, such ideas were contested by other influential writers. Francis Lieber, the editor of *Encyclopedia Americana* and a respected professor of political economy, thought well enough of Bastiat to translate him into English. But he apparently saw no contradiction in simultaneously asserting that a strong state was "essential to the full development of [man's] faculties" and that its purpose was to pursue "the highest ends of man and society."[47] "Generally speaking," Lieber wrote, the object of the state was "to aid society in obtaining the highest degree of civilization or the greatest possible development of man, both by removing obstacles, or assisting directly."[48]

All this goes to show, once again, that "classical liberalism" did not reign supreme during the nineteenth century. In fact, the concept that plays such a role in today's discussions of liberalism never actually existed during the period under consideration. Liberals held a spectrum of economic views, were often inconsistent, and themselves hardly ever even used the term "liberalism" to designate their economic views.

This fact is perhaps especially useful to know when considering German liberalism. Today Germany is often treated as an outsider to the liberal tradition, and this has much to do with German liberalism's perceived statism. But the fact is that German liberals were much like their counterparts elsewhere in Europe; they were divided on the issue of economic policy and government intervention. They could advocate laissez-faire in some cases and not in others. There were free traders among them as well as champions of protection. Most believed that economic policy should relate to specific circumstances and be adapted to particular situations.

Like liberals elsewhere, the Germans worried about the "social question." Here too advocates of strict laissez-faire were a distinct minority. German liberals knew about the deplorable conditions of workers in England and that were spreading to France. By the 1830s, the effects of industrialization were becoming visible in Germany as well, and many began to express alarm over a domestic pauperism crisis. This was the context for von Stein's *Socialism and Communism in Contemporary France*, which was meant as a warning to German liberals.

One spokesman for laissez-faire was John Prince Smith, a naturalized Prussian born of English parents. Smith moved to eastern Prussia in 1831 and became the leading figure in the German free trade movement. He was a great fan of Bastiat and wanted to establish a movement similar to the Anti-Corn Law League in Germany. Much of his work was aimed at convincing German liberals of the desirability of free trade. Other staunch advocates of laissez-faire included Karl Heinrich Rau and David Hansemann.

But most German liberals rejected extreme laissez-faire ideas. They used the derisive terms "Smithianism," "Manchesterism," and the "pseudo-system of liberty" to designate what we today call laissez-faire economics.[49] The liberal Friedrich List, who had spent time in Paris in 1830–31 and was one of the founders of the *Staats-Lexikon*, accused laissez-faire and free trade economics of being nothing but *"Individualismus,"* that is, selfishness. It sacrificed the welfare of the national community to the individual acquisition of wealth.[50]

Writers for the *Staats-Lexikon* expressed nuanced and often vague or even contradictory views. Robert von Mohl, a professor of political economy, wrote that "*laissez faire, laissez passer* must not be misunderstood. For it is one thing to interfere at the wrong place, and quite another to offer help where it is needed."[51] Limitations on freedom were perfectly acceptable when they were "for the higher purpose of the entire community." Von Mohl listed a long list of acceptable government interventions—schools for the training of workers, insurance, low-interest loans, government-sponsored savings banks, and benevolent associations. He recommended that the government outlaw child labor and excessively long working hours and suggested that the state might legitimately attempt to establish minimum wages.[52]

Nor did German liberals regard property rights as sacred or inalienable. Karl Rotteck's article on "Property" defended the rights of property, but also disapproved of "unlimited freedom of enterprise," which he equated with a "war between everyone and everyone else." Like other German liberals, Rotteck opposed the accumulation of wealth in the hands of an "ugly aristocracy of money." He advocated laws to regulate trade and industry and believed that the state had an obligation to help the poor.[53]

In other words, the great majority of nineteenth-century liberals, whether British, French, or German, were not all that adverse to government intervention. Nor did they advocate absolute property rights. And they certainly did not believe that individuals pursuing their own self-interest would spontaneously create a healthy wealth distribution or social harmony. They denounced selfishness and individualism at every opportunity. The minority of liberals who advocated strict laissez-faire principles were sternly criticized by others.

## Liberals on Colonies

Some liberals thought that the acquisition of colonies could help solve the social question. Their position on colonialism, however, is more complicated than it might at first seem. Just a glance at the attitudes of liberals in Britain and France, the two main colonizers in the mid-nineteenth century, shows this. It turns out that liberals could be both for and against the acquisition of colonies.

French liberals protested loudly when, on the eve of the Revolution of 1830, Charles X invaded Algeria in what looked like a deliberate move to curry favor with the public. They equated colonies with both aristocratic and autocratic government. The liberal deputy, Amédée Desjobert, a disciple of Jean-Baptiste Say, denounced French rule in Africa from the very beginning. In the Chamber of Deputies, he repeatedly asserted that it was morally abhorrent and fundamentally incompatible with liberal political principles. Frédéric Bastiat was also a virulent critic of colonialism, calling it "revolting." Henri Fonfrède, another leading liberal publicist, called the colonization of Algerian territory "shameful." The French were not civilizing, he said; they were exterminating.[54]

Such thinking aligned French critics of colonialism with British free traders like Richard Cobden and John Bright, leaders of the Anti-Corn Law League. They too denounced an empire based on violent conquest that served the interests of only a small minority of the population. In Bright's famous words, the empire was "a gigantic system of out-door relief for the aristocracy." Similarly, according to a writer for the *Westminster Review,* colonialism was "part and parcel of the general plot by which the aristocracy of England are to be supported by the commonality."[55] As if to confirm this liberal point of view, Tory conservatives understood the attack on Britain's colonies as attempt to "bring about [a] social revolution."[56] Liberalism was an "extensive democratic movement," an attack on the constitution, and an attempt to destroy the aristocracy.[57]

But liberals could also display a good deal of inconsistency and hypocrisy on the issue of colonies. After loudly denouncing Charles X's taking of Algeria, many of them changed their minds once they came to power. Many of them even approved of the Algerian conquest after it encountered fierce local resistance and involved the killing of innocent civilians, the expropriation of property, and the burning of farms and silos. Some publicly dismissed the brutality as "unfortunate necessities."[58] One such liberal was Alexis de Tocqueville.

Liberals justified the possession of colonies in a number of ways. Their arguments tended to differ from those of conservatives and ultra-royalists. To be sure, liberals also spoke of the honor and glory of France; but it was a different France that they claimed to be honoring. To them colonies were no longer about enhancing the status of the monarchy and aristocracy but about improving the lives of the middle and poorer classes. At least that is what they said.

Some argued that Algeria would provide expanded markets for French manufactured goods and sources of raw materials, which would aid industry. It would offer an outlet for France's urban poor and unemployed, thus lessening their threat to public order at home. Tocqueville and other liberals believed that the acquisition of colonies could serve as an antidote to the moral and physical degeneration they thought France was suffering under the July Monarchy. They argued that to survive and thrive in the colonies it was necessary to be industrious, and the culture of hard work would transform Frenchmen into manly, patriotic, and law-abiding citizens. Some liberals also spoke of France's "civilizing mission," a phrase that first appeared in French dictionaries around 1840 with specific reference to the colonization of Algeria.[59]

By the late thirties and forties, many Britons came to believe that the best way to maintain Britain's leading position in the world was not through conquest and exploitation, but with a new kind of empire based on free trade. They argued that because of England's industrial predominance, its economy would not be hurt if it gave up its colonies; on the contrary, it would allow Great Britain to achieve a virtual industrial monopoly, and to maintain it more cheaply too. Joseph Hume, a liberal member of Parliament, reasoned that there was no problem in granting Britain's colonies independence, since free trade would in any case "render all the world tributary to us."[60] Hearing such arguments, the German economist Friedrich List called free trade a neo-mercantilist strategy for British domination of the world.

Other British liberals claimed that Britain needed both an "informal" and a "formal empire," free trade as well as with "settler colonies." Many were won over by the ideas of colonial theorist Edward Gibbon Wakefield. Wakefield argued that the economies of advanced commercial states like England were in constant danger of stagnation and decline. They tended toward overpopulation, overproduction, and surplus capital. They therefore needed new lands for their populations, markets for their goods, and new territory in which to invest. Only through settler colonies (like Australia, New Zealand, and Canada) could an industrial Britain keep growing and avoid social upheaval.

Wakefield's ideas resonated broadly among British liberals. John Stuart Mill regarded himself a disciple and paid tribute to Wakefield in his *Principles of Political Economy*. If one-tenth of Britain's workers and capital were transferred to the colonies, Mill said, wages and profits would benefit.[61]

Many French liberals also favored this new kind of empire. In 1814, Say had already been pleased to predict that "the old colonial system will fall apart everywhere."[62] But this did not mean that he rejected colonialism altogether. Rather, Say favored what he and others called "true colonization"[63] based on settler colonies. He apparently thought that this new and "true" kind of colonization would not require conquest, but could be effected through their superior enlightenment. Because of their sheer entrepreneurial genius, he wrote, Europeans were destined to rule the world.

Most European liberals took for granted that they had the right to subjugate "backward" populations, which were "still barbarous." However, as Mill explained, this did not give them license to do whatever they wanted with them or to pursue limitless aggrandizement at their expense. The rule over another people, Mill wrote, was "a legitimate mode of government in dealing with barbarians, provided the end be their improvement and the means justified by actually affecting that end."[64] Moreover, the objective of colonial rule, for Mill, was the natives' self-government. It was justified if it were an educative enterprise designed to create self-governing societies everywhere, at which point there would be no need for imperial powers.

## The Liberal Battle with Religion

While socialism and demands for democracy were a growing threat, mid-nineteenth-century liberals continued to fear the

reactionary forces of the right. In France, the threat of counterrevolution remained very real, and as always, right-wing
enemies of liberalism received crucial help from traditional
churches, whether Catholic or Protestant. The period brack-
eted by the Revolutions of 1830 and 1848 was therefore one of
deep thinking about the tense and often hostile relationship
between liberalism and religion. Growing numbers of liberals
rejected the idea that traditional religions, Catholic, Protestant, or Jewish, could ever be compatible with liberal political
principles.

## LIBERALISM AND THE CATHOLIC CHURCH

The last years of the French Restoration saw a tightening of the
Throne and Altar alliance. An ultra-royalist Assembly passed
regressive laws that were deeply resented by liberals. One was
a measure that compensated former émigrés for property lost
during the revolution. Two bills legalized religious orders that
had been banned during the revolution and criminalized religious "sacrileges," very vaguely defined.

These regressive laws were very unpopular with the public
and triggered a strong backlash. Rumors spread of a plot led
by priests intent on establishing theocracy. Capitalizing on such
fears, liberals launched a major propaganda offensive. They
flooded the country with political pamphlets, cartoons, songs,
cheap books, and anticlerical tracts to denigrate and discredit
the Church. Cheap editions of Voltaire's anticlerical works and
copies of the Civil Constitution of the Clergy were disseminated.
The *Courrier français* issued a typical warning when it called
the Catholic clergy "the enemy of liberal constitutions, of social guarantees, of all that emancipates human intelligence."[65]

Popular anger over the Church's collusion with absolutism
led to repeated anticlerical outbursts during the July Revolution

and the days that followed, tacitly permitted by the liberal government. There were therefore reasons to believe that it would pursue an anticlerical course. There were hopes that it would dismantle the church-state agreement negotiated under Napoleon, the Concordat.

On this issue as well as so many others, however, the hopes of many liberals were dashed by their new, supposedly liberal government. The new constitution did downgrade Catholicism from state religion to "the religion of the majority," and promised religious toleration and freedom of association, but it did not dismantle the Concordat. The special relationship between church and state remained in place with the government maintaining its support and control of the Church. Pope Gregory XVI eventually felt satisfied enough with the July Monarchy to ask the French clergy to say prayers for the new king.

But did this mean that the pope thought Catholicism compatible with liberal principles of government? Was it possible to be a good Catholic and a liberal after all? One group of vocal Catholics answered the question with an emphatic yes. They were led by the priests Hughes-Félicité de Lamennais and Henri-Dominique de Lacordaire and the nobleman Charles de Montalembert.

Shortly after the July Days, the three men launched a newspaper called *L'Avenir* (the Future). On its masthead, the paper claimed to be both Catholic and "truly liberal." One of its earliest articles even declared that "it is contradictory not to be liberal when one is Catholic."[66] But many remained skeptical.

*L'Avenir* had three main goals: to woo the Catholic clergy away from conservatives and counterrevolutionaries, to convince Catholics that they could be liberal, and to persuade the current government to give up its control of the Church. *L'Avenir* writers accused their government of not being liberal enough. Only if left free from government control and inter-ference could Catholicism thrive. Only then could it play its destined role of bringing stability and order to France.

After all, liberal Catholics had before them the example of Catholic Belgium. Belgium's constitution, obtained during its revolution in 1830, separated church and state, and yet Cathol-icism in the country was visibly thriving. Belgium was proof that Catholics could be liberal and that the Catholic Church could prosper under a liberal system of government.

France's Church hierarchy publicly censored these views, and *L'Avenir* lasted only one year. Then, in an act that would have momentous consequences for the history of liberalism, Pope Gregory XVI released his encyclical *Mirari Vos* (1832), reprimanding all Catholic liberals. Not mincing his words, he called liberalism a deadly "pestilence" because it led to reli-gious indifference and caused people to question the obedi-ence they owed their governments. The pope explicitly con-demned the separation of church and state and freedom of conscience; he even defended book burning.

By these actions, the pope sent another powerful message around the world: liberal principles of government were fun-damentally incompatible with Roman Catholicism. The open schism between the Church and liberalism that had begun with Pope Pius VI's condemnation of the French Revolution was widened.

*Mirari Vos* struck a devastating blow to Catholic liberals everywhere. In obedience to the pope, some abandoned the fight and went quiet. But his condemnation did not quash the Catholic liberal movement forever. Montalembert eventually reemerged as one of its principal leaders. Neither Dupanloup nor Lacordaire gave up. Other prominent Catholic liberals, such as Ignaz von Döllinger in Germany, his disciple, Lord Acton, in Britain, and Orestes Brownson in the United States, came forward. Numerous Italians, Spaniards, and Spanish Americans held firm to the idea that Catholicism was compatible with liberal political principles. Some even dreamed of a more liberal pope who would reform the Church and revitalize Catholicism in a way harmonious with the liberal Zeitgeist. Although Tocqueville was hardly a believer himself, his *Democracy in America* suggested that Catholicism could survive and even prosper in a democracy.

## LIBERALISM AND PROTESTANTISM

Non-Catholic liberals subscribed to a spectrum of religious beliefs. Though few were atheists, many were fiercely anti-Catholic. Some called themselves "liberal Christians" and believed in a form of Protestantism similar to the religion championed by Villers, Constant, and de Staël. They were advocates of what the liberal political economist Jean-Charles-Léonard Sismondi, in a letter to the American Unitarian leader William Ellery Channing, called a "rational and liberal religion."[67] To Christian traditionalists, this was of course no religion at all.

The liberal battle against both Catholic and Protestant orthodoxy became particularly intense in Germany, the home of liberal theology and where the most advanced biblical criticism took place. In the 1820s, a number of provocative books appeared, often with titles referring to the life of Jesus and claiming to investigate the Bible with the goal of separating out what was historically accurate and what was not. These books caused quite a stir and inflamed relations between liberals and the orthodox.

The theologian Heinrich Eberhard Paulus authored one such book in 1828. His *Life of Jesus as the Basis of a Purely Historical Account of Early Christianity* offered rational and natural explanations of the miracles in the Bible. A few years later, his student, David Strauss, caused a bigger scandal with his *Life of Jesus Critically Examined.* The book claimed that all the significant events in Jesus' life recounted in the Bible were not only empirically inaccurate but just myths dreamed up by the early Christians.

The July Revolution convinced German rulers that such ideas were a serious threat to their authority. Ascending the Prussian throne in 1840, Frederick William IV immediately put more pressure on Protestant clergymen to declare their religious orthodoxy or step down from their positions. Ernst Wilhelm Hengstenberg of the *Evangelische Kirchenzeitung* became an enthusiastic partner in this endeavor. Together they increased their efforts to eliminate all rationalist influences in the Protestant church. Liberal pastors were threatened and harassed and eventually replaced with neo-orthodox ones. The "liberal Zeitgeist" was incessantly condemned as the work of the devil, and religious reformers were accused of encouraging all manner of sins. Germans were warned of the wrath of God should they imitate the French by trumpeting the "ideas of 89" and demanding constitutional changes.

Frederick William did not just build alliances with the Protestant churches; he also lent his support to the most conservative party in the Catholic Church. Thanks to his blessing, Germany became the venue for a large number of Catholic missions and religious pilgrimages that, to the dismay and frustration of liberals, were extremely popular. In only seven weeks in 1844, half a million pilgrims made the journey to the city of Trier to see the Holy Shroud, the cloth Jesus was supposedly wrapped in at burial, making it the largest pilgrimage in European history.

German liberals fought back despite this hostile climate. Writers of the *Staats-Lexikon* repeatedly denounced the neo-orthodox movements in the strongest of terms. They were especially severe with Catholicism. One article went so far as to call the pope the "worst enemy of the German nation," and a long entry on Jesuits accused them of attempting to impose an "empire of darkness and superstition" on the world. Their goal was to bring back "a time of barbarism, inquisition and *auto-da-fés*." But the *Staats-Lexikon* did not spare Protestant neo-orthodoxy, which was attacked for spreading "superstition, darkness, ignorance, hierarchical despotism and intolerance."

Atheism, however, was roundly rejected. Religion was crucial, said one of the writers, because it was the "moral educator of humanity." "Religion makes every civic duty a thing of the conscience,"[68] wrote another.

Rejecting atheism on the one hand and superstition on the other, the liberal authors of the *Staats-Lexikon* advocated a liberal and rational religion such as we have encountered before, namely a religion less focused on dogma, ceremony, and obedience, and more concerned with the improvement of public morals. Heinrich Paulus, author of one of the *Lives of Jesus* mentioned above, wrote the articles that dealt explicitly with the Bible. The New Testament, he said, should be read not as conveying "theological metaphysics," but rather as giving practical instructions to those who wanted to lead a moral life. True Christianity was a religion that kept up with its time, evolved, and improved itself according to the march of history. Only then could it serve its purpose, which was to moralize society.[69]

Two religious movements emerged in the 1840s that worried German authorities more than any encyclopedia ever could. In 1841, a group of Protestant clergymen founded a movement called the Protestant Friends, which also became known as the Friends of Light. The aim of the Protestant Friends was to establish a people's church free from both government and orthodox religious control. They held open-air meetings at which people of different backgrounds and faiths gathered to discuss topics of religious and political importance. Soon they began demanding freedom of the press, speech, and association, as well as a more representative government.

It did not take long for Prussian authorities to perceive the threat. They accused the leaders of the movement of being secret atheists bent on revolution. In August 1845, their meetings were forbidden by law.

In December 1844, an excommunicated Catholic priest, aided by a radical democrat, launched a second dissident movement called the "German-Catholics." The two men resented the authoritarianism and what they saw as the superstitious dogmas of the Catholic Church and had been outraged by the pilgrimages to the Holy Shroud. Soon liberal Protestants joined the German-Catholics and together they founded their own ecumenical and democratically run congregations. Some members began to speak of a "religion of humanity" that should unite and transcend all confessions. They advocated complete freedom of belief and the separation of church and state.

By 1848, membership in the German-Catholic movement had grown to an estimated one hundred fifty thousand and it was rapidly becoming the largest protest movement of any sort in prerevolutionary Germany. Elated by its successes, the liberal lawyer and politician Gustav von Struve wrote that German-Catholicism had managed to accomplish more in a matter of months than political liberalism had accomplished since the Wars of Liberation.[70]

## LIBERALISM AND JUDAISM

The reconceptualization of Christianity as a liberal and ecumenical religion had important implications for Jews. Judaism had been undergoing a liberalization of its own. Reforms of synagogue services had begun in the 1810s, and by the mid-1840s the reform movement had spread and gained adherents.

Congregations introduced changes in traditional practices and beliefs, such as mixed seating, the use of German in services, single-day observance of festivals, and the use of a cantor and choir. The reformers' goal was to revitalize and modernize Judaism; like their liberal counterparts, Jewish liberals de-emphasized what they referred to as the mere forms of religion and emphasized instead its moral essence. Bridges between liberal Jews and liberal Christians could therefore be built.[71] Many Jews were welcomed by, and joined, the Friends of Light and German-Catholics.

However, one should not exaggerate the ecumenicism of liberal Christians. Reform Judaism was closely related to the question of Jewish emancipation. Many liberal Jews longed for full civic and political equality. German liberals debated the issue, and some, like Gustav Struve and the Mannheim dissenting minister Carl Scholl, became strong advocates, Struve calling it a "false liberalism" not to support Jewish emancipation and enfranchisement. Scholl married Regine Eller, daughter of a rabbi, in a civil ceremony in 1862.[72]

A majority of German liberals were not as enthusiastic, however, and proposals to extend civil and political equality to Jews were repeatedly defeated in state diets. Jewish emancipation should be granted, some liberals said, only after the Jews had been morally "improved." Here again, many liberals wished to transcend religious differences rather than embrace them.[73] And the religion they thought could transcend the others most often looked like some version of liberal Protestantism.

## The Socialist Critique of Liberal Religion

Early socialists shared the liberals' hostility to contemporary Catholicism and, like them, yearned for a more practical and humanitarian religion. However, most were not attracted to

liberal Protestantism. They called it an excessively individualistic and intellectual religion. They were disappointed that
liberals so often denounced selfishness and spoke about the
need for reform, but in the end proposed little beyond moral
uplift and intellectual progress.

Deeply suspicious of the English established church, the followers of Robert Owen founded their own churches. Members
of the British working class movement called Chartism called
for a return to the precepts of primitive Christianity and the
values of Jesus: equality, fraternity, and solidarity. "Christ was
the first Chartist, and Democracy is the gospel carried into
practice," declared their leader, Ernest Harney.[74] The French
socialist Etienne Cabet said "Communism *is* Christianity,"
while others said it was "the Gospels in action."[75]

Liberals in the 1830s and 1840s shared a desire for reform and
progress, but they often disagreed about what that meant in
practice. How much democracy should they favor? How many
and what kinds of social reforms should they support? Was it
okay, in certain circumstances, to advocate the use of violence
against oppressive regimes? Were colonies in the country's interest? And last but not least, what about liberalism's relationship with religion?

As it turns out, many of our preconceptions about
nineteenth-century liberalism have little support in fact. Although it would be an oversimplification to say that all liberals
were antidemocratic, most were troubled by the prospect of
universal suffrage. Nor were they all laissez-faire enthusiasts
or zealous exponents of colonialism. Their religious views were
far richer and more various than is often thought. While their
heaviest guns were directed against counterrevolutionaries

and religious and political conservatives, they argued among themselves too. Liberals from all around Europe, America, and even beyond debated the meaning of "true liberalism."

One thing stands out in all these debates that may surprise us today. Like their forebears, most mid-nineteenth-century liberals did not focus as much on defending the rights and interests of the individual as we have come to believe. To them, that would have been to advocate selfishness.

Liberals always saw themselves as fighting for the common good and continued to see this common good in moral terms. Today we may think that they were naïve, deluded, or disingenuous. But to nineteenth-century liberals, being liberal meant believing in an ethical project. It meant subscribing to a moral ideal that stretched back centuries. Liberals would have agreed with Giuseppe Mazzini who, in his essay "On the Duties of Man," declared that a liberal society could not be built on a theory of rights alone. "Rights can only exist as a consequence of duties fulfilled," he wrote, or "we run the risk of producing egoists . . . [which] always leads to disastrous and deplorable results."[76]

# CHAPTER FOUR

# The Question of Character

*The degradation of public morality will shortly, very shortly*
*perhaps, bring down upon you new revolutions.*
—ALEXIS DE TOCQUEVILLE, 1848

ON JANUARY 17, 1848, Tocqueville delivered a speech in the
French National Assembly that has since become famous.
With astounding prescience, he predicted that another revolution was fast approaching. It would come, he said, because of
the many vices of the July Monarchy, its lack of true leaders,
its unwillingness to undertake reforms, and its indifference to
the plight of the poor. His fellow deputies should beware, he
added, that because of their intransigence on so many issues
and the pervasive corruption of the political system, French
workers would no longer be content with political reform alone;
they now wanted to overthrow the whole social system. "We
are sleeping on a volcano," Tocqueville said.

The volcano Tocqueville was referring to was socialism.
Less than a month after his speech, crowds filled the streets of
Paris yet another time, this time demanding a democratic *and*
*socialist* government.

## The Debacle of 1848

The year 1846 saw a severe industrial and agricultural depression that brought tremendous hardship to French workers and peasants. By the end of 1847, one-third of Parisian workers were unemployed. Meanwhile, the French government refused to undertake reforms and to extend the suffrage, while reports of government graft and corruption were widespread.[1] Criticism of the Guizot government grew louder. In a well-known passage of his *Class Struggles in France* (1850), Karl Marx described the July Monarchy as "nothing more than a joint stock company for the exploitation of France's national wealth."

For years, liberal opposition leaders had unsuccessfully lobbied the Guizot government for an expansion of the electorate and other reforms. Frustrated, they now turned to popular agitation, staging banquets in the provinces to rally support. The plan was that the meetings would culminate in one giant banquet in Paris on February 22, 1848. Fearing an uprising, the government banned this banquet and protesters were attacked by the police. Angered by such high-handed measures, crowds of people poured into the streets shouting "down with Guizot" and "long live reform" while erecting barricades. Guizot resigned; Louis Philippe abdicated and fled France.

Egged on by the crowds, the Chamber of Deputies selected a provisional government headed by nine well-known republicans and two well-known socialists: Louis Blanc and a worker named Alexandre Martin. This government promptly called for elections to a Constituent Assembly whose mandate was to draw up a new constitution based on universal manhood suffrage. Thus, in a matter of days, France transitioned from a constitutional monarchy based on a very limited suffrage to a republic based on a more democratic suffrage than existed anywhere in Europe. The electorate increased from a quarter million to close to ten million men.

As Tocqueville had predicted, however, this expansion of the electorate was not enough to pacify the crowds. On February 25, they gathered once again, this time demanding the "right to work." Responding to the relentless popular pressure, the government announced the establishment of national workshops to employ them. It also introduced such progressive social and political measures as the abolition of the death penalty for political offenses and of slavery in the colonies.

This early phase of the revolution was met mostly with sympathy in both Britain and the United States. Chartists sent their congratulations to the French people and mounted several large demonstrations, hoping to convince their own Parliament to grant all British adult males the vote as well. John Stuart Mill greeted the news with joy. "Nothing can possibly exceed the importance of it to the world or the immensity of the interest which are at stake in its success,"[2] he said. No government should expect to survive if it did not promote reform. Louis Philippe's government had been a deeply demoralizing one, motivated by the "shameless pursuit of personal gain."[3]

Celebrations were held throughout America, and the press praised the comparatively bloodless revolution and peaceful transition of power. The American minister in Paris recognized the French Republic four days after it was proclaimed, and President Polk extended his congratulations to the people of France, calling the revolution a "sublime spectacle."[4] His message was echoed by a similar one from Congress.

News of the revolution in Paris triggered upheavals in Central Europe, where liberals, supported by workers, demanded constitutional reform. When their governments refused, people rose up and rulers capitulated. The collapse of the Prussian government encouraged liberals from the various German states to come together at an assembly in Frankfurt to draft a constitution for a united Germany. Their most cherished dreams seemed to be coming true. Frederick William IV of Prussia concluded that "Satan [was] on the loose again."[5]

The reverberations did not end there. In the Italian Peninsula and Sicily, revolts forced rulers to accede to liberal reforms. Roman rebels overthrew the pope. The leader of the Italian liberation movement, Giuseppe Garibaldi, entered the city and called on Mazzini to help form a government based on more liberal principles, including religious liberty and church/state separation. Both were promptly decreed. From his exile, Pius IX fulminated against liberalism. It was "abominable, monstrous, illegal, impious, absurd, sacrilegious and outrageous to every law, human and divine."[6]

## Liberals Battle Socialism

Elections for a new French National Assembly on April 23, 1848, were the first in Europe based on universal male suffrage. Ironically, however, they brought to power a conservative majority, including many monarchists. Utterly unsympathetic to the national workshops, they closed them. Its action provoked Parisians, as many as fifty thousand, to stage another uprising, which came to be known as the June Days.

This time refusing to concede to the pressure of the crowds, the Assembly sent General Cavaignac, famous for his brutality in Algeria, to suppress the demonstration militarily. In three days of bloody fighting, some three thousand protesters were killed and fifteen thousand more arrested, many of whom were sent to prison camps in Algeria.

Newspapers in France and abroad described the battle as one between barbarism and civilization. They called the demonstrators "madmen," "savages," and "cannibals" bent on massacre and pillage. Onlookers were particularly shocked by the participation of women in the uprising and described their cruelty and barbarity as even worse than the men's. Socialism, they concluded, was threatening society with complete chaos. When it was all over the Parisian press celebrated the victory won by "the cause of order, of the family, of civilization."[7]

Most liberals now became supporters of the so-called Party of Order, also dubbed the Liberal Union. At the request of General Cavaignac, a number of them agreed to contribute to a propaganda campaign designed to protect France from the onslaught of socialism. Charles de Montalembert, who had been elected deputy, spoke for many when he denounced the workshops, financed by the government, as a flagrant attack on property rights. Adolphe Thiers, who became a leader of the Liberal Union, published a cheap edition of his tract *On Property*, in which he accused socialists of trying to abolish the "sacred"[8] right of property and, along with it, the family. Indeed, much liberal emphasis was placed on the latter.

A new constitution was published on November 4, 1848. It gave the vote to all male citizens, but its preamble now asserted their rights *and duties*. Article IV declared family, work, property, and public order the basis of the republic. Article VII affirmed the duty of all citizens to work, save for the future, and help others, while obeying moral and written laws.

On December 10, 1848, something then happened that could never have been predicted. In a landslide, voters in France's first presidential election based on universal manhood suffrage chose Louis Napoleon Bonaparte, nephew of the former emperor as their leader. Twice during the July Monarchy had he attempted coups d'état, but both had failed miserably. When the February Revolution broke out, he was living in exile in London.

Since the death of Napoleon I, however, a Napoleonic legend had lived on, and his nephew stoked it and profited from it. He returned to Paris, stood for election, and won.

The second Napoleon deliberately modeled himself on the first. He presented himself as someone above politics who would unite the country. To those on the right, he posed as the champion of order and stability. To those on the left, he styled himself as the champion of workers, a crusader against poverty, and a leader who would defend the values of the revolution. To everyone he promised prosperity and glory.

As president, Louis Napoleon aligned himself closely with the Party of Order. Symbols of the French Revolution became illegal; red caps were outlawed, liberty trees cut down. Freedoms of assembly and the press were curtailed. His government harassed journalists and political activists, driving many underground. Protesters were summarily arrested. A new suffrage law passed in 1850 disenfranchised 30 percent of the adult male population and most Parisian workers. Some historians call the form of government he installed an early version of the modern police state.

The fear of revolution led key members of the liberal Party of Order to change their minds about the Catholic Church. They now reasoned that they needed the Church in the battle against socialism. Thiers, who had never before been particularly friendly to the Church, addressed the Assembly in January 1849. "I want to make the influence of the clergy all-powerful," he declared; "I ask that the role of *curé* be strengthened, [and] made much more important than he is, because I count on him to propagate that sound philosophy which teaches man that he is here on earth to suffer."[9] Priests, Thiers continued, should tell the people that their suffering is not the fault of the rich, but the will of God, who wants thereby to incite them to work harder for their own good.[10] A year later, French troops reinstated the pope in Rome, where he remained under their protection until 1870.

Meanwhile, the liberal Party of Order passed the so-called Falloux Laws in March 1850. These laws allowed Catholics to open their own schools and also introduced Catholic religious instruction in public schools. "Today, when violent communism threatens our society," Thiers explained, "it is essential that education calls the religious sentiment to its aid in a common war to repulse the Barbarians."[11] The objective of a Christian education was "to train a child to the yoke of obedience . . . to resist his passions, accept of his own free will the law of labor and duty, and to contract habits of order and regularity."[12]

Thiers was named to a committee on public welfare and in 1850 drafted a report on the status of the social question in France. Aid to the poor was in principle commendable, he wrote, but for such help to be "virtuous" it had to be voluntary and spontaneous. Charity should never be made obligatory because it would then become self-defeating and corrupting. It would remove any sense of gratitude in the poor. The report's conclusion was that the state should always remain constrained within the strictest limits possible.[13]

In Germany as well, early victories in 1848 were followed by liberal fears, dissensions, and failures. Once their initial battle was won, liberals started arguing among themselves. Their disarray worsened when they were confronted by worker demonstrations that sometimes led to violence. All liberals wanted reform, but they meant different things by this and had different priorities. Some thought unifying Germany under one constitution was the most important goal; others wanted to establish republics; and still others wanted major social change. Some favored universal male suffrage; others did not.

The perceived threat to property struck fear in many German liberals too, pushing them to make common cause with conservatives. What John Stuart Mill said about the French bourgeoisie likely applied to the German middle classes as well: they were filled with such "insane terror" at the thought of major social changes that they were willing to throw themselves into the arms of any government that would protect them from a socialist revolution.[14]

## Retreat and Reaction

The Revolutions of 1848 left liberals across Europe scared and demoralized. Frightened by working-class activism and weakened by their inability to agree among themselves, they were led to compromise—some would say abandon—their principles, and thereby prepared the way for the ascent of two authoritarian rulers, Napoleon III in France and, some years later, Otto von Bismarck in Germany. Liberals in Germany and Italy abandoned their hopes of unification. French troops remained in Rome until 1870, thereby preventing Italy from unifying with its natural capital. In Central Europe, Habsburg power was restored, accompanied by a brutal repression.

A period of reaction followed and lasted for about ten years. Rulers revised or withdrew the liberal constitutions they had granted and replaced liberal ministers with conservatives. In some places the authorities retaliated with brutal force. In the Grand Duchy of Baden, one-tenth of the revolutionaries who surrendered were tried by military courts and executed. Others received long prison terms, and many were forced into exile or fled to avoid prosecution. In Baden alone, some eight thousand "forty-eighters" escaped to the United States, Switzerland, and elsewhere. Reactionary governments censored the press, dissolved political clubs, and subjected suspected liberals to surveillance. All of them strengthened relations with religious orthodoxy. The pope's return to power in Rome was followed by punishing repression.

Many concluded that liberalism was now over. Some said that it had in any case been a cocktail of incompatible and outdated ideas. Liberals should give up their daydreams and resolve themselves to accepting a strong man, a "Caesar."[15]

The French were soon given that opportunity. On December 2, 1851, the anniversary of the coronation of Napoleon I in 1804 and the victory at Austerlitz in 1805, his nephew orchestrated a coup d'état against the French Republic. Louis-Napoleon arrested key opposition leaders, dissolved the Assembly, and promised a new constitution modeled on his uncle's. He followed up with a period of rule by decree, during which normal laws were suspended. Thousands were imprisoned or sent to penal colonies, thousands more forced into exile. Another plebiscite on December 2, 1852, the anniversary of his own coup, made President Louis-Napoleon Bonaparte emperor of the French.

Following his uncle's precedent, Louis Napoleon created another pseudo-democratic regime. One could say that it was Constant's and Tocqueville's worst nightmare come true: another dictatorship masquerading as a democracy. Although based on popular sovereignty and representative government, the new constitution gave Napoleon far greater powers than those enjoyed by any of his predecessors.

The best interests of democracy, said Napoleon III, were always better served by one person rather than by a political body.[16] He minimized the real power of representative assemblies. He manipulated elections and used press censorship and police surveillance to prevent the spread of any opposition. He employed an unprecedented amount of propaganda to influence public opinion and plebiscites to register ostensible popular approval for his actions. A profoundly dejected Tocqueville called it "imperial despotism."[17] Filled with loathing for the emperor, Mill said hardly anything about French politics for over a decade.[18]

Observers from abroad noted the peculiar nature of the regime: Leopold von Gerlach, Frederick William's closest political advisor, called it a "vile marriage of absolutism and liberalism."[19] British newspapers declared it a new form of autocracy: democracy and imperialism combined. Neologisms were invented to designate it: "Bonapartism," "Napoleonism," and, because the new emperor liked to style himself as Julius Caesar, "Caesarism."

Some called Napoleon III a socialist. While in prison in the 1840s he had authored a book titled *The Extinction of Pauperism*. In it he declared his desire to help the working classes. As emperor, he launched a series of social reforms ostensibly aimed to improve their lives. He opened two clinics in Paris for the sick and injured, created a program of legal assistance for those unable to afford it, and extended subsidies to companies that built low-cost housing for their workers. He launched a large-scale program of public works, hiring tens of thousands of workers to improve the sanitation, water supply, and traffic circulation of Paris. Liberals despaired that he was just trying to buy the loyalty of the workers and wean them off liberal and republican politics. He also built canals, promoted railroad development, and fostered the extension of banking and credit institutions.

To the distress of many, Napoleon granted more concessions to the Catholic Church in exchange for its support. He increased the budget devoted to religion from thirty-nine to forty-eight million francs. The number of priests increased from forty-six to fifty-six thousand. Mass was made compulsory in state schools on Thursdays and Sundays, with confession once a term. Shortly before his restoration of the empire,

Napoleon set the first stone of the new cathedral in Marseilles, and soon after that the Church of Saint-Geneviève in Paris, formerly the Pantheon, was inaugurated with great fanfare. The ceremony included moving the relics of the saint back to the church in the first major religious procession in Paris since the Restoration.[20] Meanwhile French troops remained in Rome to protect the pope.

## Pius IX

Elected to the papacy in 1846, Pius IX had promptly signaled his willingness to institute liberal reforms. He released a number of political prisoners, loosened restrictions on the press, and established a lay advisory committee to help him govern. He promised additional reforms and was soon celebrated around the world as a "liberal pope".

But the Revolutions of 1848 came as a great shock and changed his mind forever. Stunned by the violence of the crowds, and outraged by what he saw as their outrageous demands, Pius now turned against liberalism and became a force for reaction for the rest of his long reign. He forged a close relationship with Jesuits sympathetic to his increasingly reactionary views. They and other Catholic spokesmen produced a spate of books, pamphlets, and articles blaming the Revolutions of 1848 on liberalism. The people had been bewildered and bewitched by the false philosophies of the modern age, they said, and liberalism was chief among them. It had eroded religion and morality. Under its influence, the masses had become selfish and materialistic. "Society is sick, very sick,"[21] wrote one Catholic publicist. Liberalism was "pure evil."[22]

A holy war against liberalism was needed, the pope's propagandists said, or the result would be a state of license and barbarism. Liberalism and socialism were virtually the same thing, they said, or one invariably led to the other. Both meant the very negation of religion. A reeducation in the Catholic dogma was urgently needed, or liberalism would kill everything—patriotism, intelligence, morality, and honor. Apocalyptic language was enlisted to instill fear. In a book translated into several languages, the Catholic publicist Juan Donoso Cortés announced that Western civilization verged on a cataclysmic crisis, the "greatest catastrophe of history."[23] All due to liberalism.

The Vatican, in partnership with reactionary governments, launched new initiatives to reeducate the European population in Catholicism. Emotional forms of popular piety, emphasizing obedience, suffering, and the miraculous, were devised to appeal especially to women. In 1854, Pius announced the doctrine of the Immaculate Conception, by which the Virgin Mary was declared free of sin. It helped generate a major outburst of religious fervor in which especially women played a large role. Marian apparitions occurred at La Salette (1846), Lourdes (1858), and Pontmain (1871). Horrified liberals despaired at the penchant for superstition in the masses and in women especially.

In Germany, too, the state and church tightened their partnership even more after the Revolutions of 1848. Together they ceaselessly attacked rationalism, liberalism, and "the ideas of 1789." They committed more resources to Catholic missions, which visited thousands of villages, towns, and major cities. Mission priests denounced the 1848 uprisings as the work of Satan and promised eternal damnation for unrepentant sinners.

Liberal distress was increased by the fact that the missions were so enormously popular. In Germany, one attracted twenty thousand faithful. Exacerbated, liberals complained that they induced "religious insanity" and mental illness. They were a pestilence at war with the most essential liberal beliefs.

Liberals denounced the Catholic Church for its ruthless campaign "against *Bildung* . . . against light and enlightenment, against the well-being of the people, against the welfare of the state and the happiness of the family."[24]

Not to be outdone, Protestant clergymen across Germany also intensified their support for reaction with more antiliberal propaganda. The Protestant state church launched a massive campaign to convince the population that the revolutions had been an assault on the God-given order, and on God himself. The newly founded *Neue Preussische Zeitung* joined the *Evangelische Kirchenzeitung* in a common effort to destroy liberalism. Practically every issue of the *Evangelische Kirchenzeitung* in 1848 attacked the revolutionaries as godless and immoral rebels against the God-given order.

Like their counterparts elsewhere, German liberals had a depressing sense that liberalism had failed and was now over. They had fought for constitutional and representative government in a peacefully united Germany, but they had secured none of these things. Instead, their enemies seemed to have grown stronger than ever. And now liberals had acquired new enemies; foremost among them were socialists. The 1853 edition of the *Brockhaus Encyclopedia* reported that since the revolution, the political label "liberal" and the term "liberalism" had "somewhat fallen out of use."[25] Friedrich Engels declared liberalism "forever impossible in Germany."[26]

## *The Problem of Selfishness*

The failed Revolutions of 1848 led European liberals to reexamine themselves and reflect deeply on what had gone so very wrong. Why had they been so unsuccessful? Why were people attracted to socialist ideas? Why were the French masses so prone to revolution?

Most liberals rejected the idea that an unjust social system was to blame. Instead, they convinced themselves that the failure of 1848 was the result of a catastrophic breakdown in public morality. Because of it, a small group of agitators had been able to mislead the people by indoctrinating them with socialism. The Revolutions of 1848, said Tocqueville, were brought about by "some general malady of men's minds," a dangerous predilection for "strange" socialist theories.[27] The public lacked the intellectual capacity and moral qualities to make responsible decisions. Instead they were attracted to selfish and materialistic philosophies like socialism. The revolution was proof of what Tocqueville had said in *Democracy in America*: the French lacked the ideas and mores needed to sustain a liberal regime.

Observers in England and America agreed about the deplorable state of French morals. Indeed, the revolution only confirmed long-held misgivings about the French national character or lack thereof. Newspapers reported that French citizens were in a state of moral and mental debasement.[28] They lacked basic self-control. Travel accounts underscored the point. The French were relentlessly mocked for lacking the manly qualities of independence and moral fortitude.

In a way, then, liberals agreed with conservative Christians and ultra-royalists: the underlying problem was moral. The public was uneducated, selfish, and materialistic and this is what is what had caused them to embrace socialist ideas. Unlike conservatives, however, most liberals did not think that the long-term answer was a return to traditional churches, Catholic or Protestant. They did not believe that the answer to the problem lay in teaching the population religious doctrine or more respect for authority. Rather, they reasoned that the populations needed to acquire *character*. Indeed, after 1848 the problem of character became a virtual obsession for liberals.

In Britain, the disparaging depiction of French character was often accompanied by a very favorable view of their own. Britons found reasons to be proud that they were *not French.* The *Edinburgh Review* noted that, in order to function, a liberal system of government needed patriotic citizens.[29] The British were patriotic; they had a sense of community and responsibility nonexistent in France. The British also displayed a capacity for independent thought, which saved them from being duped by the propaganda of despots. In short, if Britain had avoided revolution, it was in large part due to its national character. "Thank God! We are Saxons!" exclaimed one journalist.[30]

## *The Rise of the British Liberal Party*

Right around this time, and as if to confirm this Anglo-Saxon superiority, the Liberal Party came into existence in England and went on to thrive. What did this Liberal Party stand for? What made the party "liberal"? After all, in Britain liberals did not have to fight for constitutional or representative government, since these were generally accepted even by conservatives. Being liberal in Britain largely meant what it had during the years leading up to the Revolutions of 1848, namely favoring "improvement," "reform," and "progress"—words increasingly heard during these years. It was only in 1859, however, that several parliamentary groupings joined together and officially created the British Liberal Party. Under the leadership of William Gladstone, it would dominate British politics for the rest of the century.

In mid-nineteenth century Britain, progress and reform generally meant the dismantling of aristocratic privileges, monopolies, and vested interests—including that of the Anglican Church. Liberals frequently complained that conservatives just wanted to defend ideas and practices that had outlived their usefulness. The Tory, liberals said, was a person who protected his privileges and badges of status. He felt entitled and regarded other people as subordinate and inferior. The liberal, on the other hand, was more democratically inclined. The *Bristol Gazette* explained the difference between liberals and conservatives like this: "The former are for extending the privileges of the people, the latter are for contracting them."[31] As we know, however, this did not mean that liberals stood for universal suffrage.

Beyond this commitment to reform, there were sharp divisions among members of the Liberal Party. There was no national liberal organization yet and no specific legislative program. There were liberals who favored the expansion of the franchise, others who did not. While liberals often stood for freer trade, the Liberal Party was never doctrinaire about laissez-faire. Most liberals continued to support intervention in some areas, and not in others. In retrospect, and as other historians have argued, what identified liberals was not so much any united party platform but the emphasis they placed on improving the morals of the British population.

The duty of a state, declared the *Edinburgh Review*, was to inculcate religion and morality in the population. It was the government's responsibility to raise the energy, tone, and moral character of the British population. This, then, was a principal ingredient in the Liberal Party's self-definition: the importance it accorded to the inculcation of civic responsibility, public spirit, and patriotism. Despite all the confident talk about the Anglo-Saxon race's character and capacity for self-discipline and self-government, it appears that these needed fostering and encouraging. Anglo-Saxon manliness required constant maintenance and fortification. And this was an important role of government.

## *Laissez-Faire versus* Bildung

After 1848, European liberals became virtually obsessed with educating and moralizing the public. They debated how to do it. Some advocated the dissemination and implementation of laissez-faire principles. In fact, some became very doctrinaire about it. These were the liberals who, after the experience of 1848, claimed that workers had behaved poorly because they did not understand the "laws of the economy." The workers' ignorance had made them vulnerable to chimerical and absurd ideas peddled by charlatans.[32] One of the most urgent tasks of political economists, therefore, was to disseminate a proper understanding of economics to the public at large. It was crucial to prevent socialist ideas from spreading and to counter them with the salutary lessons of laissez-faire. Workers needed to know that government efforts to overcome or even tame the laws of the economy were always doomed to failure. "Legal charity" *caused* pauperism; it didn't prevent it.

And so a number of political economists set out to do just this, in newspapers and journals, dictionaries, pamphlets, and books. The French *Dictionary of Political Economy* is one example. It was a grand illusion, it said, to think that socialism could abolish poverty. State intervention in the economy was ineffective and could actually be dangerous. Perhaps liberals should even stop using the word "social" because it inspired so many crazy ideas.[33]

After 1848, the free trader and laissez-faire ideologist Frédéric Bastiat devoted all his efforts to the struggle against socialism, rehearsing his previous ideas in ever more strident language. Giving in to the workers' demands should not be called legal charity, he wrote, since it was really "legal plunder." The problem of poverty was not due to too little government intervention, but too much. Government should provide only physical protection and justice. Beyond that, it should allow the free play of the "laws of harmony," which God himself had provided for the progress of mankind. The unobstructed competition of individual interests would generate the wealth that would flow downward to the poor. In the meantime, workers should learn to accept that their pain and suffering were "part of the providential plan."[34]

French political economists like Bastiat continued to propagate the idea that the poverty and misery of the working classes were mainly their own fault. They were lazy, irresponsible, and prone to prodigality. To pull themselves out of poverty, they needed to learn good habits: regularity, diligence, and sobriety. They needed to learn the value of hard work, responsibility, and self-reliance—all of which were taught by the market and religion. Most importantly, workers needed to understand that the government had nothing to do with their hardship. Nature assigned each person to his position in society, and the only way to better one's condition was by improving one's own character.

John Smith Prince was a great fan of Bastiat and translated his *Economic Harmonies* into German in 1850. Smith denied that there even was a "social question." The economy was subject to certain unalterable laws. To disregard these laws in search of a solution to social discontent would do more harm than good. The only way to diminish the level of suffering was to grow the economy through the free operation of the market. Workers should be made to understand that their distress was due mainly to their own failings. Self-help and personal responsibility were the only solution.

But such extreme laissez-faire ideas were far from representative of liberal opinion in Germany. Liberals there worried more than ever that industrial development under conditions of laissez-faire would lead to the emergence of a proletariat, that is, to a group of people sunk in material poverty and spiritual degradation. Most of them rejected doctrinaire laissez-fairism and continued to use the pejorative terms "Smithianism" and "Manchesterism" to indicate that such ideas were impracticable, ineffective, and even immoral.

John Stuart Mill also rejected any doctrinaire or extremist adherence to laissez-faire principles. Ever the Francophile, he even wrote to the socialist Louis Blanc to express sympathy with certain socialist ideas in 1848. As Mill later explained, he and his wife gave much time "to the study of the best Socialist writers on the continent."[35]

Mill's attraction to aspects of socialism only grew over time, as can be seen in the changes he made to the second and third editions of his *Principles of Political Economy*. He became ever more sensitive to social problems and receptive to the idea that poverty had little to do with the moral failings of the poor, and more with the "grand failure of the existing arrangement of society." What was needed, Mill came to believe, was "social transformation."[36] In 1866, he entered Parliament as a Liberal and fought hard against any policies based on the principles of laissez-faire.[37]

Over the course of the fifties and sixties French commentators increasingly spread the idea that a middle way had to be forged between laissez-faire and socialism. The liberalism of the laissez-faire economists, wrote one publicist, was a *false* liberalism that only encouraged social atomism.[38] What was needed was "liberal socialism."[39] The state should become an "instrument of civilization."[40]

Mill's French friend and translator Charles Dupont-White used the derogative term "individualist" to refer to those who preached laissez-faire. A system based solely on competition and self-interest was, in his mind, completely unsustainable. The state should step in to protect and promote the public good. Progress required more, not less, action by the government. What was needed now, he said, was "legal charity." And although he favored free trade in principle, he insisted that "there is no liberty without regulation."[41]

Like many other liberals at the time, Dupont-White worried less about government intervention than the sorts of human beings modern society was creating. Tocqueville's *Democracy in America* warned its readers that democratic society had a tendency to encourage selfishness. Mill, who reviewed both volumes of Tocqueville's book, agreed. Democracy had a natural propensity to erode character. Modern men, he wrote, were susceptible to becoming narrow-minded and egoistical. It was important to cultivate a different spirit to counter this tendency to moral degradation. This was the proposition of his famous essay *On Liberty* (1859), in which Mill expressed worries not so much about the dangers of state interventionism, but about how to encourage the moral education of mankind.

## The Role of the Family

To speak of the moralization of mankind invariably meant to speak of women. For centuries, theologians, jurists, and political thinkers had contended that women played crucial roles as the socializers and moralizers of their families. Having a wife and family was said to tame and civilize men who were otherwise prone to selfish, irritable, and even violent behavior. A widespread consensus held that women were more loving, compassionate, and giving than men, and that they taught the values on which any social order depended: self-sacrifice, discipline, and compassion for others. Such values were important in democracies, where men ran an especially high risk of losing their character. "No free communities ever existed without morals," said Tocqueville: "morals are the work of woman."[42] Indeed women were one of the secrets of America's success, he wrote in *Democracy in America*.

Thus it was especially disturbing for liberals to see women participating in uprisings. During the Revolutions of 1848, newspapers as far away as the United States expressed shock over the involvement of women in the upheaval. It was reported that they had been as angry, violent, and vindictive as the men, a clear reversal of the moral and natural order. French women had "unsexed" themselves by their conduct.[43] Newspapers also reported that women and girls had been raped and tortured in the streets, all of which reinforced the message that women's participation in contentious politics was disastrous to public morals.

People across the political spectrum agreed that the moral health of a nation depended to a large extent on women playing their designated domestic role. Where there was disagreement was not over the importance of women, but over *what* moral values they should teach their families. The Catholic Church decreed that women should teach traditional Christian values: humility, piety, and obedience to authority. Liberals said that they should teach character and manliness, qualities essential to responsible citizenship. Having a wife and family taught men sobriety, industriousness, and personal responsibility. In the bosom of the family, and under the influence of their wives, men acquired the habit of regulating themselves. They learned self-command.

Many liberals also advocated a different kind of marriage, based not on patriarchy but on companionship. Giuseppe Mazzini called the family "the cradle of Humanity," but said that it could inspire the right values only if it was based on mutual love and respect, not male authority. He asked men to think of women as partners, not subordinates.[44] For John Stuart Mill, the family, as presently construed, was a "school of despotism"; as such, it could never mold children into responsible citizens. The only way the family could teach morals was if it was a partnership of equals.[45]

Most liberally inclined women did not deny their "natural" difference, nor their primary role as wives and mothers. In this, they were no different from their eighteenth-century forebears. The Parisian newspaper *Voix des femmes*, launched in 1848, echoed Tocqueville when it said that the morality of a nation depended on the morality of women. When women asked for reforms, it was so that they could better fulfill their duties; they wanted to participate more fully in "the regeneration of humanity." How could they be expected to educate their families properly if their own minds were "debase[d] and enslave[d]"?[46] To do their job, they needed first to raise themselves intellectually and morally.

Liberals, whether male or female, differed on the question of the vote. Very few followed the lead of American feminists Elizabeth Cady Stanton and Lucretia Mott, who campaigned for women's suffrage. Undeterred by the negative newspaper accounts of female participation in the European revolutions, Stanton and Mott organized the first national women's convention in Seneca Falls, New York, less than a month after the notorious June Days in Paris. They issued a Declaration of Sentiments modeled on the Declaration of Independence, proclaiming "all men *and women* are created equal," and added a list of grievances to the declaration's second part.

The British philosopher and women's rights advocate Harriet Taylor was also an outspoken advocate of the female vote. Her essay on "The Enfranchisement of Women," published in the *Westminster Review* in July 1851, promoted full equality for women in all rights, political, civil, and social. Until women possessed such rights, she said, they would remain the slaves of men. No individual should be allowed to decide for another what was in his or her proper sphere. Every occupation should be open to all, with complete liberty of choice for everyone. Following Taylor, her husband, John Stuart Mill, also argued for the full equality of women, including the franchise. He took the additional step of questioning whether women's natures were, in actual fact, so different from men's. "What is now called the nature of women," he reasoned, "is an eminently artificial thing—the result of forced repression in some directions, unnatural stimulation in others."[47]

Mill had many disciples and admirers, including Louis Dittmar in Germany. Dittmar agreed that a properly constituted family was essential to the health of a liberal state, and that keeping women in a state of legal subordination would fail to moralize society. Women needed the vote as well as access to better education and economic independence. Only then could there be the happy and morally sound families upon which a successful liberal society depended. Women's "slave-chains" had to be broken.

Liberals who advocated the female vote were in a distinct minority, however. Most liberals at the time ridiculed the idea. The German jurist and liberal politician Johann Bluntschli spoke for many when he declared that granting women political rights would be both "dangerous for the state and ruinous for women."[48] Women were sentimental beings and their judgments were flawed. Their health would be ruined if they left the confines of their homes. Women's supposed emotionalism, weakness, and irrationality led liberals like Bluntschli to maintain that they needed to be governed by men.

## *The Religion of Humanity*

Questions of morals were also, as always, closely intertwined with those of religion. The failure of the Revolutions of 1848 only reinforced the liberal belief that a religious reformation was necessary before any real political progress could be made.

For Mill, one of the main lessons of the revolutions was that the minds of the community had to be changed before any new and socialist ideas had a chance of succeeding. A "real amelioration in the intellectual and moral state" of mankind was necessary. One way was through more equitable marriages; another was a liberal education that taught students "ethics and politics, in the largest sense."[49] But Mill also thought that changing the minds of modern men required a change in religion. Christianity fixed people's thoughts on their own salvation, making them selfish and disconnected from any sense of duty to their fellow men. What was needed, Mill wrote, was a "Religion of Humanity" that would cultivate in individuals "a deep feeling for the general good."[50]

As we have seen, since the very conception of liberalism, reforming religion had been a liberal concern. Constant and de Staël had argued for the need of a new and enlightened version of Protestantism. Now, growing numbers of liberals across Europe adopted the term "Religion of Humanity" for what they had in mind. What was needed, they said, was "a new and benign gospel" to inspire devotion to the common good.[51] Bluntschli also called it the "Religion of Jesus," stripped of dogmas and dedicated to the teaching of morals.[52]

French liberals, who lived in an overwhelmingly Catholic country, were the most prolific on the topic. Historian and professor Edgar Quinet, an admirer of Benjamin Constant's writings on religion, agreed with him that a liberal form of Protestantism would be best. It would help France transition out of Catholicism. In his 1856 book *A Letter on the Religious and Moral Situation in Europe*, Quinet reasoned that centuries of Catholicism in collusion with absolute rule had made the French indolent, servile, selfish, and materialistic. They harbored an unhealthy respect for authority and a complete disregard for individual responsibility. But the problem was that they were unlikely to give up their Catholicism all at once. It would be impossible to convert them to "the pure light of reason" overnight. What was needed, then, was an interim religion that would help the French to transition. That religion, Quinet thought, could be the Unitarianism of the American preacher William Ellery Channing.

Other French liberals spoke similarly of the need for a transition religion. In his *Letters on the Religious Question*, the popular novelist Eugene Sue wrote that the population could not be expected to renounce Catholicism in one fell swoop. Unitarianism was an acceptable interim faith because it taught civic virtue, patriotism, and hatred of despotism. It could be a path toward natural religion.[53] Some liberals said that Unitarianism could lead people to an even better religion, namely the "Religion of Humanity"; others said that it *was* the Religion of Humanity.[54] Admirers of Channing began to disseminate his ideas through articles in journals like *Journal des Débats* and by translating his writings into French.

Many liberals elsewhere in Europe also remained very critical of Catholicism. The German *Staats-Lexikon* was generally hostile and, when it came to the Jesuit Order, positively vituperative. Jesuits, it said, had declared an all-out war "against *Bildung* and the humanity of our time, against light and enlightenment, against the well-being of the people, against the welfare of the state and the happiness of the family."[55] They were a disease that endangered the most sacred liberal beliefs. The self-declared enemies of human progress, Jesuits were "criminals against mankind."[56] One could hardly be more hostile.

German liberals did not just abhor Catholicism, however; orthodox versions of Protestantism were almost equally abhorrent to them. In 1863 Bluntschli helped form the Protestant Association, whose aim was to combat reactionary religion whether Catholic or Protestant. Every year or two, his association held conferences to promote the separation of church and state. One speaker defined the association's target as "Jesuitism of the Catholic *and Protestant* varieties."[57]

On the other hand, Bluntschli was relatively welcoming to liberal Jews. His article on Judaism in the *Staatsworterbuch* maintained that modern Jews had "stopped being a particular people." They had shown by their recent behavior a desire to belong to the European population. Jews were therefore no longer foreigners in Germany, but compatriots.[58] Of course, not all liberals were this friendly.

Many liberals thought that Freemasonry was another way to teach the Religion of Humanity. Throughout Europe and America, they joined Masonic lodges in droves. Lodge speeches often trumpeted the brotherhood's goal of inculcating inner virtue and uprightness. Freemasonry's aim, it was said, was "moral *Bildung.*" In Masonic lodges, men learned how to govern themselves and acquired "true masculinity." Bluntschli called the lodges "schools of humanity." Masons, he said, advocated a human religion that taught "noble morals."[59] While they were very anti-Catholic, lodges in Hamburg, Leipzig, and Frankfurt began admitting Jews in the 1840s, and soon lodges elsewhere followed suit.

Masonic rituals were described as a kind of baptism during which men were spiritually reborn. One mason recounted: "I noticed that I had now been taken up into a community of men, of brothers, of magnanimous souls. . . . I had become another human being."[60] This is no doubt one reason why Pope Pius IX sharply condemned Masonic lodges, calling them the "Synagogue[s] of Satan." In total, the Catholic Church condemned Freemasonry eight times during the nineteenth century (in 1846, 1849, 1854, 1863, 1864, 1865, 1873, and 1875).

Not all liberals sought new religions to promote their moralizing and educational goals. In England, many liberals thought they could work within the established Anglican Church. There also remained Catholics who believed that Catholicism and liberal politics could be compatible and mutually reinforcing. The historian and politician John Acton, later Lord Acton, was one such Catholic. He belonged to what he called the Catholic "liberal party" and became a close friend and advisor of William Gladstone. Acton admired Catholic liberals like Montalembert. But Catholicism, Acton said, should be reformed if it hoped to remain vital in the modern world. It should be more open to science and new knowledge. Some temporary, or merely outward, elements of dogma should be revised and the obligation to blindly obey the pope rejected.[61]

{≈≈≈⊙w⊙≈≈≈}

The Revolutions of 1848 were a great shock and setback for liberals. It forced them to realize that they had new and powerful enemies. Absolute monarchists and Catholic counterrevolutionaries remained a major threat. But they now faced new threats from the left as well: a host of political tendencies such as radical democracy, republicanism, and even socialism.

Once they had recovered, liberals thought long and hard about why the revolutions had occurred. They placed the blame on neither an unjust political system nor an exploitative economy. Instead, they blamed the morals—or lack thereof—of the public. The poor had been seduced by socialism; they had been tricked into believing in a selfish and materialistic ideology that threatened the entire social and political order, including their own lives and livelihoods. In this, liberals in fact agreed with conservatives: social problems were essentially moral problems. They became more than ever obsessed with the need to moralize and educate the public. This led them to a renewed emphasis on the family and the need for religious reform.

CHAPTER FIVE

# Caesarism and Liberal Democracy

## NAPOLEON III, LINCOLN, GLADSTONE, AND BISMARCK

*The first duty imposed on those who now direct society is to educate democracy.*

—ALEXIS DE TOCQUEVILLE, 1835

TOCQUEVILLE WAS ONLY one among many liberals who blamed the Revolutions of 1848 on widespread moral degeneration. The revolution, they concluded, had been caused by the materialism, selfishness, and irrationality of the French people. The masses were easy prey for demagogues who peddled crazy ideas.

Such negative views of the public were the reason why the term "liberal democracy" would have seemed self-contradictory to most liberals in the nineteenth century. Successive revolutions and the reigns of two Napoleons had made it clear how very easily democracy could ally itself with despotism. Democracy, it was plain to see, was naturally *illiberal.*

But liberals also knew that the problem was not just the public. There was an issue of leadership as well. The first duty of those who directed society, wrote Tocqueville in *Democracy of America,* was to "educate democracy." The leaders of the July Monarchy had abdicated this responsibility; they had been indifferent and selfish, and this had led to an unnecessary revolution followed by another dictatorship.

Were democracies doomed to being illiberal? Could they, with the right leadership, become liberal? In the 1850s and 1860s, the emergence of four powerful leaders aroused reflections on that question.

## Napoleon III and Caesarism

As both a person and a leader, Napoleon III was the target of an enormous amount of mockery and disdain. Karl Marx called him "a grotesque mediocrity" and ridiculed his reign as a pathetic farce. Others called him a "dwarf," a "disgusting dwarf," a "scoundrel," a "thief," a "tyrant," and even a "murderer." Perhaps the most famous insult came from one of France's greatest writers, Victor Hugo, who ridiculed the emperor with the title "Napoleon the Little." He was, said the liberal politician Charles de Rémusat, an "idiot" beneath contempt. But Rémusat also recognized that Napoleon III "changed the course of history."[1]

The second Napoleonic regime, deliberately modeled on the first, attracted much commentary from around the world. Foreign observers noted with dismay that a revolution followed by a democratic election had once again yielded a dictator. The *Living Age,* a New York City journal, reasoned that universal suffrage in France was impossible since the only thing the French ever voted for was "their own subjection to a new master."[2] US Secretary of State Daniel Webster called Louis Napoleon's rule a catastrophe that might weaken everyone's faith in the future of democracy.[3] Once again, the public had voted for a dictator and demagogue.

Louis Napoleon's regime was very much the kind of government that Benjamin Constant had tried so hard to prevent fifty years earlier: an authoritarian government based on universal manhood suffrage. Claiming to represent the people, the emperor exploited their worst instincts for his own benefit. It was a kind of déjà vu, although in some ways even worse. This time, a popular election had served to establish a despotism more absolute than any in French history. It only confirmed Tocqueville's insight that democratic societies were especially vulnerable to new and more insidious forms of oppression. Over time, and thanks partly to the second Napoleon, Tocqueville became more pessimistic about the prospects of democracy.[4]

Interest in Napoleon III's form of government was especially intense because it seemed to constitute a new and hybrid type of rule—economically progressive yet socially conservative, popular but authoritarian. Modern scholars have likened it to both a police state and a welfare state, although those terms and concepts did not yet exist. While the emperor imposed new authoritarian measures and used censorship and surveillance to stifle any opposition, he offered workers an unprecedented range of relief measures: soup kitchens, price controls on bread, insurance schemes, retirement plans, orphanages, nurseries, and hospitals. He subsidized workers' banquets, festivals, and prize-giving ceremonies. He offered tax relief and grants to developers willing to build inexpensive housing. He sponsored a delegation of French workers to the

London Exposition of 1862. And all of it was widely reported in the state-controlled press. Tocqueville thought the words "despotism" and "tyranny" inadequate for this kind of rule. "The thing itself is new," he said, setting out to analyze it.[5] In the end, the word adopted to describe this kind of despotism was "Caesarism."

Caesarism became the name for a modern form of democratic dictatorship, the rule of a military strongman who centralized power in his own hands, while claiming to embody the will of the people. The word was used interchangeably with "Napoleonism" or "bonapartism" and was not necessarily a term of abuse. The first sustained theory of Caesarism was actually developed by Auguste Romieu, an admirer of Napoleon III, in a short treatise called *The Age of Caesars* in 1850. Some conservatives thanked Napoleon III's Caesarism for restoring order. Some socialists praised him for his Caesarism too.

Caesarism was an appropriate label for Napoleon III's form of government for several reasons. The original Napoleon had modeled himself on the Roman dictator, and the second Napoleon emulated his uncle in every way possible. He owed his power and prestige to his uncle's name and to the myth it evoked, so he used allusions to both Napoleon I and Caesar to portray himself as a similarly heroic and inspirational leader. His coup d'état on December 2, 1851, was code-named "operation Rubicon." He even published a *History of Julius Caesar* in which he described the Roman dictator as a "superior man" guided by "elevated motives" whose rule was the "path [the French] ought to follow."[6]

References to Caesar and Caesarism multiplied during the 1860s. Criticizing Caesar, lamenting the decline of the Roman Republic, or just evoking the name Brutus became ways to criticize Napoleon.

In the 1860s, following a number of personal setbacks, the emperor began to liberalize his regime. He gave the National Assembly the right to review and approve the budget and allowed Adolphe Thiers, who had been exiled in 1851, to return to France. He relaxed press controls and this triggered a flood of articles, pamphlets, and books calling for more reforms. They carried titles such as *Liberal Politics*, *The Liberal Opposition*, *The Liberal Program*, or *The Liberal Party*.[7] Thiers became the leader of what some people again called the Liberal Union. In the 1869 elections, liberals received almost 45 percent of the vote. Liberalism, it seemed, was back.

But what exactly did it mean? What did being liberal signify in France in the 1860s? Once again, the Liberal Party was not unified. Some thought it not much more than an umbrella term for people who wanted reform. "Everybody calls himself liberal,"[8] complained Jules Simon, a leading liberal politician. The dissensions made it hard to come up with a platform with which everyone could agree. There were Bonapartist liberals, Orleanist liberals, and republican liberals. There were even liberal legitimists. When it came to economic policy, there were sharp divisions. Some were for tariffs; others were not. Some were antisocialist; others held more nuanced views. Some favored reforms for women, but they argued over which ones. This is why liberals called themselves a loose coalition or union. Edouard de Laboulaye, who emerged as one of the most influential liberal theorists of his day, referred to them as "a universal church where there is room for whoever believes in liberty."[9]

To Laboulaye, and to a sizable group of others, being liberal meant working with the emperor to introduce reform. They insisted again and again that they had no wish to provoke a revolution or topple the government. They sought gradual reforms to institute a genuinely representative system with real elections and a responsible ministry. They wanted power decentralized and individual rights enshrined in law, among which they regarded a free press as particularly important.

Liberals often pointed to the English and American constitutions as models from which the French should learn. "We have before our eyes two great nations that possess sincerely liberal institutions," said one pamphlet, "England and the United States." It didn't matter so much that one was a monarchy and the other a republic; France could learn from both.[10]

As always, most liberals were mistrustful, and often even hostile to democracy; but now they were also resigned to its inevitability. As Tocqueville had said, there was no way of stopping what was willed by Providence. This realization made it ever more pressing to channel it, contain it, and make it *safe*. And to make democracy safe meant educating and moralizing the public.

It was to educate the electorate that Auguste Nefftzer founded the newspaper *Le Temps* in 1861. A liberal Protestant from the Alsace region of France, Nefftzer had previously worked on several newspapers and had served a month in prison for publishing an article critical of Napoleon III. Nefftzer had also studied theology in Germany and in 1858 had cofounded the French-language *Revue Germanique*, whose purpose was to bring German thought and culture to France.

As stated on the front page of *Le Temps*'s first issue, the goal of the Liberal Party was to enlighten democracy, to elevate it and give it "capacity." This was also a main point of a remarkable article on liberalism written by Nefftzer and published in his paper. Public instruction, said Nefftzer, was the most important goal of any liberal agenda.[11] Without it, democracy would inevitably slide down the slippery slope to Caesarism.

A liberal democracy, Nefftzer explained, was a special kind of democracy. It was one that placed constitutional limits on state power and guaranteed certain fundamental individual freedoms. Foremost among these guarantees was freedom of thought, from which all other freedoms derived: freedoms of religion, teaching, association, and the press. These were the freedoms that would save democracy from its inherently despotic tendencies.

It was largely to convey this same lesson that Edouard Laboulaye brought out a new edition of Benjamin Constant's *Course in Constitutional Politics* in 1861. Today, Laboulaye is best known as the person who organized the gift of the Statue of Liberty to America. In 1861, he was professor of comparative law at the Collège de France and the country's foremost authority on the United States. Like Tocqueville, whom he admired greatly, Laboulaye thought France had much to learn from America.

Making a new edition of Constant's major writings available to the general public made a lot of sense. After all, Constant's liberalism was conceived in reaction to the despotism of the first Napoleon, and he had helped the emperor liberalize his regime in 1815. Perhaps Laboulaye hoped to convince the second Napoleon to accept Constant's liberal principles, as his uncle had fifty years before.

It is no accident that Laboulaye's introduction contained long passages about the Roman emperor, Julius Caesar. His rise to power, Laboulaye asserted, had been facilitated by the Roman people's moral debasement. By contrast, Laboulaye evoked favorably the "German spirit" exhibited by the brave and freedom-loving barbarians, who resisted the emperor. Any reader would easily have known to whom he was referring.

It was in this context that the expression "liberal democracy" came into existence. One of the first persons to use it was Charles de Montalembert. As we recall, Montalembert was the Catholic nobleman who had been reprimanded by the pope for his liberalism in 1830. In 1858, he had been imprisoned by Napoleon for an article praising England's constitutional system. Now, in 1863, Montalembert once again defied authorities, both political and religious, by delivering two very public and controversial speeches in Malines, Belgium. The speeches were then published and disseminated widely.

Next to France, Belgium was perhaps the only other success story of the 1830 Revolutions. An uprising in August of that year had led to the establishment of an independent country, with a lasting constitutional parliamentary monarchy. And despite the fact that Belgium was predominantly Catholic, its constitution guaranteed religious freedom and recognized the separation of church and state.

The first controversial thing Montalembert did in his speech was to ask Catholics around the world to heed Belgium's example. They should surrender their support for absolute monarchy and accept the separation of church and state. The old regime was dead, Montalembert said, and Catholics should stop dreaming of its restoration. A "free church in a free state" should be their goal. There was not a single modern freedom that could not be useful to the Catholic Church, he insisted, going so far as to say that freedom of conscience was the most necessary, precious, and "sacred" right of all.[12]

Montalembert also spoke to liberals. Democracy was unstoppable, he said, so there was no sense trying to resist it. Instead, they should fight to make democracy *become* liberal. They could do this by fighting for the recognition of essential freedoms, such as freedoms of thought, press, and teaching as well as the separation of church and state. Resisting an "anti-liberal" democracy, and fighting instead to help "democracy become liberal," should be the liberals' goal. Turning an "imperial democracy" into a liberal one was the crucial task at hand.

To Montalembert, the term "liberal democracy" was clearly an aspirational rather than descriptive term. It was something liberals should fight for, a goal to be attained. It was different from pure democracy or imperial democracy in that it was a genuinely representative form of government that placed limits on the government's powers and recognized certain essential liberties. Among these, the most important were, once again, freedoms to think, read, criticize, and publish freely. But these freedoms were necessary not for the sake of freedom itself, nor for the mere protection of the rights or interests of citizens, but to enable their education and moral improvement. Making democracy liberal meant battling against the selfishness and materialism that so often accompanied it, and that made it vulnerable to Caesarism.[13]

Montalembert thought that liberals needed to learn another lesson as well. Catholicism need not be their enemy, he said. On the contrary, Catholicism was ideally suited to help democracies become liberal because it encouraged people to lead a moral life. Catholicism served as an antidote to the "passion for well-being" that overwhelmed and eventually corrupted democratic societies.

In the years to come, the concept of Caesarism helped liberals understand and confront the dangers of modern democracy. Closely identified with the reign of Napoleon III, it caused them to focus, once again, on the interlinked problems of public education and public morals. In an 1865 article for the *Economist* titled "Caesarianism as It Now Exists," a British journalist went to the heart of the matter. Napoleon III was deliberately preventing the dissemination of information to the public to keep the French in a state of intellectual and political immaturity. This was the most dangerous and indeed tragic aspect of his form of rule. Napoleon allowed no individual thought, no criticism.[14]

An entry on Caesarism in the 1867 Larousse *Dictionary* reiterated the point. Caesarism was a form of rule that both encouraged and profited from the ignorance of the masses. According to Littré's *Dictionary* of 1873, the word applied to "those peoples who cannot or do not know how to govern themselves."[15]

In fact, Montalembert was only reiterating what liberals from Constant and Madame de Staël to Mill and Tocqueville had repeatedly stressed: the need for education and moral improvement. Laboulaye admired the fact that Constant, like other liberal Protestants of his day, viewed liberty as connected to the idea of human "perfectibility." The liberty that these liberals sought had nothing to do with egoism, or the pursuit of material pleasures, for which Laboulaye, Montalembert, and any number of them showed only contempt. That is why they spoke so often of the need to foster "individuality" instead of "individualism." The true source of man's right to liberty was his duty to improve himself. This also meant imbibing the values of patriotism, dedication, and self-sacrifice, in short, what a liberal like Nefftzer called civic virtue, and which the French so sorely lacked. Only then could they hope to govern themselves in a "liberal democracy."

"The supreme goal," wrote Laboulaye, "the most elevated goal a man can propose here below, is to develop the whole of his faculties; to improve himself, even at the cost of suffering." In a similar vein, Nefftzer wrote that liberalism was dependent upon generosity and public spirit. Liberalism depended on the awareness that "a free man has his rights, but also duties."[16]

Montalembert's speeches drew a prompt and stinging rebuke from Pius IX. The pope reacted much the same way his predecessors had: by issuing a sternly denunciating encyclical. His *Quanta Cura*, with its attached *Syllabus of Errors*, condemned liberalism wholesale. He decreed, as a matter of official Catholic doctrine, that liberalism was fundamentally incompatible with Catholicism. He explicitly denounced church and state separation, popular sovereignty, freedom of conscience, and freedom of the press. He rejected eighty such liberal propositions, declaring it a "monstrous error" to believe that the Church could reconcile itself with liberalism. There could be no accommodation between the Church and modern culture, ideas, or politics. Catholicism should *not* be called on to make democracies liberal.

Over time, the *Quanta Cura* and *Syllabus of Errors* would become the most frequently cited and discussed Catholic documents of all time. Catholic propagandists reinforced their message, often in strident and unforgiving terms. They loudly proclaimed the Church's implacable opposition to any compromise with liberal values, ceaselessly denouncing liberals as anti-Christian and immoral. By weakening the Church vis-à-vis the state, it was the liberal Catholics themselves who were responsible for Caesarism, one such publicist claimed.[17]

The pope's pronouncements were yet another blow for the many Catholics who considered themselves liberal. One of them was the American Orestes Brownson, a notorious weathervane when it came to religion. Baptized into the Presbyterian Church as a teenager, he converted to Universalism, and later embraced Unitarianism, followed by Transcendentalism, before converting to Catholicism in 1844. From that point on, Brownson was a tireless and vocal defender of the Catholic Church. But he also supported the attempts of Catholic liberals in Europe to demonstrate the mutually sustaining relationship between Catholicism and political liberalism.

The problem, Brownson tried to explain, was that most Catholics did not understand the fundamental difference between *religious* and *political* liberalism. They mistakenly rejected liberalism wholesale. Brownson agreed that religious liberalism was a very bad thing. Based on rationalism, it inevitably led to the denial of revelation, which in turn encouraged a sinful disrespect for all authority. Liberalism of the religious sort inevitably led to permissiveness, moral chaos, and eventually society's ruin. Political liberalism, on the other hand, was another word for the American constitutional system, for which Brownson expressed only approval and even reverence.

The *Syllabus of Errors* of 1864 reinforced the conviction of many liberals that Catholicism was among their most formidable foes. It triggered a spate of publications advocating church-state separation and promoting liberal Christianity and liberal Protestantism. The works of the American Unitarian preacher William Ellery Channing were translated and disseminated.

One of the leading French advocates of the separation of church and state was Edouard de Laboulaye. In his opening series of lectures at the Collège de France in 1849, he had praised the "absolute freedom of religion" that he believed was guaranteed by the American Constitution, and that contrasted so starkly with the situation in France. Laboulaye had Channing's works translated and disseminated, thereby helping to initiate a wave of enthusiasm for American Unitarianism among French liberal intellectuals. The more radical ideas of Theodore Parker, Channing's disciple, were also translated and published, often in the form of excerpts. What France needed, admirers of both Channing and Parker said, was an entirely nondogmatic, unorthodox religion that promoted morality. This religion should accept within its fold everyone, Catholics, Protestants, Jews, and perhaps even atheists, as long as they were committed to the higher purpose of perfecting man and humanity. Some called this ecumenical religion the "Religion of Jesus Christ."

The Protestant theologian Albert Réville, professor of the history of religion at the prestigious Collège de France, recommended Parker's liberal religion, which he said was enlightened and moralizing, in harmony with the institutions, liberties, and new needs of modern society. It was, said Réville, an eminently practical religion, which encouraged men to be industrious, inspired the domestic and social virtues, and supported republican and democratic values. Quoting Parker, Réville wrote that a religion like Unitarianism was "a marvelous instrument of political liberalism," because "all liberalisms are interrelated."[18]

The time must have seemed propitious to French liberals. Not only was Napoleon liberalizing his political regime, but his relations with the pope were souring. During the first decade of his rule, the ties between Church and state had strengthened. The Church had strongly supported his coup d'état and had been rewarded with significant concessions. By the 1860s, however, tensions had begun to appear. Liberals seized on the growing rift to lobby for the separation of Church and state, and they became more insistent over time.

Like his uncle, however, Napoleon was unwilling to promote liberal Protestantism. In any case, the Franco-Prussian War soon removed him from power. The project of moralizing France and liberalizing democracy was put on hold, but only temporarily.

## Abraham Lincoln and His Liberal Friends throughout the World

While French liberals struggled to liberalize their Caesarian democracy, a leader emerged across the Atlantic who came to symbolize the kind of ruler for whom they yearned. That leader was Abraham Lincoln, who is one of the most admired presidents in US history.

It's not that Lincoln wasn't accused of Caesarism, because he was. There were those who charged him with deliberately amassing despotic powers, violating civil liberties, provoking the Civil War, and destroying the republic. Because of this, calls were issued for people to learn from Roman history, resist Lincoln's usurpations of power, and even assassinate him. After firing his gun in the theater's presidential box and leaping down to the stage, assassin John Wilkes Booth waved his weapon and cried out to the audience, "Sic semper tyrannis. The South is avenged."

There were also Europeans who accused Lincoln of Caesarism. They saw the United States under Lincoln as another example of a democracy degenerating into military despotism. Many in Britain—including numerous liberals—regarded the American president as nothing more than an aspiring tyrant, a demagogue who hypocritically used the issue of slavery to exert the North's authority over the South. From history, they knew that democracies were destined to failure.

On the other hand, there were also many European liberals who admired the American president, seeing in him the very opposite of a demagogue or despot. To them, he was a leader who disproved the notion that modern democracies were doomed and who showed, rather, that democracies could be liberal.

French liberals' admiration for Lincoln had much to do with his abolitionism. Going back to Benjamin Constant and Madame de Staël, they saw slavery as a stain on America's national character, and many worked to end it by joining various antislavery societies, making speeches, and publishing books and articles. In fact, all the French liberals named in this book were adamantly opposed to both the slave trade and slavery itself, which had been abolished on French territory in 1848.

Well before the outbreak of the Civil War, Lincoln was aware of European liberals' support for abolition. He read European newspapers and took an interest in the activities of European reformers. In a speech given in Peoria, Illinois, in 1854, he recognized those he called "the liberal party throughout the world," who disapproved of slavery and thought it contradicted the principles of the American Constitution. Their reproaches, Lincoln said, "are not the taunt of enemies . . . but the warning of friends."[19]

Lincoln may very well have read the open letter Tocqueville published in the American abolitionist newspaper the *Liberty Bell* in 1856. Describing himself as "the persevering enemy of despotism everywhere," Tocqueville said that he was pained by the fact that the freest people in the world maintained slavery. Calling himself an old and sincere friend of America, he hoped to see the day when the law would grant equal civil liberty to all. The prominent American journalist and abolitionist William Lloyd Garrison reprinted the letter in his paper the *Liberator*.

Lincoln also corresponded with French liberal Agénor de Gasparin. In 1861, Gasparin published a book asking how it could be that a liberal people like the Americans maintained slavery. The next year, he followed up with another book, which was translated into English. By electing Lincoln, Gasparin said, a liberal and generous people had cast off material self-interest to fight for the noble cause of emancipation. Lincoln's battle against slavery was, to Gasparin as to many French liberals, "the greatest liberal contest of our times."[20] Lincoln responded with a letter of thanks, telling Gasparin that he was "much admired in America . . . and much loved for your generosity to us, and your devotion to liberal principles generally."[21] The two men corresponded throughout the war.

Such shared liberal values were the basis of a transatlantic network of men who admired Lincoln greatly and viewed the Civil War similarly. Members included John Stuart Mill, Edouard de Laboulaye, Charles de Montalembert, and a number of influential American and British journalists, editors, and public intellectuals. Charles Eliot Norton, editor of the most influential transatlantic journal, the *North American Review*, was a member of the group, as was Norton's friend, Goldwin Smith, a professor of history at Oxford University. Smith later became president of the American Historical Association. Another friend of Norton's, Edwin L. Godkin, editor of New York City's the *Nation*, also belonged to the circle. Godkin's father had been an advisor to William Gladstone, the British Liberal prime minister. Finally, one must include George William Curtis, an editor at *Harper's Weekly*.

United by what they called their "political liberality of thought," these gentlemen, from Britain, France, and America, believed that men like themselves were the trustees of political progress. They supported Lincoln and the North in the Civil War, but to them the battle was about not just the abolition of slavery. It was about the viability of democracies. As one member of the network later remembered, before the American Civil War it was commonplace to think of democracies as "incapable of the sentiment of loyalty, of concentrated and prolonged effort, of far-reaching conceptions." Everyone knew how vulnerable they were to despots. There was therefore a widespread belief that the North would not only lose the war, but fall prey to a kind of Bonaparte, a Caesar.

The central question posed by the Civil War thus resembled the one Tocqueville had asked several years previously and

that now became so timely in France: Could their democracy
become liberal? In other words, could it protect individual liberties and pursue high-minded, noble objectives—or would it
show itself to be materialistic and ignoble by remaining attracted to despotism? Could Americans dedicate themselves
to such a noble ideal as the abolition of slavery and pursue it to
the end? Were they capable of sustained courage, patriotism,
and self-sacrifice? Through his inspired leadership, Lincoln
proved that they could. Under the right leadership, a liberal
democracy was possible.

The Civil War, to liberals across Europe, was a momentous
conflict not just for America, but for the whole world. Liberals
in Britain, France, and elsewhere believed that the prospects
for democracy in their own countries were linked to the fate
of the Union. Norton declared that the triumph of the North
"will be shared by our foreign friends, who are fighting the battle
of liberal principles and equal rights in the Old World." Smith
responded that the "effect of [America's] example may enable
European society finally to emerge from feudalism." Another
member of the liberal network believed that America's example
and ideas would "hasten incalculably the progress of equaliza-
tion over the whole earth." On the other hand, if the North lost,
"European democracy would be silenced and dumbfounded
forever." In 1865, amid the celebrations of Union victory, Curtis
saluted the North's foreign friends. The war had shown that "all
believers in a true popular government . . . in whatever country they live" were members of the "great liberal party of the
world."[22] By his example, Lincoln proved that with the right
leadership, a great democracy could be liberal. He was educating the American population, moralizing them, elevating them,
the way a truly liberal leader should.

The publications of these admirers of Lincoln helped to
transform the president into a transnational figure who was

engaged in a noble struggle on behalf of all people against privilege and despotism. European liberals admired his moral strength and statesmanship. They respected the fact that he knew how to inspire the American people with uplifting language.

Lincoln offered a stark contrast to Napoleon III. He spoke to Americans not as a demagogue, but in a way that appealed to their best instincts and most admirable qualities. In so doing, he encouraged the people to be liberal like him, that is, to love freedom, to be generous, moral, and manly.

Liberals would have been aware that their irreconcilable enemy, the Vatican, favored the South. Officially the Church hierarchy was neutral, but the pope's sympathies were no secret. Like many people, he saw the South as a more traditional and aristocratic society compared to the North, which seemed more modern and democratic, prone to anarchy and all the problems associated with liberalism. The Jesuit publication *Civilta Cattolica* traced the origins of the Civil War to the mania for liberty and disrespect for all authority endemic in democratic political culture. The slavery issue, this Catholic newspaper argued, was not a humanitarian cause, but a pretext for underlying selfish motives.

After the Emancipation Proclamation of 1863, the *Civilta Cattolica* showed even more hostility to the North, calling Lincoln a double-dealing politician and his government a political dictatorship. It accused him of engaging in an unjust war for "uncivilized motives."[23] In a letter that was widely publicized the same year, the pope recognized Jefferson Davis as the "Illustrious and Honorable President of the Confederate States of America."[24] In 1866, he issued a statement in which he declared that, subject to certain conditions, it was "not at all contrary to the natural and divine law for a slave to be sold, bought or exchanged."

Very few prominent Catholics vocalized support for Lincoln, the North, or abolitionism. But most of those who did were also French and included not only Tocqueville but Laboulaye and Montalembert. The American Catholic Orestes Brownson, a supporter of the North, took note of this fact. In a very positive review of Montalembert's speeches in Belgium, Brownson remarked on how rarely European Catholics supported abolition and thanked the liberal Catholics of France, "the only Catholics in Europe who sympathize with the loyal people of the Union."[25]

Lincoln's death in 1865 triggered another surge in his popularity across Europe. Tributes linked his leadership and the Union victory with the prospects of liberal democracy around the world. Laboulaye wrote a moving eulogy that was widely disseminated. He celebrated the president's services not just to America, but to the cause of all of humanity. Goldwin Smith wrote that English liberals, too, had reason to be thankful for the heroism and determination of the American people. The Union victory demonstrated that the "great liberal party of the world" was triumphing over the forces of illiberalism.

Such sentiments were echoed widely and sometimes in the loftiest of terms. Montalembert was effusive—Lincoln had acted not only like a champion of liberty, but like a true Christian. His leadership and the victory of the North showed that America was now superior to most European societies and should take its rank among the first peoples of the world.[26] Giuseppe Mazzini believed that America's heroic deeds proved that its destiny was to become the whole world's guiding light. "You have become a leading Nation," he gushed. "You must come forth and take your part in this battle. It is God's battle."[27]

Norton summarized this liberal optimism about the Union victory in an article titled "American Political Ideas" for the *North American Review* in 1865.[28] The Civil War, he wrote, proved that selfishness, ignorance, and corruption could be defeated. America had demonstrated itself to be a true community, a liberal republic. This was what "We, the people" meant. The country was now poised to realize "the most inspiring and most promising idea of modern Christian civilization—the true brotherhood of man." That same year, Laboulaye conceived the idea of a monument to the United States—the Statue of Liberty.

It is worth pausing for a moment to consider the fact that Lincoln's liberal credentials had little to do with "small government" principles or laissez-faire. Instead, they had everything to do with his moral principles and ability to inspire patriotism, courage, and devotion to noble goals. His admirers in Europe were apparently not all that worried about the fact that he suspended the writ of habeas corpus, ordered the arrest and military detention of suspected traitors, spent money without congressional approval, and ignored many constitutional provisions, justifying such actions by citing emergency powers granted to him by the people.[29]

In fact, Lincoln's use of emergency authority was analyzed carefully by Laboulaye. It was, he concluded, the very model of crisis government. Lincoln had responded to the emergency without undermining the Constitution or the rule of law. He had suspended habeas corpus, but only to save the Constitution. Most importantly, Lincoln had engaged in moral uplift. In all these ways, then, Lincoln was a great leader of liberal democracy. In making such a man president, the United States had vindicated not only its Constitution, but liberty, democracy, and humanity itself.

## The Liberal Republican Party

The euphoria would not last long. Only a few years after publishing his glowing tribute to American political ideals, Charles

Norton found himself deeply disappointed in his country. He was distressed by what he saw as the baseness of American life, the loss of honor, manners, and moral principles. True gentlemen were nowhere to be found and money ruled. The leadership of President Ulysses Grant contrasted glaringly with that of Abraham Lincoln.

Like Norton, Charles Schurz was exasperated by what he saw as the demoralization of political life under President Grant. An émigré from Germany, Schurz had fought in the Revolutions of 1848. Upon arriving in the United States, he had gravitated to the Republican Party, becoming something of a liaison for the German American community. Appointed minister to Spain, he later served as a major general in the Union Army. After the war, he became the first German-born member of the US Senate and eventually served as secretary of the interior.

Initially, both Schurz and Norton hoped that Grant would reform the bureaucracy that had grown during the Civil War and get rid of the corruption that accompanied it. But it soon became clear that nothing of the sort would happen: Grant was even exacerbating the situation. A number of well-publicized scandals furnished proof that he was using the power of his office for personal advantage. There were even worries that he might overthrow the republic and install a military dictatorship if he lost the election in 1872. His was a "species of Caesarism" utterly abhorrent to republican institutions, declared Charles Sumner, senator from Massachusetts, on the Senate floor.

Such feelings and fears lay behind the creation of a new but short-lived political party in 1872. An offshoot of the Republican Party, it was founded by Schurz, with the support of Norton and Sumner. It called itself the Liberal Republican Party, no doubt to signal its opposition to Caesarism and devotion to high moral principles. Beyond that, there was a great deal of disagreement about the specific policies the Liberal Republicans stood for. Even on key issues such as free trade, and the paper currency there were diverse opinions. Indeed, members' divisions eventually led to the failure and dissolution of the party.

But Liberal Republicans were united on one important point: their desire to "infuse a higher moral spirit into our political life."[30] They loudly denounced "greedy politicians" who treated the electorate like a flock of sheep and practiced dirty tricks on them in order to line their own pockets. They called for more integrity, patriotism, and manliness in public life. These were the leadership qualities necessary if American democracy was to survive the dangers posed by Caesarism. They were the characteristics of liberalism.

## Gladstone, Liberal Icon

Like Lincoln, William Gladstone became an internationally famous symbol of liberal principles and values. Leader of the British Liberal Party and prime minister four times between 1868 and 1895, he came to personify the values of Victorian liberalism. But what, might we now ask, did that actually mean? What was liberal about Gladstone?

It was not that he supported Lincoln and the North during the Civil War, because he did not. Like a majority of British liberals, Gladstone supported the South, a fact that irritated John Stuart Mill greatly and caused the American abolitionist paper the *Liberator* to denounce his "sham liberalism."[31] But many British liberals reasoned that the North was not so much concerned with emancipating the slaves as with subjecting the South to the authority of the central government. Slavery was more of an excuse than the real reason for the war.

Over time, Gladstone came to regret his initial sympathy for the Confederacy, going so far as to call it "a mistake of incredible grossness." The war and the Union victory ended up having the same effect on him as on other liberals. It reduced his fear of democracy. In a Liverpool speech on electoral reform in 1866, he declared that America illustrated the virtues of a more extended franchise and expressed admiration for the "self-command, self-denial, and forethought" of its citizens.[32] In response, the *New York Times* reported that "Mr. Gladstone's is a name held in the highest esteem by intelligent and high minded Liberals all over the world."[33] Over time, Gladstone became easily the most admired Englishman in America.

Like all liberals, Gladstone subscribed to a number of core principles. He was deeply committed to civil equality and parliamentary government, and had a profound aversion to aristocratic privileges and prejudices. He believed in the individual freedoms of religion, speech, and the press. Like other liberals, he also stood for reform, improvement, and progress; however, and again like other liberals, he was not always clear or consistent about what these beliefs meant in practice. As we have seen, the British Liberal Party was rife with internal disputes. It was *not* committed, as it is sometimes thought, to a doctrinaire policy of laissez-faire.

Some say Gladstone was an advocate of "small government," and in a way this is true, especially of his early years in politics; however, his second government was characterized as socialist by many people at the time. Gladstone's own politics, historians have found, are in reality very hard to pin down. The truth is that his opinions on specific legislative issues were inconsistent and changed over time. He never quite succeeded in uniting the party behind a strictly defined or consistent legislative agenda.

Why Gladstone was perceived as a great liberal leader, then, has little to do with any particular legislation or political agenda that he promoted, but more to do with his character and personality. The great pioneer of sociology and German liberal Max Weber noted that Gladstone had great personal charisma. He appealed to the British population's high moral principles, and they in turn trusted the ethical substance of his policy. What brought Gladstone to power and kept him there was "the firm belief of the masses in the moral rightness of his policy and especially in the man's own moral qualities."[34]

Gladstone's reputation owes much to what was seen as his commitment to educating and uplifting Britain's citizenry, both intellectually and morally. He was regarded as a principled leader fighting for the whole community and not beholden to any selfish interest. This was particularly important at a time when there remained deep worries about democracy and its tendency to devolve into despotism or socialism. Between 1886 and 1914, Germany, France, and Italy saw the rise of socialist and workers' parties; by contrast, in Britain the Liberals remained the only mass party on the left. Many attributed this fact to the leadership of Gladstone. Like Lincoln, he was perceived as guiding, educating, and moralizing democracy. A person of high moral principle, Gladstone brought workers into the Liberal Party and could make democracy safe.

Like Lincoln, Gladstone was admired for the way he addressed and inspired the masses. In countless soaring and sermon-like speeches, he appealed to their moral sense, reason, and intelligence. Always, he exhorted them to selflessness, patriotism, and devotion to the common good. Workers came in droves and listened for hours. He seemed to hear them, to know and respect them—and they responded with trust and admiration. From the very beginning of his leadership of the Liberal Party, workers supported the liberals at the polls.

The Liberal Party program, Gladstone often said, was aimed at "the general benefit of the whole mass of the people."

Its goal was "to bind together the whole of the country in harmony and concord."[35] At the same time, Gladstone was not adverse to criticizing the wealthier members of society. The most dangerous threat confronting England, he liked to say, was not the advent of democracy but the likelihood of plutocracy. The danger came not from the lower classes, but from the selfishness of the upper classes, who were sometimes inclined to put their private interests before their public duties.

The modern, industrializing economy was making matters worse. "You are threatened, gentlemen," he told a group of workers in 1876, "in the foundations of national character by the rapid creation and extension of wealth in this country." But *they* were not the danger, he said; rather, it was the wealthy classes who were enriching themselves at an unprecedented rate and changing their values. They were becoming interested more in their own pleasures at the expense of "the inward health, the manhood, the vigour" of the country. The nineteenth century, Gladstone lamented in 1880, was an "age of sham." Affluence, leisure, and the pursuit of luxury were corrupting the nation.[36]

This kind of populist moralism incensed Gladstone's upper-class critics. They denounced him for using "ultra-democratic" language and behaving like a demagogue. Queen Victoria called him a "half-mad firebrand." Even an admirer like Max Weber likened him to a dictator and "Caesarist plebiscatorian." But Gladstone was no democrat, at least not in our sense of the word, nor was nineteenth-century Britain anything close to a democracy. Even the so-called Third Reform Act of 1884, which added 1.7 million voters to the rolls, excluded at least 40 percent of English men and all women from the suffrage.[37] Gladstone's rhetoric about trusting "the people" masked this fact. Like almost all liberals, he believed in the concept of capacity.

Enfranchised voters, he said, must always show evidence of "self-command, self-control, respect for order, patience under suffering" and regard for their superiors. These were also the values he sought to inspire in his audiences.

Character was particularly important to Gladstone. He spoke frequently of the need for voters to exercise self-command, so as not to vote in narrow and self-interested ways. It was legitimate, he conceded, in a speech delivered in 1877, for a man to pursue his own interests, but he should always "test his interests by his duties."[38] When voting, it was necessary to rid oneself of "all selfish and narrow ends." And voting, Gladstone liked to say, was an ennobling experience, an act of individual responsibility before God. "The conscientious exercise of important duties," Gladstone told a working-class audience in 1890, "is a function that tends to elevate a man."[39] But to exercise such important duties required real manliness. In preparation, they must cultivate public spiritedness and virtue. They must also educate themselves in issues of politics. Gladstone encouraged his listeners to read newspapers as well as his speeches, which were printed in cheap editions and were veritable political treatises.

While not everybody appreciated Gladstone's style of leadership and brand of populism, he was enormously admired. He was, said John Stuart Mill, a "great modern statesman," an honest and sincere man who always fought for "the public good . . . especially of the poorer classes."[40] Max Weber, in his famous essay *Politics as a Vocation*, admired him as an early master of "leadership democracy" and compared him to Lincoln. By the respect Gladstone showed for the working man, and the way the working man responded to him, he seemed to suggest that a liberal democracy—one of patriotic and civic-minded citizens aware of their rights and duties—was possible, and that Britain, under the right leadership, could cultivate it gradually and safely.

## Bismarck, Liberalism's Gravedigger

Certainly nobody ever thought of Otto von Bismarck as a liberal leader. Many have described him as a cynical despot who ruined the prospects of both democracy and liberalism in Germany. He practiced what liberals at the time called Bonapartism or Caesarism: he manipulated democracy for illiberal ends.[41] In the history of liberalism, Bismarck therefore serves mainly as a foil for those leaders, like Lincoln and Gladstone, who worked to enlighten, educate, and elevate democracy.

Foreign minister and minister-president of Prussia during the 1860s, architect of German unification in 1871, and chancellor of a unified German Empire from 1871 to 1890, Bismarck was a larger-than-life figure like Lincoln and Gladstone, but he displayed none of their virtues. Historian and politician Heinrich von Treitschke was shocked when he first met him: "Of the moral powers in the world he has not the slightest notion." Bismarck was deceitful and vindictive, even demonic, according to some. An astute Austrian diplomat commented on his manner of governing: "He reckons on the lower motivations of human nature: avarice, cowardice, confusion, indolence, indecision and narrow-mindedness."[42] Nothing could be more illiberal.

A confluence of circumstances brought Bismarck to power. In the late 1850s, the Prussian government's reactionary policies began to ease. The new King William I promised to grant more freedoms and, most importantly, to institute the rule of law. A number of liberal politicians responded by creating the German Progress Party, and between 1861 and 1865 they were the largest group in the Prussian Lower House.

Disagreement with the king ushered in a standoff and constitutional crisis in 1862. It was provoked by the king's plans to push through reforms that would have increased his control over the army. Parliamentary liberals refused to approve the funds needed, resulting in a deadlock. Refusing to compromise, in 1862 the king appointed Otto von Bismarck as head of his ministry. Bismarck was at the time a convinced absolutist and a member of the Prussian Junker (land-owning) class, most of whose members were adamantly opposed to liberalizing reforms of any kind.

Bismarck's first move was to announce that he would operate without constitutional authorization, and he proceeded to do so for the next four years. He simply ignored liberal opposition and never hid his contempt for liberals. In a speech that has since become famous, he starkly declared that he would never indulge them: "The position of Prussia in Germany will not be determined by its liberalism but by its power. . . . Not through speeches and majority decisions will the great questions of the day be decided—that was the great mistake of *1848 and 1849*—but by iron and blood."

Bismarck chose advisors who were openly disdainful of liberalism. One of the most important was Hermann Wagener.[43] Wagener was the founder and chief editor of a newspaper called the *New Prussian Newspaper to Save the Monarchy* (*Kreuzzeitung*) and the editor of the *Staats-und Gesellschafts lexikon*, an encyclopedia with a strong conservative bias. Its entry on liberalism was slashing. Liberalism, said Wagener, was an evil, entirely negative force that had done immeasurable harm to humanity. Beholden to the "ideas of 1789," it was spread by Freemasons bent on wreaking havoc.

Wagener conceded that the word came from the Latin and originally had a noble meaning. It referred to laudable personal qualities, such as benevolence, generosity, tolerance, and enlightenment. But the French Revolution had changed all that. The word now meant the loosening of all restraints, the releasing of all bonds, and the rule of unbounded self-interest. It was nothing more than shameful individualism. For rulers to embrace liberalism would be inexcusably reckless.[44]

The same year Wagener published this article, Bismarck struck against the Progressive Party by restricting freedom of the press, refusing to confirm the election of Progressive mayors, and banning the discussion of political matters in municipal council meetings. Given all of this, one might ask why a sizable group of German liberals agreed to support and work with him, as many did. It has led historians to ask whether German liberals were really liberal. Was German liberalism defective, weak, even *illiberal*?

Heinrich von Treitschke's 1861 article on "freedom" sheds light on the question. When he wrote the piece, von Treitschke was a university professor, liberal politician, and editor of the liberal journal *Preussische Jahrbucher*. German liberals, he argued, were not so different from French or British ones. They shared many of the same ideals and values. Like John Stuart Mill and Edouard de Laboulaye, German liberals believed in the inviolability of personal freedom. The differences between the Germans and the others had more to do with their circumstances. Given their situation, it was understandable to von Treitschke that Laboulaye should worry about the power of the state. German liberals, however, did not *have* a state. And how could any progressive goals be achieved while Germany was divided into thirty-nine separate states, each with different governments. How to bring about a German state was the most pressing question.

Frustrated by their inability to see any effective way forward, some German liberals began to long for a strongman who might accomplish from above what they had failed to achieve from below. Germany needed "one decisive man at the top," one liberal said. Another admitted that "one would like to go with a Caesar, if we had one." Using biblical allusions, the liberal Karl Bollman expressed what many other liberals felt when he said that Germany was in need of an "armed redeemer to lead it to the promised land of national unity and independence." Germans should accept such a leader, Bollman continued, even if it meant that they had to "go through the Red Sea of an all-out war."[45]

When Bismarck appeared and successfully united Germany, many must have seen him as that longed-for Caesar. Two successful wars, the first with Denmark in 1864, the second with Austria and other German states in 1866, led to the creation of the North German Confederation under Prussian leadership in 1867. Shortly afterward, the chancellor seemed to extend an olive branch to liberals when he asked Parliament to pass a law that recognized its power of the purse. Everything they had wished for seemed to be coming true.

But it wasn't so simple. The bill also approved his unconstitutional spending between 1862 and 1866. This part of the law caused many liberals great consternation and ultimately split the liberal party in two. Despite their euphoria over unification, many simply could not condone his unconstitutional behavior. But one group of liberals decided to support the bill and left the Progressive Party to form the National Liberal Party. The remaining group retained the Progressive Party name and refused to compromise. During the ensuing debates, denunciations of Caesarism reached a fever pitch. "Everyone now speaks of Caesarism," grumbled National Liberal Party member Ludwig Bamberger.[46]

Hermann Baumgarten was instrumental in convincing liberals to leave the Progressive Party and join the National

Liberals in support of Bismarck. Born in the Duchy of Bruns-wick, Baumgarten had studied history at the University of Jena before becoming a liberal journalist and eventually a professor of history. In 1866 he published *A Self-Criticism of German Liberalism*, in which he explained his point of view. Liberals should be more pragmatic than they had been in the past, he said. They should face the fact that before any progress could be made, they needed a unified Germany. Mere rhetoric in opposition to Bismarck was leading them nowhere: "For men to work in the state they must above all have a state." It was better to work with Bismarck and obtain gradual gains than remain powerless in perpetual opposition. In response, other liberals questioned whether liberal principles could be ob-tained by illiberal means. Was it possible to compromise with Caesar?

The constitution promulgated by Bismarck in 1871 was nei-ther liberal nor democratic according to its time or ours but combined semblances of both. Rather than being drafted by an elected assembly, it was granted to the German people as a gift from their emperor. It instituted a national representative body, the Reichstag, which was elected by universal manhood suffrage, but its powers were severely circumscribed. In the end, it was a system that had some democratic and some par-liamentary features, but in reality gave enormous power to a small aristocratic group. It contained no references to liberty of speech or person.

The National Liberals harbored no illusions about how dif-ficult it would be to work with Bismarck. Most thought that they were engaging in a tactical compromise and hoped that they would eventually win concessions. After all, they had be-fore them the example of France, where Louis Napoleon was working with liberals to reform his regime. They may well have hoped that Bismarck would behave first like Lincoln and unify Germany, and then like Napoleon III and liberalize his regime.

In any case, the National Liberals did not abandon their battle against Prussian authoritarianism. During their collaboration with Bismarck, they continued to fight for many of the same things liberals in Britain and France had. They advocated broadening and strengthening the powers of Parliament and sought legislation to ensure personal freedoms, equality before the law, and a long list of economic reforms, including dismantling antiquated feudal regulations.

In some ways, the liberals were successful. They did, in fact, win substantial concessions. Freedoms of parliamentary debate, association, and press were broadened. Laws guaranteeing personal and civil rights were passed, restrictions on travel within the country removed. The requirement of official permission to change residence or marry was eliminated. A new criminal code was passed and judicial reforms instituted. Liberals also obtained uniform coinage, weights, and measures, a new commercial code, an imperial bank, and freer trade. They did not get everything they wanted, but for a time they seemed vindicated in their decision to collaborate with Bismarck.

It is indisputable, however, that the liberals committed some grave errors. One was their enthusiastic support of Bismarck's Kulturkampf. The word, translated as the "War for Civilization," refers to a series of laws passed between 1871 and 1877, whose ostensible purpose was to curtail the power of the Catholic Church. Critics then and now have denounced the policy as a clear violation of the liberal principle of religious toleration. To be fair, the situation was not quite as clear.

On July 18, 1870, the Vatican had announced the doctrine of Papal Infallibility. The dogma held that in virtue of a promise made to Peter by Jesus, the pope was preserved from error when speaking "ex cathedra," that is, when he was defining a doctrine regarding faith or morals. This can actually sound quite restrictive—the pope is said to be infallible only when it comes to Christian *doctrine*. However, the *political* import of Papal Infallibility, if any, has been debated ever since. Critics at the time, including quite a few Catholics, believed that it compromised their loyalty to the state or could at least be interpreted that way.

Papal Infallibility attracted widespread condemnation from liberals everywhere. It was, the *New York Times* declared, "a denial of the principles upon which the liberties of all free nations of the world are founded." The acceptance of Papal Infallibility, the *New York Tribune* reasoned, had built a "Chinese wall between the world of modern progressive thought and the Roman Catholic Church."[47] The conclusion of many was that Catholics had once again rejected the opportunity to reconcile themselves with the modern age. Gladstone himself was moved to write two pamphlets denouncing "Vaticanism" and refuting the idea that British Catholics could be loyal to the papacy and the nation simultaneously. Accepting Papal Infallibility would be to renounce one's "moral and mental freedom" and transfer one's civil loyalty to Rome. The first of Gladstone's pamphlets sold 150,000 copies and was translated into many languages.

In the same period, the question of the status of the Papal States caused a focus on the Church's alleged quest for political domination. The issue was particularly pressing for France, whose troops had restored Pius IX to the Holy See in 1849, and whose garrison continued to maintain his control over Rome until 1870. The pope's refusal to cede authority over his remaining territory to a movement proclaiming the principles of national unity and democracy was seen in America as further proof of the fundamental schism between his Church and the age. In 1860, a letter from Pius IX to Napoleon III in which the pontiff characterized the principles of the advocates of Italian unity as immoral was widely published in the American press.

The first piece of German anti-Church legislation was the so-called pulpit paragraph in December 1871. It prohibited "misuses of the pulpit for political purposes." In 1872, Church supervision of schools was abolished. The following year, the first of the "May Laws" revised the Prussian Constitution that since 1850 had granted churches the right to manage their own affairs. All aspiring clergymen were now required to attend German universities or pass a cultural examination designed by state officials. Government approval was also required for any ecclesiastical appointment, and Catholic priests were no longer permitted to give religious instruction in the public schools. A Royal Court of Ecclesiastical Affairs was established which claimed final jurisdiction over all matters of Church discipline, and the Jesuits were expelled from the country.

When the Catholic Church hierarchy refused to accept these laws, Bismarck imposed penalties against violators and more extreme measures. Two laws in 1874 gave the Prussian government authority to expel all clergy who refused to comply, and to confiscate the property of a parish that had no legally appointed priest. Lower clergy were fined or jailed in thousands of cases. By 1876, a total of fourteen hundred parishes—almost a third of those in Prussia—were without priests.

Most German liberals gave wholehearted support to the Kulturkampf. Johann Bluntschli denounced Catholicism as "a menace to manhood," asserting that Germany "must defend itself against this terrible power . . . with every permissible *and impermissible* means." Wherever the Catholic Church exerted power, he declared, "the state is castrated and devalued." The liberal Eduard Windhorst apparently saw no contradiction in arguing that "the burning hate with which the German Empire persecutes Jesuitism" was justified because it was "the land of toleration and enlightenment."

German liberals insisted that their support of the Kulturkampf upheld the liberal principles of freedom and progress. Their commitment to *Bildung*, the modern state, and German unity required it. Freedom, Windhorst explained, "protects everything except unfreedom, and tolerance endures everything except intolerance."[48] It was, said the liberal deputy Rudolf Virchow, a crucial part of a great struggle for civilization in the interest of humanity.

The Kulturkampf was initially met with support from liberals in other countries as well. Much of the British press saw the laws as essentially defensive measures. In March 1872 the *London Times* agreed that the papacy was trying to overthrow the German Empire. It offered the German people and government the support "of all friends of intellectual, moral and spiritual freedom."[49] British papers singled out the Jesuits as advocates of "Papal absolutism" and "missionaries of sedition."[50] The dogma of Papal Infallibility was described as a naked attempt by the pope to increase his own power through the use of superstitious, obscurantist, and obsolete dogmas. As such he constituted a great threat to the pillars of liberal society.

In America, the doctrine of Papal Infallibility and Kulturkampf triggered another surge of anti-Catholic sentiment. Critics of the Church said that America was now threatened by a government of priests. At the height of the Kulturkampf, the American ambassador to Germany, George Bancroft, sent reports back to the State Department defending Bismarck's "firmness and moderation," and warning that "the selfsame malign [Catholic] influence is at work" in many countries around the world, including the United States. New York publishers reissued Gladstone's *Vatican Decrees*, and the American press applauded him for having "struck the Romish despotism." The leading American church historian, Philip Schaff, added a commentary to one edition denouncing the Vatican's "direct antagonism to the liberal tendencies of the age."[51]

In President Grant's December 1871 message to Congress, he warned that America had to protect itself against "superstition, ambition and ignorance," an obvious attack on the Catholic Church. He urged the passage of a constitutional amendment banning government aid to religious schools, a measure that would affect Catholic schools especially. A German Catholic newspaper concluded that the president had "inaugurated the Kulturkampf" in America. Jesuits decried the growing influence of liberalism in the United States, equating it with a "war on Catholicism."[52]

Liberals differed on how and how far state power should be used to oppose the pope and his Church. American measures against Catholicism were a far cry from imprisonment. Many liberals withdrew their support of the Kulturkampf when Bismarck started to enforce his laws in a heavy-handed manner. Gladstone privately observed that "Bismarck's ideas and methods are not ours."[53] The *Spectator* was anti-papal and anti-infallibilist, but also anti-Bismarckian, and regarded the whole Kulturkampf as illiberal. "The so-called 'Liberals' of Prussia," it wrote, seem to have lost all confidence in the power of light to fight Roman Catholic authoritarianism. . . . Liberalism cannot afford to exchange arms with its enemies and to persecute in the name of progress." The *Guardian* declared that "we decline to regard it as a policy of Liberalism to punish by persecution even bigoted churches and reactionary creeds."[54] With the passage of the Falk Laws in May 1873 and their enforcement through the ensuing three years, British writers began to split over the issue. A large majority of them continued to be anti-papal and some were pro-Bismarckian, but most drew a distinction between the abstract aims of the Kulturkampf and the method of enforcement of the Falk Laws.

In the end, the Kulturkampf backfired against German liberals. Germany's Catholic Center Party only grew stronger in defiance, and because of the animosity it had fueled, a future liberal-Catholic coalition became virtually impossible. In 1879, the unscrupulous dictator ended his alliance with the National Liberals by working out an agreement on tax reforms with the Center Party.

In 1878, German liberals were led to support another policy that backfired, namely Bismarck's infamous antisocialist laws. In 1869, various left-wing groups had joined together to establish the SPD, the Socialist Party of Germany. A few years later it drew up its program at a party congress at Gotha. It called for the state to take over industry and for profits to be shared among workers. In 1878, the SPD had twelve seats in the Reichstag. That year there were two attempts on the life of the kaiser.

Using the assassination attempts as an excuse, Bismarck introduced his antisocialist laws. The measures did not ban the SPD outright, but made any organization that was spreading social democratic principles illegal, outlawed trade unions, and shut down many newspapers. German liberals mostly supported the laws.

Like the Kulturkampf, the antisocialist laws failed catastrophically. The SPD kept growing despite them. The laws also divided, weakened, and discredited German liberals and made it very difficult for them to collaborate with socialists in the future. The party split again and again. While Gladstone brought workers into the Liberal Party, the German liberals under Bismarck failed to do so.

An aura of disrepute hovered over the National Liberals for a long time and to some extent taints German liberalism even today. In 1907, the two factions of liberals were still trading insults, the Progressive Party accusing the National Liberals of betraying liberal principles due to their lack of character, cowardice, and manliness.[55] Today, there are those who say that Bismarck *destroyed* liberalism.

Max Weber placed much blame on a leader who never respected parliamentary government. A Caesarist despot, Bismarck destroyed political parties and any individual who threatened his authority, and he used demagoguery to advance his interests. In 1918, when contemplating Bismarck's legacy, Weber made an observation that is worth quoting at length: "He left a *nation totally without political education* . . . accustomed to expect that the great man at the top would provide their politics for them . . . [Germany] had grown accustomed to *submit patiently* and fatalistically to whatever was decided for it in the name of 'monarchical government.'" Bismarck bequeathed to his successors "a nation without any political sophistication" and "without any political will of its own." He created a pseudo-democracy that he manipulated to pursue illiberal goals. "Egoism," he said, was "the only sound basis for a large state."[56]

# CHAPTER SIX

# The Battle to
# Secularize Education

*The snake in Paradise already spoke the temptations and
false promise of liberalism.*

—CATHOLIC CHURCH LEXICON, 1891

IN 1870 BISMARCK goaded Napoleon III into declaring war
on Prussia and the Second Empire came to a sudden and humiliating end. It took Prussia a mere six months to defeat
France, which until then had been regarded the strongest
power in Europe. When Napoleon III was captured at Sedan
on September 2, 1870, France became a de facto republic.

The shock of the French defeat was compounded by a rebellion in Paris, where a large portion of the population, refusing to accept the peace terms imposed by Germany and agreed
to by their own government, rose up in anger and set up the
so-called Commune.

While the provisional national government at Versailles
assembled the forces necessary to put down the uprising, the

Commune took a series of actions that stunned the world. It adopted the red flag as its symbol. It sent delegates to other French cities encouraging them to establish their own communes. It issued a Declaration to the French People promising to implement measures to improve the "social welfare" and began legislating in the name of the working classes. It voted the separation of church and state and the elimination of the ecclesiastical budget. It closed many Catholic schools and churches. Some two hundred priests, nuns, and monks were arrested. A feminist movement demanded wage equality, the right to divorce, and secular and professional education.

The astonishing defeat of the French army, followed by what seemed like another revolution and a communist takeover in Paris, sent shockwaves through Europe and beyond. Liberals were yet again forced to contemplate what had gone so horribly wrong. They of course had no way of knowing that France's humiliation at the hands of Prussia would help prepare it for what liberals had fought for so long: a "liberal educational system" and the separation of church and state.

## What's Wrong with the French?

Horrified observers of the Parisian uprising of 1870 reported that barbarians and savages had once again taken control of the city. The fault lay with the "Reds" who preached class hatred and violence. They were "brigands," "outlaws," "vermin." The pope called them "beastly, God-forsaken scum."[1] Newspapers reported on the role of women in the uprising, calling them debased and debauched "furies."

Fear spread that this revolution, like previous ones, would export its ideas across France's borders. The *New York Times* predicted that the Commune was only "the first muttering of that social storm which shall yet shake every capital of Europe."[2] Repeatedly calling the insurgents "communists" bent on overturning the existing order of society, the paper warned of a coming revolution that would nationalize all property.

The French government at Versailles blamed the revolution on a conspiracy masterminded by the International Working Men's Association and its leader, Karl Marx, and this idea spread. Edwin Godkin, editor of the American journal the *Nation*, warned that the Commune would "give the civilization of the Western world a severe shaking."[3]

Many were therefore relieved when, on May 21, 1871, the French National Assembly, led by Adolphe Thiers, ordered an army into Paris to retake the city. The battle was brutal, with many atrocities committed on both sides. The Versailles troops killed several thousand suspects without trial, including many women and children. The Communards executed hostages, including the archbishop, Monseigneur Darboy, and set fires to symbols of the national government, among which was Thiers's home.

Although it is always difficult to know exact numbers, it is estimated that by the end of "Bloody Week," twenty to twenty-five thousand people had been killed, most of them Communards or innocent victims, and many by summary execution. Some forty thousand were also arrested, including a great number of trade union and socialist activists as well as feminists, many of whom were deported to a penal colony in New Caledonia.

The military defeat, a "communist" uprising, and a brutal repression provoked yet another period of deep reflection and soul searching in France. What or who was to blame? Catholic royalists said it was divine punishment for the sin of liberalism. The pope set the tone when he denounced liberalism as "the epitome of satanic subversion." Liberals should have known that banishing God from society would lead straight to disorder, anarchy, and death. They had only themselves to blame for the curse of socialism, to which their ideas inevitably led. Using all the propaganda at their disposal, Catholic royalists unleashed a fierce attack on liberal principles, directing their ire especially at popular sovereignty, representative government, and freedom of religion.

The debates over the causes of the humiliating defeat and the Commune were especially intense at a time when opposed camps were battling over what kind of government should be established, a monarchy or a republic. In 1871, elections based on universal male suffrage returned a majority of monarchists, but they were divided among themselves. Legitimists, Orleanists, and Bonapartists could not agree about who should be king. Not until 1879, after elections returned a republican majority and the monarchist president MacMahon resigned, was it clear that France would remain a republic.

A devout Catholic, famous for having crushed the Commune, General MacMahon welcomed the help of the Church in combating liberalism. The principal aim of his government, he said, was the restoration of moral order in the country. For this he needed Catholicism. Public prayers in Parliament were introduced. The construction of a Basilica of the Sacred Heart in the left-wing area of Montmartre was approved to expiate the crimes of the Commune. Since 1789, the Sacred Heart had been a symbol of royal and Catholic counterrevolution. Pilgrimages to Lourdes were organized at which royalist hymns were sung.

All of this was exceedingly frustrating to those who thought that Catholicism was France's problem and not the solution to the problem. But they also agreed with the royalists that a deep moral and intellectual crisis had caused France's fourth revolution. In a widely read book, the historian and theorist Ernest Renan placed the blame squarely on Catholicism. Thanks to the Catholic Church, he wrote, France had become a second-rate

country, a society of weaklings. Other books and articles followed. That the French army had been defeated by the Prussian
schoolmaster became a frequently heard refrain. Catholicism,
it was endlessly repeated, made French soldiers not only superstitious and submissive, but unpatriotic. Alfred Fouillée, one
of France's most respected philosophers, said that French soldiers were selfish and materialistic. France desperately needed
intellectual and moral reform.[4]

Foreign onlookers weighed in, once again attributing
France's problems to a giant moral failure. British commentators blamed them on a lack of manliness. The French were
infested with a love of luxury and material enjoyment. John
Stuart Mill thought their troubles had to do with the infirmity
of the French mind. Once again, the French had shown their
lack of character.[5] Americans reasoned that the French were
"ignorant, priestridden and emasculated,"[6] Germans that they
were debilitatingly frivolous.

The widespread disdain for the Catholic Church was only
magnified by the Vatican's declaration of Papal Infallibility on
the eve of the Franco-Prussian War. French critics saw it as
yet another affront to rational thinking and encouragement of
superstition. Like liberals elsewhere, they interpreted it as an
attack on the sovereignty of their nation. The pope seemed
to be requiring Catholics to pledge allegiance to him and
his Church rather than to their own country. This weakened
France, as was shown when it faced a Protestant enemy on the
battlefield.

Charles Renouvier, another influential French philosopher,
weighed in as well. After the war, he founded *La Critique phil-
osophique* and its supplement *La Critique religieuse*, in large
part to denounce the danger posed by the Catholic Church and
to promote Protestantism and civic education instead. During the short-lived Second Republic, he had served as minister

of public instruction and had produced a manual for promoting republican values. What was needed, he now demanded, was a campaign to stamp out once and for all the "slave-religion," that had weakened the moral fiber of the nation. This meant separating church and state, and instituting a free, compulsory, and lay educational system. Civic education, he wrote, should deliver men from the yoke of theocracy.

Renouvier was only one voice among many who contended that the French population desperately needed to be weaned off Catholicism. Public education thus became a key and fiercely debated issue of the Third Republic. The battle culminated in the so-called Ferry Laws of 1881 and 1882 and in church/state separation in 1905, after which the Republican victors boasted that France possessed "the most liberal, the most modern [system of education] in the civilized world."[7]

## A Liberal Public School System

Named after the prime minister and minister of public instruction Jules Ferry, the Ferry Laws were later seen as the most significant and lasting reform of the Third Republic. They made public primary education free, compulsory, and secular. The architects and supporters of this system were certain that it would create a much-needed "moral and social revolution" in France.[8]

The Ferry Laws were supplemented by a third law in 1886, sometimes called the Goblet Law, after the prime minister, René Goblet, who served as minister of the interior and minister of worship between 1886 and 1887. The law forbade the employment of members of religious teaching orders in public schools. When it encountered difficulties in the Senate, the Lower Chamber retaliated by calling upon the government to dissolve the Jesuit order. Jesuits were ordered to leave their houses within three months, while the other named orders were given six months to seek government authorization.

It is not hard to see that the liberal system of education championed by the educational reformers was overtly anti-Catholic. Its designers never hid the fact that its purpose was to detach the population from priests. Nor did they make a secret of the fact that this meant forcing through a kind of Protestant Reformation. A *Le Temps* article in 1879 explained their thinking: "Catholic societies have a difficult time. The work of moral secularization that they didn't accomplish in the sixteenth century through an ecclesiastical or religious reform, they try to accomplish by way of school reform."[9]

In the passing of these laws, it helped that so many Protestants occupied prominent positions in government—in fact, all out of proportion to their numerical strength in the country. Between 1879 and 1890 five cabinets had Protestant premiers. In one of these, the Waddington cabinet of 1879, half of the minsters were Protestants. Many of them were also Freemasons and admirers of the "Religion of Humanity." Some no longer believed in God.

The principal architect of the French school reforms was Ferdinand Buisson, who became director of primary education in 1879 and retained that position for seventeen years. Buisson later went on to preside over the League of Education from 1902 to 1906 and the League of Human Rights from 1914 to 1926. In 1905, he chaired the parliamentary committee that implemented the separation of church and state. In 1927, he was awarded the Nobel Peace Prize (jointly with Ludwig Quidde).

Buisson was a liberal Protestant and, like Ferry and Goblet, a Freemason. During the Second Empire, he published several books and articles with titles like *Liberal Christianity* (1865) and *The Principles of Liberal Christianity* (1869), which explained his religious views. He also created an organization called the Union of Liberal Christianity to help propagate them.

The religion Buisson professed was one without dogmas, miracles, or priests. It subordinated everything to morality and had as its goal "the spiritual perfecting of man and of humanity." It was a universal church that welcomed all people, of whatever denomination, including deists and even atheists. Only such a church, Buisson reasoned, could bring about the reign of fraternity and human solidarity that men like he sought.[10] What was needed, he said, was "a human church, lay, [and] liberal." It would be "like a vast Freemasonry out in the open."[11]

As director of primary education, Buisson was well positioned to implement his religious and educational ideas. His mammoth *Dictionary of Pedagogy and Primary Education* (1880–87) was meant to serve as a guide for all those engaged in primary instruction. A public school system, Buisson said, should not just teach the usual subjects. Its most important goal was to produce "good men and good citizens." It should teach boys to "think and act like a man."[12] To that end, it should wean them off Catholicism and teach them the educational principles advocated by liberal Protestants instead. Most importantly, French schools should teach morals rather than obedience to the pope.[13]

Buisson especially admired the American public school system. His *Dictionary* contains long and complimentary articles on the United States and its method of educating citizens. He appreciated the fact that in US schools no particular religious doctrines were taught, only Christianity "in general." The *Dictionary* includes laudatory articles on not only the Unitarian leader William Ellery Channing, but also Theodore Parker, Channing's more radical disciple, and their mutual friend, the educational reformer Horace Mann.[14]

It is easy to understand why Buisson admired these Americans so. They shared his aversion to Catholicism and preference for a liberal kind of Protestantism. Mann himself had Unitarian sympathies. Parker, who was familiar with Benjamin Constant's writings on religion, began as a Unitarian, but eventually left the movement because it was not liberal enough. It was standing still, he said, becoming narrow and bigoted. All Christian churches, he argued, were straying too far away from the teachings of Jesus. Religions should teach self-improvement and moral comportment, not dogma.

Catholicism, as propagated by the Vatican, was enemy number one. It would not allow men to think for themselves. When Protestantism arose, wrote Mann, it brought in its wake freedom of thought and toleration. Parker was even more blunt. Catholicism was positively harmful to children of a republic, he said, because it was "the foe of all progress [and] deadly hostile to democracy." The natural ally of tyrants, it was an irreconcilable enemy of freedom.[15]

Mann thought American public schools should teach children a generalized form of Christianity that focused on morality. Children should learn the principles common to all Christians, and not those doctrines about which different sects disagreed. As secretary to the Massachusetts Board of Education in 1837, he designed a free and "nonsectarian" school system that he thought would teach the civic virtues and values needed to sustain a republic. It was important, most of all, to cultivate self-discipline and judgment. Morality and intelligence were essential in a republic.

Buisson and his collaborators believed that similar principles should be introduced in France. Paul Bert, for example, agreed that a main goal—perhaps *the* main goal—of France's educational system should be to liberate the minds of boys from what he thought were the absurd and terrifying beliefs that were taught in Catholic schools. Instead, public education should transmit basic public and private virtues, a boy's duties to his family and his fatherland.[16] Himself a Freemason, Bert served for a while as minister of education and authored one of the handbooks used in the primary education course on morals.

The goal of the new French school system would be twofold. First, by encouraging free thought and discussion, it would teach young boys how to think and judge for themselves. Second, by the inculcation of what Buisson called "liberal discipline,"[17] it would teach them self-command and self-direction, both of which could be summed up by the term "self-government." In order to be a proper adult and a man, it was often repeated, a boy must learn how to govern himself. Once again, this meant liberating him from Catholic priests and Christian dogma, and instead teaching him liberal or generalized Christian moral principles. If the Bible itself was taught, it should be approached strictly as a historical document that could help instruct morals.

Buisson admired the fact that Americans understood the necessity of propagating an appropriate intellectual culture. They knew the value of teaching young students the moral precepts of justice and piety, on which every republican constitution depended. Patriotism was exceptionally important. According to the educational system he helped design, French preschoolers learned patriotic songs and poems on moral themes. Between the ages of nine and eleven, they learned the obligation to pay taxes and serve in the army. Between eleven and thirteen, their instruction emphasized the importance of military service, respect for the flag, obedience to the law, as well as elementary notions of political economy.[18]

The educational reforms did not concern just boys. Girls, the reformers said, should also receive a liberal education. And here, as well, they took inspiration from America. In 1870, after a visit to the country, educational reformer Célestin Hippeau published *Public Education in America*. In it, he argued that America proved the benefits of giving girls a liberal education. Only that way could they become patriotic contributors to a democratic society. France, he regretted, had utterly failed to rescue women from the grip of the church, with devastating consequences.

The liberal theorist Jules Simon considered even the best French boarding schools completely useless in the way they educated girls. The principles they imparted were frivolous; there was nothing serious or elevating about them.[19] A long article on girls in Buisson's *Dictionary* concurred. Buisson regretted that his compatriots had given such low priority to girls' education and that it had been so focused on religion. Girls and boys had the same right to an elementary primary education, he said, because they had an "equal intelligence and equivalent duties as members of the State and of a family." He gave a long list of topics that girls, just the same as boys, should be taught, with moral and civic instruction at the top, but also including French language and literature, geography, some law, and political economy. The point was not to make girls "argumentative [*raisonneuses*]," he insisted; but girls, like boys, should be made to understand their duties to their fatherland, the constitution, and the laws. It wasn't that girls should be turned into bluestockings, another reformer asserted, but neither should they "remain strangers to the intellectual life of the modern world."[20]

The educational reformers did not question the idea that a girl's natural vocation was to become a wife and mother. Their main goal was to make girls *better* wives and mothers. Henri Marion, who was at the time considered an expert on girls' education, composed a lecture series on this topic that he delivered at the Sorbonne. Relations between husband and wife, Marion explained, were an example of the mutual dependence and solidarity that characterized all forms of social life. Women and men had different roles to play in society, but they were complementary and equal in importance: "women's proper role is to perfect and soften life, private life above all, but by way of that, at least indirectly, public life as well."[21]

Reformers like Marion often pointed to the way girls were educated in America as an example to be emulated. Marriages in America were more equitable, they said, and the authority of parents over their children more reasonable; this was how American children learned democratic values.[22] The idea that husbands and wives were mutually dependent and worked in solidarity with each other was of course quite different from the patriarchal view of marriage usually propagated by the Catholic Church.

The truth is that in America, the "nonsectarian," liberal, or secular public school system was controversial as well. Like their French counterparts, American Catholics objected that it wasn't truly nonsectarian; the schools actually taught a liberal version of Protestantism. Catholics therefore demanded the right to open their own publicly funded schools.

In 1876, a debate was organized on this issue. It was advertised as a discussion between "a Catholic American citizen" and "a liberal American citizen." Afterward, the debate was published as a pamphlet. The Catholic citizen was Bishop McQuaid of Rochester, a strong advocate of Catholic education, and the liberal citizen was Francis Ellingwood Abbot, a notorious freethinker and self-proclaimed "anti-Christian."

McQuaid laid out the Catholic objections to American public schools. First, they were not, in fact, nonsectarian. They imparted a form of liberal Protestantism, which violated the rights of Catholics under the Constitution and Bill of Rights. Second, the schools violated parental rights to decide the religion of their children. Finally, it was wrong for Catholics to have to pay for schools meant to lead their children away from their religion. McQuaid also rejected the notion that morals could be taught without religion, which to him would be the same as basing morals on selfishness, a clear contradiction in terms.

In his response to Bishop McQuaid, Abbot did not deny that the schools were anti-Catholic. The goal of the American public school system, he said, was not to teach religion but to develop "individuality." The parental rights to which McQuaid referred were a mere relic of "primeval barbarism." Their real purpose was to give despotic authority to fathers and, beyond them, to the pope. Catholicism, and the kind of family it advocated, bound women and children to domestic servitude. In modern America, Abbot noted approvingly, people were coming to recognize women as the equals of men before the law. The woman's movement, Abbot added, again approvingly, "aims to establish and protect a woman's right to the enjoyment of her own free individuality."[23]

This discussion between a Catholic and a liberal should not mislead one into believing that only Catholics objected to the American public school system. Many conservative Protestants denounced it in the most virulent terms. Seeing no difference between liberal Christianity and rank infidelity, they called Horace Mann's schools anti-Christian hotbeds of immorality. According to Congregationalist minister Noah Porter, liberalism was even more dangerous than outright atheism because it was so seductive. A conspiracy against scriptural truth, it was also a clear and present danger to traditional notions of the family. Were it to be allowed to spread further, it would invariably overturn society and bring chaos to the world.

Traditionalist proponents of religious orthodoxy, whether Catholic or Protestant, were especially alarmed by the connection between liberal religion and feminism. From Mary Woll-stonecraft, who came from a Dissenting background, to Lou-ise Otto, who was close to the German-Catholic movement,[24] and the militantly anticlerical French feminists, these advo-cates of women's rights denounced "priestcraft and supersti-tion" and often blamed traditional churches for women's low status. Like their male counterparts, many of them also be-lieved that, for significant reforms to occur, either the Chris-tian churches had to become more liberal or a new religion had to be invented.

Few feminists were more radical than the American Eliza-beth Cady Stanton, who denounced the Bible itself for its blatant sexism and coauthored a *Woman's Bible* to replace it. "The Bible and the Church," she declared, "have been the greatest stum-bling blocks in the way of women's emancipation." Thankfully, however, "more liberal minds" were now producing "higher and purer expositions of the Scriptures."[25] Stanton, like oth-ers, hoped for the advent of a new religion, more tolerant, more open to science, and more conducive to political, economic, and social reform—including the emancipation of women.

## The National Liberal League, Free Thought, and Free Love

Bishop McQuaid would certainly have been incensed by an or-ganization called the National Liberal League. It was formed the same year that his debate with Abbot, one of its founders, took place. The goal of the league was the total separation of church and state, something that its members thought was not clearly enough stated in the Constitution. To achieve its goal, the league endorsed the Nine Demands of Liberalism.

The Nine Demands attacked all government appropria-tions for religious educational and charitable institutions, and all religious services and uses of religious artifacts in government procedures. They demanded that the government no longer recognize religious days and occasions, that Sunday laws be repealed, that oaths be replaced by simple affirmation, that laws enforcing Christian morality be revoked, and that government favoritism to any religion come to an end.

The National Liberal League welcomed men of all religious backgrounds, whether Christian, Jewish, Muslim, Buddhist, Brahman, or even atheist. Liberal Jews came to occupy prominent positions of its leadership. In 1879 both Rabbi Isaac Wise, of the *American Israelite* and a founder of American Reform Judaism, and Moritz Ellinger, of the *Jewish Times*, served as national vice presidents.

While the league's principal goal was the separation of church and state, a related goal was to combat "spiritual slavery" and "superstition," code words for Catholicism or, in fact, for any religion based on unchanging dogma. The league aimed to encourage free thought and to promote a rational and nonsectarian religion committed to spreading "a sense of brotherhood."[26]

Abbot and other prominent league members advocated a secular religion, or what they called the religion of humanity. Of course to the religious traditionalists, conservatives, and all those who considered themselves orthodox, this "religion of humanity" was no religion at all. It is no wonder, then, that Bishop McQuaid, in his communications with the Vatican, ranted against the liberalism that was spreading.[27]

By the end of the nineteenth century, the word "liberal" in a religious context could mean several different things in America. It could mean tolerant, in the way George Washington used the term. It could mean a variety of Unitarianism, such as preached by William Channing or any number of his disciples. Or it could also mean an advocate of the strict separation of church and state and a "nonsectarian" public school system.

And, finally, liberal might also mean a freethinker, which itself could mean any number of positions on religion.

By the early twentieth century, there existed many clubs with the word "liberal" in their titles, all catering to freethinking men. In New York was the Harlem Liberal Alliance, in Boston the Friendship Liberal League, in Los Angeles the Liberal Club. There was even a town in Missouri called Liberal. Founded in 1881 for liberal-minded people, it grew by 1885 to an active business town of five hundred inhabitants who wished to live free from church dogma. There was also a Liberal University and numerous newspapers with the word in their titles. In fact, the *Kansas Liberal* thought the word "liberal" so overused that it changed its name to *Lucifer, the Light Bearer* in 1883. Those who considered liberalism the work of the devil now had a suitably named periodical to attack.

Some self-designated religious liberals rejected Christianity altogether. Abbot confessed that he was not only not a Christian, but a determined *anti*-Christian. According to the Boston journal the *Free Religious Index*, "The word 'liberal' in this country today means one who does not acknowledge the authority of the Bible or admit the supernatural character of the Christian system." Robert Ingersoll, a famous lawyer, popular orator, and member of the National Liberal League, liked to make fun of religion in his widely attended lectures.

David M. Bennett, the founder of the magazine *Truth Seeker* and another member of the National Liberal League, called Christianity the "greatest sham in the world."[28] It was "a curse to the human race," he said, because it "fostered ignorance, superstition and falsehood." The *Truth Seeker*'s professed mission was to communicate to "the Liberals of the country . . . information, entertainment and support against religious error and mental slavery." On the masthead of its first issue, David Bennett and his wife, Mary, announced that their magazine would devote itself to propagating liberalism, identifying it by name, meaning "whatever tends to elevate and emancipate the human race." A long list of topics included science, morals, labor reform, free thought, free education, sexual equality, and free love.

Liberalism's association with "free love" became a particularly controversial issue. Although there were disagreements among them, many free-lovers advocated voting rights for women, property rights, and the right to divorce. What distinguished free-lovers from other champions of women's rights was their outspoken critique of marriage. Some called it legalized prostitution, others sexual slavery, still others a system of rape. Neither the church nor the state, they said, should have the right to regulate sexual relations. Divorce should be easy to obtain and marriages based on mutual love and sexual attraction. Before entering into any relationship, women, as well as men, should be taught about sexuality and then entrusted with the regulation of their own sexual conduct. Women should be permitted to control their reproduction and to refuse intercourse with their husbands if they so wished.

Free-lovers sometimes referred to this as a woman having rights over her own body.[29] Ezra Heywood, the president of New England's Free-Love Association, advocated a "Woman's Natural Right to ownership and control over her own body-self, a right inseparable," she said, from "Woman's intelligent existence."[30] Some free-lovers even spoke of a woman's right to sexual gratification.

As if its association with atheism and free love were not bad enough, a highly publicized trial tainted liberalism further in the eyes of traditionalists. At the same time as Bennett began publishing his *Truth Seeker*, free speech was coming under attack by the US postal inspector and politician Anthony Comstock. In 1873, Congress passed the so-called Comstock Act, named after him, and whose ostensible purpose was the "Suppression of, Trade in, and Circulation of, Obscene Literature and Articles of Immoral Use." The act criminalized the use of the US Postal Service to send any item deemed "obscene." It also radically broadened the government's power to regulate printed material by expanding the materials that could be deemed obscene to include newspapers, advertisements, and a variety of products to do with contraception. It also defined obscenity in such vague terms as to include any kind of sexual information, including basic physiological facts. Freethought attacks on the Bible could be regarded as obscene as well. Comstock used the obscenity laws to arrest and imprison both freethinkers and free-love advocates.

A number of high-profile liberals intentionally broke the Comstock Laws to provoke a legal battle. In 1877, David Bennett published an "Open Letter to Jesus Christ" in the *Truth Seeker* and then sold it as a pamphlet on the side. Addressing Jesus directly, the "Open Letter" asked: "Has not the religion called after your name caused more bloodshed, more persecution, and more suffering than all the other religions of the world?" Bennett was arrested but the charges against him were dropped after Robert Ingersoll, a man with broad connections, interceded on his behalf. But Bennett was arrested a second time and then a third, and on this last occasion the case led to trial, conviction, and imprisonment.

The second and third arrests of Bennett concerned the free-love pamphlet *Cupid's Yokes*, authored by Ezra Heywood. The pamphlet mocked Comstock's anti-vice campaign as a species of "lascivious fanaticism" and openly supported many free-love principles. It called for an end to any church or state regulation of marriage, adultery, and birth control, which it said should be replaced by "sexual self-government." Divorce should be easy to obtain; and both men and women should be permitted to love whom they wanted and for as long as they wanted.

Soon the National Liberal League got involved. Heywood and Bennett were arrested on obscenity charges, one for authoring the pamphlet, the other for selling it. But the first time Bennett's case never went trial. He was then arrested for mailing a copy across state borders, this time landing in jail. Their prosecutions prompted the National Liberal League to petition Congress against the Comstock Act. In February 1878, it submitted a petition signed by over fifty and perhaps as many as seventy thousand people asserting that the law was serving as an instrument of religious persecution. It was being used to intimidate editors, publishers, and writers of antireligious works unjustly labelled as obscene. A House Committee nevertheless upheld the constitutionality of the law.

In the end, debate over the Comstock Act produced a schism within the National Liberal League convention. Ingersoll, Abbot, and other leaders resigned. They considered the obscenity law a side issue that distracted from the more central concerns of the league. For some liberals, however, free discussion of sexual matters was of central importance.

Meanwhile, publicity generated by the campaign to repeal or revise the Comstock laws helped blur the distinction in the public mind between liberalism, atheism, sexual freedom, and obscenity. Critics who attended meetings of the National Liberal League reported that atheism was being preached there and that free-love fests were taking place. They accused liberalism of encouraging "rampant individualism," and of denying God and the sanctity of marriage. If the trend continued, one commentator warned, and the free-lovers had their way, the pleasure of the individual would replace the stability of the family, and the disintegration of society would inevitably ensue.[31] Liberals were sinful and lascivious atheists bent on peddling obscenity and destroying the family.

## The Pope Strikes Back

Pope Leo XIII was not wrong to see the Ferry Laws as a direct attack on his Church and teachings. He responded with two encyclicals. On February 8, 1884, he issued *On the Religious Question in France*, which condemned the laws unequivocally. They were "perverse," "vicious," and "criminal." Two months later, he issued *Humanum Genus*, in which he anathemized Freemasons in identical terms; their principles, he said, were perverse, vicious, and criminal. Masons, whom we know were very prominent in the Third Republic and especially in the design and implementation of the school laws, "attack with impunity the very foundations of the Catholic religion." Their brotherhood was a "foul plague creeping through the veins of the body politic," and France's educational reforms were nothing but a malicious conspiracy that would spell the end of all social order. French bishops and Catholic propagandists repeated these charges.

The Church was especially outraged by the reformed system of education for girls.[32] As always, it saw its control over the education of future wives and mothers as a way to re-Catholicize the nation. The liberal educational system was clearly a threat to that goal. While the liberal press celebrated the "release of women from the yoke of ridiculous superstition," conservative and Catholic newspapers declared the changes disastrous. Priests tried to dissuade Catholic girls from enrolling in the new courses by saying that they would endanger their souls. They warned that if the state were to assume the education of all girls, it would expose each one to "radical impiety, atheism, materialism and the most subversive theories of all morality."[33]

Catholic spokesmen categorically rejected the idea that changes in the education of girls would improve marriages and produce happier, more moral and patriotic families. Instead, they would "excite [girls] to a certain spirit of independence" and cause a revolution in the French family. Women would lose their taste for domesticity and motherhood. They would become unruly and disobedient. Tragically, this would also mean that they would have difficulties finding a husband in the first place. There would be additional dangers if young girls attended courses taught by unmarried professors.[34]

Catholic propagandists reinforced and spread the pope's attack on liberalism, often in the most virulent terms. A pamphlet by the Spanish priest Don Felix Sarda y Salvany, titled *Liberalism Is a Sin*, was first published in Spanish in 1886 and then quickly translated into other European languages. Liberalism, the book declared, was "a greater sin than blasphemy, theft, adultery, homicide, or any other violation of the law of God." It was "the evil of all evils," the "offspring of Satan and the enemy of mankind."[35]

Two years later, in 1886, the pope issued yet another damning encyclical, *On the Nature of Human Liberty*. Liberals who supported the separation of church and state, he now said, "follow in the footsteps of Lucifer." Those who subscribed to the principle of popular sovereignty were denying the existence of God. Such liberal principles would inevitably lead to corruption, turmoil, confusion, and ultimately the overthrow of all states. Somewhat contradictorily, the pope also said that the separation of church and state would lead to state tyranny. If there was no authority above the individual except the state, the state would become omnipotent.

The papal attack was not only on liberalism, but also "Americanism," which around this time became a virtual synonym for liberalism in the Vatican's lexicon. Americanism was regularly denounced in the most strident of terms by spokesmen for the pope. According to the Jesuit journal *Civilta Cattolica* the United States breathed in "the infected air" of liberalism and Americanism threatened Catholicism everywhere. Another Roman paper attacked Americans' "Satanic spirit" and "blasphemous theories."[36]

The pope and his close supporters would, of course, have been well aware of the American inspiration behind the Ferry Laws, and of the ongoing battle in America over its public schools. He would also have known that many Catholics in America—including some prominent Catholic leaders—were not opposed to democracy, nor to the separation of church and state, nor to many other liberal principles. Examples are Archbishops John Ireland, John Keane, and Dennis J. O'Connell as well as Cardinal James Gibbons. Some were even accommodating to the public school system. In a letter to Cardinal Miecislaus Ledochowski, prefect of Vatican Propaganda, Bishop McQuaid characterized the whole trend within the American Catholic Church as a pernicious "liberalism."[37]

As we know, Catholic liberals had existed since the very inception of liberalism and throughout the nineteenth century. They saw themselves as part of an international movement that wished to demonstrate the compatibility of Catholicism with modern civilization. The so-called Americanists felt the same way. Ireland, Kean, and Gibbons were well received in France, especially by those who wanted to mend relations between their republican government and the Church. They had some of Ireland's most famous speeches translated into French. More conservative Catholics, like Bishop McQuaid, despaired over the "liberalism that if not checked in time will bring disaster on the Church."[38]

In 1892, the pope made a sudden about-face. Only four years after his encyclical condemning popular sovereignty, he reversed himself in a new encyclical, *Inter innumeras sollicitudines*. It carried as its subtitle "Church and State in France." In a major revision of the Church's teaching, he asked French Catholics to cease identifying the Catholic cause with that of monarchy and to accept the republic. This policy came to be known as "rallying" to the republic—the *ralliement*.

Rallying to the republic was not the same thing as accepting "liberalism," however. As the ultramontane author of a diatribe against liberal Catholicism repeated in 1897, "liberalism is, in itself, a mortal sin."[39] Instead, rallying to the republic meant using republican and liberal means to *combat* liberalism.

The *ralliement* certainly did not mean accepting the non-sectarian teaching in public schools—or the secularizing laws. These continued to be denounced by the pope and his close supporters as a pernicious "Americanism."[40] What Catholics were asked to do was to adopt modern methods, such as the press and propaganda, social movements, and clubs, to convey and spread the Catholic message and re-Catholicize the French nation. In a very real sense, then, the pope was asking the French to use liberal methods to combat religious liberalism.

The Vatican's ostensible ability to accept certain liberal principles, notably in the realm of electoral politics, led to the formation, at the pope's suggestion, of a French Catholic political party named Action Libérale Populaire (ALP) in 1901. Created by two former monarchists, Albert de Mun and Jacques Piou, it was most likely funded by the Vatican.[41] The party published a newspaper called the *Bulletin Action Libérale*, whose first issue appeared on November 20, 1901.

It is worth pausing a moment to consider the fact that a word historically used to describe a movement *opposed* to the

Catholic Church was now appropriated to designate a *pro-*Church party. The ALP's object was to use the liberal system—its free elections, press, and media—to defend the rights of the Church against what it called the menace of "Masonic . . . Jacobin and socialist tyranny." The ALP was fiercely pro-Church and pro-Concordat; it fought tooth and nail against all the secularizing laws, and especially against the project to separate church and state.

If, however, the ALP thought that it would be able to pressure the government to revoke the Ferry Laws, it was sorely disappointed. More secularizing laws followed. In 1901, the Law of Associations granted expanded freedom to groups such as labor unions and political parties to organize, but limited sharply the freedom of religious congregations by forcing them to obtain government authorization if they wished to remain in France or to expand.

The administration of Emile Combes, prime minister from 1902 to 1905, and a Freemason with staunchly anticlerical convictions, applied the law strictly, and religious orders found it next to impossible to gain legal authorization. By 1903, over fourteen thousand schools run by unauthorized orders were closed. In 1904, members of religious orders were forbidden to teach and almost all religious orders in France were banned and their property sold. Between thirty and sixty thousand priests and nuns were exiled. And all of this culminated in the Law of Separation of 1905, which suppressed all public financing and recognition of the Catholic Church.

As it protested fiercely against each one of these measures, the ALP's membership grew, reaching two hundred thousand dues-paying persons and twelve hundred local election committees in 1906. At its peak, the party had seventy deputies in the Chamber and constituted a real threat to the liberal agenda. At one point Combes singled it out for opprobrium in a series of speeches, calling out "L'Action Libérale Populaire, here is the enemy!"

Since the word's inception in the second decade of the nineteenth century, "liberalism" had been closely associated with the Revolution of 1789 and a posture explicitly hostile to the Catholic Church. Being liberal meant advocating freedom of thought, religion, and church-state separation, principles that the papacy firmly and repeatedly rejected over the course of the nineteenth century. The word stood for other things as well, including civil equality for women and the right to divorce. These were also principles rejected by the Catholic Church.

By the late nineteenth century, such liberal causes remained controversial around the world, but in the United States they had taken a particularly radical turn. There, the word "liberal" was also used to describe someone who was openly atheist, or who advocated the right to sexual freedom and contraception, or defended the right to publish obscene literature. To traditionalists, what they had predicted for over a century was coming true: liberalism was leading to complete moral degeneracy and chaos.

Meanwhile, in France, Church advocates capitalized on the word's associations with freedom and toleration to establish the ALP. Subsidized by the Vatican, it fought to *protect* Church rights against the secularizing reforms in the French Chamber of Deputies. "What did it really mean to be liberal?," asked the group's leader, Piou. "The word needs to be defined," he explained, before offering a definition that conscripted it for what was a Catholic and essentially right-of-center movement. Being liberal, Piou said, meant protecting French men and women from the menace of Jacobinism, Freemasonry, and "socialist tyranny." Curiously then, in France by the beginning of the twentieth century, being liberal could mean being socially and religiously conservative, while in America it generally meant the opposite.

# CHAPTER SEVEN

# Two Liberalisms

## OLD AND NEW

*We do not regard state welfare as an emergency measure or
as an unavoidable evil, but as the fulfillment of one of the
highest tasks of our time and nation.*
— VEREIN FÜR SOZIALPOLITIK, 1873

LIBERALS PLACED MUCH of the blame for France's defeat in
the Franco-Prussian War on its poor educational system and
the debilitating influence of Church teachings. They realized,
however, that there were additional reasons for France's humiliation. It was easy to see that German soldiers were physically stronger and healthier than their French counterparts.
Over the course of the war, the French army lost the equivalent of an entire division to smallpox and perhaps five times as
many fell ill. The Prussian army was inoculated and therefore
suffered many fewer casualties. Here, then, was clear evidence
of the benefits of government intervention.

After the war, the Prussian government followed up with
more initiatives. In 1874, it imposed a program of obligatory

vaccination against smallpox on all German citizens. It created a department of health to study infectious diseases and find effective treatments. In 1876, it passed a law requiring all industrial workers over sixteen years of age to enroll in a medical plan unless otherwise covered. Bismarck appeared to be engaging in "state socialism," and liberals everywhere took notice.

Over the course of the following few years, the Prussian government embarked on several more pathbreaking endeavors. It created a full and compulsory insurance system for German workers, including insurance against sickness, industrial accidents, old age, and disability. Bismarck himself did not hesitate to call these measures socialist and promised workers more legislation. Some liberals denounced the measures as just another example of Caesarism, but others approved of them. Soon, a transatlantic debate began over the relationship between "true liberalism" and state socialism.

Historians tend to neglect the role that Germany played in the history of liberalism. But German ideas had an enormous impact from the very beginning. German liberal theology influenced the liberal view of religion for over a century. And now, in the late nineteenth century, German ideas of political economy caused liberalism to split in two, one stream favoring laissez-faire and the other government intervention. Both called themselves liberal.

## *The Role of the State Reimagined*

German measures on behalf of its poor were especially striking at a time when so many studies were revealing the grave problems afflicting all industrializing countries. Although great wealth was being created and standards of living were generally rising, large numbers of poor people were being left behind.

Slums, overcrowding, and disease were rampant. Labor unrest was growing, and workers, unions, and parties were organizing. Socialism, in its various forms and manifestations, was spreading. This caused increasing numbers of liberals to believe that governments should do more to help the poor and they found inspiration in what was going on in Germany.

Worried liberals in France, Britain and the United States now became receptive to the ideas of a new school of German economists. The pathbreakers were economics professors like Wilhelm Roscher, Bruno Hildebrand, and Karl Knies, who were influential in their own day but have been forgotten in ours. At midcentury they launched a full-scale attack on the doctrine of laissez-faire. Laissez-faire ideas, they said, were too abstract and theoretical to be of any use. They were also unethical because they allowed for the exploitation of workers and did nothing to remedy endemic poverty.

What was necessary was a more practical and results-oriented political economy based on empirical data. And so they began collecting evidence that proved that laissez-faire was making life worse, not better, for the majority of the inhabitants of industrializing countries. They predicted that conditions would only deteriorate and spread if governments took no action.

For men like Roscher, the errors of laissez-faire were not only empirical, but moral. Man was not just a solitary, self-interested individual; he was a social being with ethical obligations that he could both understand and fulfill. It was morally abhorrent, they said, to claim that egoism and unbounded competition could serve as the basis for any viable and just economy. Such views caused some people to deride Roscher and his colleagues with labels like "ethical economists" and "socialists of the chair," and they stuck. In return, the ethical economists continued to accuse their adversaries of "Manchesterism," an equally if not more derisive term.

In 1872, the ethical economists founded the Association for a Social Politics (Verein für Sozialpolitik). Their mission statement affirmed the view that the state had a moral obligation to tend to the common welfare. It declared unequivocally: "We do not regard state welfare as an emergency measure or as an unavoidable evil, but as the fulfillment of one of the highest tasks of our time and nation. In the serious execution of this task, the egoism of individuals and the narrow interest of classes will be subordinated to the lasting and higher destiny of the whole."[1]

Slowly, but surely, the ideas of the ethical economists spread, triggering heated debate across Europe and beyond. Philosophers, political scientists, journalists, and politicians weighed in, taking sides on whether to support government intervention or laissez-faire. Some liberals welcomed and absorbed the ideas enthusiastically; others rejected them. Observers began to speak of a crisis in political economy. Future president Woodrow Wilson, who was well versed in the German ideas, called it a "war between the political economists."[2] It resulted in the creation of what the American philosopher John Dewey would later call "two streams" of liberalism, one favoring interventionism and the other laissez-faire.

In France, the debates over German political economy pitted men like Charles Gide and Alfred Fouillée against Léon Say, the son of Jean-Baptiste, who served as French finance minister from 1872 to 1883. Say and other political economists close to the government dismissed the ideas coming from Germany as an abominable "statism" and a kind of "idolatry."[3] "True liberalism," they said, meant adhering to the principles of laissez-faire.

Thanks largely to men like Say, the official stance of French governments during the 1870s was to do as little as possible in terms of direct aid to the poor. Except for the Lois Roussel of 1874 regulating wet nursing and the care of foundling children, very little happened in the realm of poor relief in France during this time. Government officials advanced the same arguments as they had before: "public charity" was harmful since it encouraged the laziness and irresponsibility of workers. It also pushed them to think of aid as a right and not an act of charity. Paul Ceré, a prominent intellectual who served briefly as a prefect during the Second Republic, went so far as to propose that hospices and other "magnificent dormitories for pauperism" should be closed. The old and the sick should be sent back to their homes and the idle enrolled in the army.[4]

But a new class of political economists was rising to challenge this laissez-faire ideology. Charles Gide belonged to this group. Professor at the Universities of Bordeaux and Paris, and later at the Collège de France, Gide published a book in 1883 which championed the new ideas. It was translated into English as *Principles of Political Economy* in 1892. Two years earlier, an article summarizing Gide's ideas for an American audience was published in the *Political Science Quarterly*.[5]

It was high time, Gide said, to look to the new school of German political economy for guidance. The Franco-Prussian War, he argued, had been a defeat of not just France's military but also its policy of laissez-faire. Once upon a time, France had been a leader in the field of political economy. Men like François Quesnay, Dupont de Nemours, Turgot, and Condorcet, to whom even Adam Smith acknowledged his debt, had been at the forefront of their field. But now, Gide lamented, leading French economists like Frédéric Bastiat and Léon Say had become complacent, conservative, and even callous about the misery of the poor. Perhaps they shouldn't be allowed to call themselves liberal any longer, Gide suggested, since they advocated a reprehensible kind of selfishness that was blind to the public good. Perhaps they should be called "modern hedonists" instead. Gide resolved to name them "classical" or "orthodox" liberals, perhaps coining those terms. Orthodox liberals were stuck in the past, he said, unwilling to face up to the new realities. Thankfully, their ideas were being replaced by healthier ones coming from Germany.

The German ideas made headway in Britain as well. While the sudden defeat of France in the Franco-Prussian War and the Commune had served as a stark warning, a severe economic downturn had created massive unemployment and misery. Competition from Germany and the United States also made Britons worry about their country's leadership position as workshop of the world while growing numbers of people were losing faith in the "free market."

Liberal anxieties intensified when in 1874 their party suffered a sudden defeat in the elections and the conservatives gained a parliamentary majority for the first time in over thirty years. Benjamin Disraeli replaced Gladstone as prime minister. In his winning election campaign, Disraeli had reached out to workers and promised them legislation. Once in power, the conservatives pushed through a number of reforms, causing Alexander MacDonald, one of the first working-class members elected to Parliament, to note in 1879 that "the Conservative party have done more for the working classes in five years than the Liberals have in fifty."

All of this left many in the British Liberal Party feeling disoriented and confused. They began to complain about their party's aimlessness. They seemed no longer to have a unifying message or purpose. Vague incantations of improvement and talk of character and self-sacrifice were obviously no longer working. It was not even possible, some complained, to arrive at a definition of a liberal. Pamphlets and articles with titles like "What Are Liberal Principles?" proliferated.

The situation led a growing number of British liberals to become receptive to the new ideas coming from Germany, as can be seen by the plethora of articles and translations of German works of political economy that began to appear. As early as 1875, the *Fortnightly Review*, one of the most influential and reform-minded magazines in nineteenth-century Britain, joyfully announced the fall of "the old orthodox creed," which had proved so incapable of solving the problems plaguing industrializing nations. In 1879, the same review published John Stuart Mill's "Chapters on Socialism," in which he argued that socialist ideas should be given full consideration because they could supply the guiding principles for reform.

Over the course of the next few decades, a growing number of British liberals began to favor a new type of liberalism that advocated more government intervention on behalf of the poor. They called for the state to take action to eliminate poverty, ignorance and disease, and the excessive inequality in the distribution of wealth. They began to say that people should be accorded not just freedom, but the *conditions* of freedom. They began to call this "new liberalism."

In America, the new ideas of political economy were introduced by way of the many young men who went to study at German universities and came back to take leading positions in American colleges. In Germany, they were immersed in ethical economics and witnessed firsthand what a state could do for its poor. Like their British and French counterparts, they became increasingly certain that laissez-faire was simply wrong, both morally and empirically, and they began to advocate more government intervention in the economy.

As elsewhere, profound changes were transforming the economy in America. The country was rapidly industrializing, such that at the turn of the twentieth century, its production surpassed the combined total of Great Britain, Germany, and France. The changes in the economy caused unprecedented disparities of wealth. Prolonged depressions in the 1870s and 1890s caused millions of Americans to lose their jobs.

When American workers, like those elsewhere, asked the government for help, they were refused. Authorities used armed forces to put down the Great Strike of 1877, the first nationwide labor dispute in US history. Anxious observers thought the Paris Commune had crossed the Atlantic.[6]

The next year, the House of Representatives resolved it to be their solemn duty to inquire into the causes of worker distress and to devise remedies. In the end, however, none were recommended. The consensus appears to have remained the same as before: government intervention would violate the laws of the market. Workingmen should learn these laws and acquire the right habits: the values of hard work, saving, and manliness.

Several Americans who studied ethical economics in Germany became leading figures in the emerging disciplines of economics, political science, history, and sociology. They founded a host of professional academic associations, the American Historical Association (1884), American Economic Association (1885), American Political Science Association (1903), and American Sociology Society (1905). Five of the American Economic Association's six original officers had studied in Germany, as had twenty of its first twenty-six presidents.

One of the most important disseminators of the new ideas in America was the economist Richard Ely. Ely earned a PhD in economics from Heidelberg University, where he studied under ethical economists Karl Knies and Johann Bluntschli. Ely came back to accept a teaching position in the Department of Political Economy at Johns Hopkins University in 1881. He soon became a prolific writer of books and articles. Americans, he said, should heed the German example and learn from German ideas.

It was under Ely's leadership that a group of young American economists in 1885 founded the American Economic Association. Its charter reiterated the German association's founding ideal. The state, it said, was "an educational and ethical agency" whose aid was necessary for humanity to progress. Political economy should no longer be used as a tool in the hands of the greedy or as an excuse "for doing nothing while people starve."[7]

British and American encyclopedias testify to the influence of German ethical economics. The 1885 edition of the *Encyclopædia Britannica*'s article on political economy informed its readers that a new school was rising. The *Cyclopaedia of Political Science, Political Economy, and of the Political History of the United States* announced that political science was in a chaotic state. A rebellion, it said, was taking place against the doctrine of laissez-faire, which the Germans had proved to be so utterly false. Most people now realized that the state was morally obliged to step in on behalf of the helpless and oppressed. It had nobler ends to pursue than the mere creation of material wealth. The citizens' improvement in "intelligence and happiness" was of far greater importance. This was what distinguished civilization from barbarism.[8]

Such German ideas exerted a powerful effect on the history of liberalism. They triggered a great debate—often a vituperative one—between advocates of the "old," "classical," or "orthodox" ideas of political economy and the "new," "progressive," or "constructive" ones. As a result, political economy was split in two. The two sides would battle it out for the next century and, to a certain extent, continue to do so today.

Resistance to the new liberalism was considerable. The orthodox school fought back. One of its strongest and most influential voices was Herbert Spencer, perhaps the most widely read English-language philosopher of his age. Now most famously known for the expression "survival of the fittest," Spencer was an authority in a wide range of fields, including ethics, biology, philosophy, and economics.

In 1884, Spencer weighed in with a highly polemical work titled *Man versus the State*. The advocates of "new liberalism," he charged, were not really liberal at all. "True liberalism" meant nothing more than freedom from restraint or interference. In the past, liberalism had opposed the unlimited authority of monarchs; in the present, liberalism should oppose the unlimited power of parliaments.[9]

Spencer's most important American disciple, William Graham Sumner, dismissed the German ideas as nothing but "social quackery." Sumner taught social science at Yale University and, like his mentor, believed in a strict policy of laissez-faire. There simply was no such thing as a "social question," he said; what the working man needed was to be left alone.[10] Similar ideas were advanced by J. Laurence Laughlin, then at Harvard University. In 1884, Laughlin published an abridgement of John Stuart Mill's *Principles of Political Economy* for use in American schools, from which, however, he removed Mill's references to the benefits of state intervention.[11] Five years after Mill's Socialist Essays had been published in England, he was turned into an advocate of unfettered free markets in America.

Neither Sumner nor Laughlin could stem the tide. By 1903, Charles Merriam, professor of political science at the University of Chicago, proclaimed the victory of the German ideas. His *History of American Political Theories* tracked the evolution that American political thinking had undergone since the founding. Modern ideas about the purpose of the state had radically changed, he said. Political scientists in America were now ready for the state to assume more extensive powers.

They no longer believed that the government should limit itself to playing a negative role, but that it should advance the general welfare. Merriam himself had been trained in Germany.

While British liberals argued among themselves about the nature of true liberalism, Gladstone continued to offer little leadership on the question. He turned to Home Rule for Ireland as an issue around which all liberals could rally. Instead, however, the party split over the question and liberals fell from office in 1885. By that year, liberal disunity and confusion reached a peak. Liberals remained out of power for the next twenty years, except for a short period between 1892 and 1895. According to the *Daily Chronicle*, the Liberal Party was in a state of crisis; it was "incoherent, apathetic, disorganized and dumb."[12] Liberals had no idea what they stood for anymore.

Meanwhile, many British newspapers demanded that more attention be paid to social and economic matters. With an increasing sense of urgency they said that liberals must discard "old liberalism," to give way to the new. In 1906, one of the most original political theorists of the time, John A. Hobson, starkly announced that "the old *laissez-faire* liberalism is dead." More progressive measures should be passed to extirpate the roots of poverty and the diseases that accompanied it. Only then could real "equality of economic and intellectual opportunity" exist.[13]

## Liberal Socialism

Many proponents of the new liberalism admitted that they could be seen as preaching socialism, but they didn't mind. In 1893 a leading liberal weekly in Britain wrote that "if it be Socialism to have generous and hopeful sentiments with regard to the lot of those who work . . . we are all Socialists in that sense."[14] A few years later, the future prime minster, Winston

Churchill, delivered a speech in which he specifically urged liberals not to worry about the socialist label. "The cause of the Liberal Party is the cause of the left-out millions," he said, and it should favor state intervention on their behalf. It was through the agency of a new and "socialistic" form of liberalism that society would evolve "to a more equal foundation."[15]

To be sure, openness to socialism also depended on the way socialism was defined. Here, too, there were disagreements. The word meant different things to different people. For Churchill, being "socialistic" did not have to mean that one advocated revolution or something as radical as the nationalization of private industry. He favored gradual, nonviolent reforms. The American economist Francis Amasa Walker asserted that one could apply the term "socialist" to "all efforts, under popular impulse, to enlarge the functions of government" for the public good.[16] Bluntschli's *Staatsworterbuch* acknowledged that socialism meant different things to different people, but that it was, in his mind, perfectly appropriate to refer to gradual social reform as socialism.[17]

In France, the middle way between liberalism and socialism was often called "solidarism." Its leading proponent was Léon Bourgeois, who became prime minister in 1895 and published a book titled *Solidarity* the following year. Some preferred to called it "liberal socialism,"[18] and in fact Bourgeois was happy to call himself a "liberal socialist."[19] The French Republic had a duty to promote solidarity among its citizens, he said, and it should do so not only by teaching them patriotism in public schools, but by reducing the inequality that divided them. In response, Léon Say and his colleagues insisted that the government remain faithful to *true* liberalism, by which they meant laissez-faire.

Solidarism provided the rationale for a collaboration between the French radical republican party and a group of socialists in Parliament. Together they pushed through a program of reforms, including the limitation of the workday and the provision of pensions and public assistance to be paid for by a progressive income tax. The duty of social solidarity required such intervention by the state, said Bourgeois. A republic should not be just a certain kind of political institution, he declared, but the instrument of moral and social progress. Such ideas infuriated liberal political economists like Say.

The liberals' increasing friendliness toward socialism no doubt had something to do with the socialists' increasing friendliness toward them. Late nineteenth-century socialists did not necessarily advocate revolution or the abolition of capitalism. France's first socialist party, the Federation of the Socialist Workers of France, founded in 1879, advocated gradual reforms passed by Parliament. In Germany, too, the electoral success of their party caused many Social Democrats to believe that socialism could be achieved by peaceful reform and legislation. These developments encouraged liberals to think that they could collaborate with socialists to pass progressive laws. In 1901, the liberal leader Friedrich Naumann proposed a grand electoral coalition from "Bassermann to Bebel," in other words, from the National Liberal right to the Social Democratic left.

Eduard Bernstein, a German political theorist and member of the Social Democratic Party, emerged as a leader in this revision of socialist doctrine. In a series of articles in *Die Neue Zeit*, Bernstein proposed that socialists tone down their rhetoric against liberalism since liberalism was anyway evolving in the right direction. Socialism, Bernstein said, was the heir and fulfillment of liberalism, and democracy enabled the realization of socialism by peaceful and gradual means. A revolution was not necessary.

Such socialist attitudes help to explain why Leonard Hobhouse, a leading English publicist of the new liberalism, could assert that "true Socialism serves to complete rather than to destroy the leading Liberal ideals."[20] His friend John Hobson called it "practicable socialism."[21] Unsurprisingly, however, old-school liberals continued to denounce any collusion with socialism. In France, self-titled "men of order" and "sincere conservatives" created a Liberal Republican Union to fight for "*true* liberalism."[22] To these men, as to the members of the Action Libérale Populaire, being liberal now meant being conservative.

## A Moral Way of Life

From the very inception of liberalism, liberals saw their cause as a moral one. They were fighting not just for their rights, but for the means to better fulfill their moral duties. New liberals spoke that way too. They championed not individual rights so much as moral self-development as a way to further the public good. A good example is T. H. Green's lecture "Liberal Legislation and Freedom of Contract," delivered in 1880 and thereafter published and widely read. Green, who had studied philosophy and theology in Germany, was a professor of moral philosophy at Oxford University. His lecture was very influential in its time and has since been regarded as the very quintessence of the British new liberalism.

Every human being, Green claimed, had a moral obligation to make the best of himself. And making the best of yourself meant performing certain duties to your fellow citizens. Not just the wealthy or well-off, but everyone had such duties. But how, he asked, could the poor and sick possibly fulfill their duties to society given the miserable conditions in which they found themselves? Circumstances beyond their control, Green argued, prevented the majority of the poor from fulfilling their moral obligations. Such reasoning led him to advocate a slew of measures including sanitary laws, factory inspections, and public education. Other liberals would add to this list.

It is in fact impossible to understand new liberalism apart from the primacy its advocates gave to ethics. It was a passion for improving mankind that drove them. New Liberals often spoke of the need for individuals to develop their "higher faculties." Self-development for the sake of others, Ely believed, was the aim of social ethics. In lay sermons at Balliol College, Green urged people to strive for their better selves. For this, he said, they should cultivate the spirit of self-sacrifice. Liberalism's most important task, said one German liberal, was to help workers to lead a moral way of life. Others called it a "human life" or "the best life."

One way that governments could provide people with the opportunity to lead a moral life was through public education. We have seen how much effort liberals devoted to it. According to the French Solidarist Léon Bourgeois, it was up to the public school system to "elevate men to the notion of social duty."[23] The new French schools made it their mission to mold students into good citizens—to teach them, in other words, solidarity. It was an improved public education system, said Hobson, that would precipitate the necessary "revolution . . . in the minds of men."[24] Woodrow Wilson declared that the sentiments of generosity and humanity needed to be cultivated and he believed that the role of a liberal arts education should be to develop such sentiments.[25]

Educational and moral reform was, as always, intimately related to religion. Unsurprisingly, many of the new liberals were either Protestant or had Protestant backgrounds, and most of these were favorable to a variety of "liberal Protestantism" that we have encountered before. T. H. Green was the son of an Evangelical minister and had studied liberal theology at Tübingen.[26] The American Economic Association included twenty-three clergymen among its charter members, many of whom had studied in Germany. Liberal Protestants and Freemasons played a disproportionately large role in the French Solidarity movement. Both Hobson and Hobhouse imbibed much of their moral perspective from their work in the British ethical societies.

According to its advocates, "liberal Christianity" showed itself in altruism and good works. By the end of the nineteenth century, Englishmen called it a "generalized" or "common Christianity." The liberal MP and Congregational minister Edward Miall wanted British schoolchildren to imbibe a "broader, more liberal, and perhaps, in some respects, a more *indistinct* doctrinal creed."[27]

The widely read Unitarian manual *Our Liberal Movement in Theology* described this "generalized" Christianity. Above all, it should disseminate a system of morality that would have a practical effect on life.[28] This idea that religion should be practical was often repeated. Friedrich Naumann called it "practical Christianity."[29] For Richard Ely, a "Christianity which is not practical is not Christianity at all."[30] Each one of these liberal Protestants believed that the Christian religion should rid itself of what they thought was a narrow, negative, and excessively individualistic attitude that focused on saving each person's soul, and devote itself instead to bettering the lives of all people.

## Liberal Eugenics

Such lofty words about human betterment and self-perfection leave us unprepared for a stunning fact: many of the same people who championed an expanded role for the state to help the poor were also enthusiastic proponents of "race science" and eugenics. As shocking as it seems to us today, many liberals saw these as entirely consistent with their mission to further the common good.

The term "eugenics" was coined in 1881 by the British naturalist and mathematician Francis Galton, a cousin of Charles Darwin. The leading American eugenicist, Charles B. Davenport, described it as "the science of the improvement of the human race by better breeding." There was "positive" eugenics, which aimed to encourage more prolific procreation by the fit. Positive measures typically involved legislation to promote healthy mothers and newborns. There was also "negative" eugenics, which aimed to encourage those deemed "unfit" to breed less or, even better, not at all.

Many eugenicists expected their program of race improvement, whether positive or negative, to be voluntary. They stressed education, moral injunction, and contraception. Some also favored forced sterilization or the prohibition of marriage for the "unfit." These included, among others, the insane, the feeble-minded, and epileptics. And because it was commonly thought that a relationship existed between low intelligence and immorality and crime, and that criminals bred criminals and paupers bred paupers, some advocated the restriction of marriage to them as well.

Not only liberals were enthusiastic proponents of eugenics. Belief in eugenics and "race science" was widespread across the political spectrum in all the countries we have considered. It was fueled by the fears of degeneration that were growing in industrializing countries, not just in France after the Franco-Prussian War, but in the United States, Britain, and Germany too. In France, concerns about the degeneration of the "race" led to the formation of a League of Human Regeneration in

1896. A few years later, Léon Bourgeois became honorary president of the newly created French Eugenics Society. The French, historians have noted, tended to prefer positive methods to negative ones.

In 1903, the British Parliament was moved to establish a commission on national deterioration. The "fiber" of the nation—its moral character, intelligence, and capacity to compete in the world—was thought to be in decline. To counter the problem, social and political reforms were insufficient.

Hobson, one of the most respected liberal theorists of his time, supported the prevention of "anti-social procreation." "Selection of the fittest, or at least, rejection of the unfittest" was essential to all progress: "To abandon the production of children to unrestricted private enterprise is the most dangerous abnegation of its functions which any Government can practise."[31]

In America too, progressives from Richard Ely and Herbert Croly to Woodrow Wilson were enthusiastic advocates of eugenics. Ely urged the embrace of artificial selection to avoid the birth of "vicious progeny" and favored laws denying certain people the right to marry. There were some human beings, he wrote, "who are absolutely unfit and should be prevented from a continuation of their kind." Ely also supported segregating the "unemployable" in labor colonies, and when that was not enough, proposed more drastic remedies. "The morally incurable" and those "who will not work and will not obey," Ely asserted, "should not be allowed to propagate their kind."[32] In 1911, then New Jersey governor Wilson signed the state's forcible sterilization legislation, which targeted "the hopelessly defective and criminal classes."[33]

Many, if not most, eugenicists were also overtly racist. Ely wrote that blacks were "for the most part grownup children, and should be treated as such." The racism of his student, Wilson, is of course well known. As professor, Wilson told his

*Atlantic Monthly* readers that freed slaves and their descendants were "indolent and aggressive, sick of work, [and] covetous of pleasure."[34] But such ideas were common. Blacks, it was said, lacked the capacity to govern themselves and therefore should not be permitted to vote.

## *Feminism and Liberalism at the End of the Nineteenth Century*

Eugenics also informed liberal attitudes toward women. As the biologically weaker sex, women were said to need special protection from the rigors of employment outside the home. This is mainly why liberal legislators favored such things as restrictions on hours of work or bans on night work for women. After all, women played an especially important role in the preservation of human heredity and should not be allowed to risk the race's health by overwork and fatigue. Any type of employment "injurious to the female organism" should be forbidden, wrote Ely.[35]

Such ideas were common among French liberals too, especially in the wake of the Franco-Prussian War, when fears of population decline and degeneration ran high. In his *On the Female Laborer*, Jules Simon wrote that women who worked outside the home produced weak and malformed babies. Their breast milk was corrupted. Anxieties such as these lay behind French liberal welfare reforms that targeted women especially. The new laws had much to do with encouraging healthy child bearing.[36]

When it came to extending the vote to women, most liberals continued to be opposed. Like African Americans, women were said to lack the necessary capacity. They were not only physically weaker, but more impressionable and less rational than men. Their natures made them less capable of forming sound judgments. They lacked common sense. Such ideas of course only reinforced the idea that their proper role was within the home, where they could be overseen by their husbands and encouraged to produce healthy children.

In France, there was the additional fear that giving women the vote would favor Catholic candidates. Women were naturally superstitious, liberals said, and thus susceptible to the manipulation of priests. This was the main reason why Alfred Fouillée, otherwise an advocate of what he called a "progressive" and "reforming liberalism," opposed the enfranchisement of women. They needed more education before it should even be considered. In the meantime, their contribution to the public good was to produce healthy offspring and maintain happy homes.

Liberals proffered additional reasons for depriving women of the vote. Because they were so emotional and unreasonable, giving women the vote would encourage over-legislation. Liberal member of Parliament Herbert Samuel conceded that government might perhaps become "more humane," but it would be at the cost of efficiency, principle, and "true statesmanship." If women were granted the franchise, government would be overwhelmed by "unpractical idealism." A spirit of effeminacy would infiltrate government, "silently sapping the foundations of both national and imperial greatness." Sex, Samuel concluded, "fixes a line of political capacity beyond which it is not safe to go."[37]

Despite the growth of women's suffrage movements, William Gladstone unequivocally opposed women's suffrage. So did the Women's Liberal Federation, formed in 1886 under the presidency of Mrs. Gladstone. The purpose of the federation was to promote the interests of the Liberal Party, or, as Mrs. Gladstone put it, "to help our husbands."[38] Giving women equal rights, some liberals continued to say, would not improve but endanger marriage and the family, the all-important institutions that moralized and prepared men for citizenship.[39] In Germany, the National Liberal Party handbook of 1897 spoke for many liberals when it declared that domestic life "can only develop in a healthy way . . . when the man is the head of the family."[40] Echoing one of Samuel's points, inviting women into government might "effeminate" the state.[41]

Some arguments were blatantly contradictory. While it was said that granting women the vote would cause "over-legislation" in favor of humane and idealistic causes, it was also said to be unnecessary since their husbands voted for them. Granting women the suffrage would simply double the number of votes, which would be pointless. On the other hand, political disagreement within a couple would create disharmony within the family. Samuel added that women's various grievances in matters of divorce, inheritance, "and so forth" were in any case "not serious" and were being addressed. Remaining issues could be remedied by their husbands.[42]

Some liberals thought that women might *eventually* acquire the vote. "Let us wait a while," Samuel suggested, since with time women might gain the fitness needed.[43] In fact, many liberals said that the time just wasn't right for their enfranchisement. Women needed to acquire, and show, their "capacity" first. When German feminists appealed to Friedrich Naumann for support, he responded that women "would do better to demonstrate their accomplishments in public affairs" before requesting the vote. Their first priority should be suffrage reform for Prussian men. Women should help men gain their "full political manhood" and then "the question of woman suffrage will solve itself."[44]

A growing number of liberal women and men disputed such arguments, insisting that the liberals were contradicting their own principles. German feminists complained that the recent and much vaunted "new liberalism" had brought women nothing, or next to nothing. Alice Salomon tried to convince liberals that feminism "sprouted on the same ground" as liberalism and shared a similarity of worldview.[45] What women were asking for was simply a "broadened liberalism" that would include them.[46]

Many feminists began to say that "true liberalism" should now support voting rights for women. Among a new generation of men, such as the German Young Liberals, there was a growing number of voices who agreed. Protestant theologian Rudolf Wielandt was one of them. "The women's movement in its noblest and finest motives is a sister to liberalism," he declared. "Woman only wants the right to . . . utilize her particular nature" for the public good, and women should be encouraged to do so.[47]

For their part, the British Women's Liberal Federation grew unsatisfied with the narrow mission of "helping their husbands," and demanded that they themselves be given voting rights. In 1911 the *Manchester Guardian* proclaimed that the exclusion of women was "an outrage. . . . No Government calling itself Liberal could so far betray Liberal principles without incurring deep and lasting discredit and ultimate disaster."[48]

Some women asserted that it was precisely their special "natures" that made their full political participation so important to the state. An example is the German feminist Gertrude Bäumer, who in 1910 was invited to deliver a keynote address titled "Women and the Future of Liberalism" to a conference of German progressives. Women's uniqueness, she said, made it imperative for them to have the vote. Women's suffrage would ensure the influence of "feminine talents and energies" on society.

This, however, is precisely what Bäumer's adversaries worried about: the effeminization of the state. The official National Liberal position in 1908 rejected her arguments, continuing the charge, endlessly repeated for over a hundred years, that granting women the vote was to deny "the difference between the sexes that Nature intended."[49]

Rights-based arguments remained rare among late nineteenth-century campaigners for female suffrage. American suffragettes Susan B. Anthony and Elizabeth Cady Stanton had been true pioneers—and outliers—in that regard. On November 5, 1872, Anthony and fifteen other women in Rochester, New York, cast a ballot in the presidential election, although women were prohibited from doing so. Two weeks later they were arrested; Anthony was tried and found guilty of voting illegally. Her actions were said to threaten marriage, the family, the church, and the constitution. She, in turn, accused the authorities of "trampl[ing] under foot every vital principle of our government. My natural rights, my civil rights, my political rights, my judicial rights, are all alike ignored. Robbed of the fundamental privilege of citizenship, I am degraded from the status of a citizen to that of a subject; and not only myself individually, but all of my sex, are, by your honor's verdict, doomed to political subjection under this, so-called, form of government."

Such arguments, based on a woman's individual rights, were rarely heard elsewhere. In his Liberal Party handbook, Samuel explained that it was pointless for people to speak about a "natural right" to the vote since no such right existed. Fitness was an absolute condition of enfranchisement. Because the English woman, like the English child or the Indian man, lacked the required "fitness," it was ridiculous to think that she should be granted the vote. Likewise, the *National Liberal News* hoped that German women would avoid allowing themselves to be "Americanized." Good German women rejected any "Suffragette idiocy."[50]

More often, women continued to argue that they wanted a change in the laws so that they could better perform their duties as wives, mothers, and citizens and produce healthier children.

Most feminists did not deny their special natures or their domestic vocations. They believed that men and women had different but *complementary* natures and duties; they should work together to raise families in ways that contributed to the public good. Some even used eugenic arguments to further their cause. The notorious American free-lover and suffragette Victoria Woodhull, who ran for president in the 1870, argued that more liberal divorce laws would regenerate "the race." Free-lovers often said that making divorce easier, marriages more loving, and sex more pleasurable for women would translate into better mothers, better families, and healthier babies.

By the end of the nineteenth century, when it came to the role of government, there existed two varieties of liberals: the new and the old, the interventionists and the laissez-fairists. Both insisted that *they* were the *true* liberals.

Eventually, the new liberals dropped the qualifying word "new" and just called themselves liberals. Like Green, many of them thought that there was in any case little new about their version of liberalism. Liberals, Green said, had for fifty years been fighting for the same thing: the social good. Hobson insisted that liberals had *never* subscribed to a policy of narrow laissez-faire or conceived of liberty in a purely negative way. Incorporating the views of German ethical economists was entirely compatible with liberal principles, since they were constantly being adjusted to deal with the problems of the times.

The battle between new and old liberals was also about how to read the founders of the liberal school. New liberals claimed that the laissez-fairists were misreading economists like Adam Smith. It was they who were "doing the work which Adam Smith began."[51] After all, Smith had been sensitive to historical circumstances, wrote the *Encyclopædia Britannica*; in the fifth book of the *Wealth of Nations*, he had recognized the need for government interference. Likewise, Alfred Fouillée dismissed the "laissez-fairists' economism"; Smith had meant nothing of the sort.[52]

The Fabian socialist Beatrice Webb mused over the irony of it all: "The Political Economy of Adam Smith was the scientific expression of the impassioned crusade of the 18th century against class tyranny and the oppression of the Many by the Few. By what silent revolution of events, by what unselfconscious transformation of thought, did it change itself into the 'Employers' Gospel' of the 19th century?"[53]

# CHAPTER EIGHT

# Liberalism Becomes the American Creed

*In the United States at this time liberalism is not only the dominant but even the sole intellectual tradition.*

—LIONEL TRILLING, 1950

HOW DID LIBERALISM become such a key and ubiquitous term in the American political vocabulary? The *Encyclopaedia Americana* of 1831 did not contain an entry on liberalism, and the one on "liberal" explained that its political meaning came from France. Only half a century later did liberalism receive an entry in the American *Cyclopaedia of Political Science*, and it was a translation of a French article that equated liberalism with the "principles of 89." During the closing years of the nineteenth century, "liberalism" remained a rare word in the language of American politics and, when it was used, it was most often to designate a European, if not *French*, cluster of ideas.

How, then, did liberalism become so Americanized? According to the noted intellectual and political commentator Walter Lippman, the word first came into common usage thanks to a group of reformers who were Republican Progressives in 1912 and Wilsonian Democrats from around 1916.[1] It is indicative that Woodrow Wilson called himself "progressive" in 1916 and "liberal" in 1917.[2] But what did the president mean? What did being liberal mean to Wilson?

By 1917, the meaning of the term had evolved significantly from its origins in the French Revolution and its century-long association with French political developments. Toward the end of the nineteenth century, the French influence had receded and German ideas were exerting a growing influence.

In England, this led to the conception of "new liberalism." Thanks largely to the travails of the British Liberal Party, liberal newspapers, and liberal theorists like Leonard Hobhouse, this new form of liberalism spread, and by the second decade of the twentieth century, its advocates felt secure enough to drop the "new" and just call it liberalism. Herbert Samuel's liberal handbook, published in 1902 with an introduction by future prime minister H. H. Asquith, was titled *Liberalism: An Attempt to State the Principles and Proposals of Contemporary Liberalism in England*. Lyon Blease, another Liberal Party politician, published a book in 1913 simply titled *Short History of English Liberalism*. It was this liberalism that was imported into America around 1914–17 by Republican Progressives and Wilsonian Democrats.

Herbert Croly, one of most influential public intellectuals of the Progressive movement and cofounder of the flagship progressive magazine the *New Republic* in 1914, was one of those responsible for dissemination of the term in America. His enormously influential book, *The Promise of American Life* of 1909, delivered a stinging indictment of laissez-faire economics and a strong argument for government intervention. It is more than likely that Croly adopted the term to show solidarity with the liberal government and liberal thinkers in Britain, with whom he sympathized. By 1914 Croly had begun calling his own ideas liberal, and by mid-1916 the term was in common use in the *New Republic* as another way to describe progressive legislation. After all, as Woodrow Wilson explained in his *Constitutional Government in the United States* of 1908, Americans "borrowed our whole political language from England."[3]

## A Liberal Empire

President Wilson may also have been one of the first Americans to use the word "liberal" to describe a certain foreign policy agenda. During his famous Peace without Victory address in January 1917, he claimed to be "speaking for liberals and friends of humanity." While en route to the Paris Peace conference to sell his Fourteen Points, he declared that "liberalism is the only thing that can save civilization from chaos."

Of course, liberalism had always been about more than domestic politics. From Lafayette, who boasted that liberalism was a vast movement radiating outward from France, to those who feared a "universal liberalism" with reverberations as far away as India, the idea of spreading liberalism internationally had a long history, at least some of which President Wilson was surely aware. On his way to Paris, he visited Genoa and paid tribute to Mazzini in front of his monument. Wilson professed to have studied Mazzini's writings closely and to have derived guidance from them. The president added that with the end of the First World War, he hoped to contribute to "the realization of the ideals to which his [Mazzini's] life and thought were devoted."[4]

Wilson most likely also knew that liberalism was closely intertwined with the idea of empire. Many of the British liberals with whom American progressives sympathized spoke of empire as a way of spreading liberal values around the world.

Indeed, many of them saw no contradiction in approving of empire and while at the same time believing that "the root principle of Liberalism [was] a passionate attachment to the ideal of self-government."[5] Empire was a "truly liberal foreign policy" that would spread civilization and the "arts of government" around the world.[6]

It may seem curious today that they spoke this way about empire when they simultaneously denounced "imperialism." To take just one example, John Hobson, in a highly revered book on imperialism, called it a "disease" spread by economic parasites who preyed on the poor. The liberal statesman Robert Lowe called it the very "apotheosis of violence . . . the oppression of the weak by the strong, and the triumph of power over justice."[7]

In Britain, during the election campaign of 1872 that pitted the Tory Benjamin Disraeli against the liberal William Gladstone, the subject of empire became highly politicized. Liberals repeatedly accused Disraeli of imperialism in a concerted attempt to besmirch and defame him. In return, Disraeli exploited the empire's popularity with the British people to denigrate the liberals. He suggested that they were weak and unpatriotic and could not be trusted with safekeeping Britain's colonies. Liberals, he warned, would ruin the empire. In his famous Crystal Palace speech of June 24, the aspiring prime minister claimed that throughout British history there "has been no effort so continuous, so subtle, supported by so much energy, and carried on with so much ability and acumen as the attempts of Liberalism to effect the disintegration of the Empire."

Disraeli's rhetoric was clearly a winning tactic. During his premiership, he engineered the purchase of the Suez Canal shares, took his government into Egyptian affairs, supported Turkey against Russia, and adopted an aggressive stance in both southern Africa and Afghanistan. In 1876, he proclaimed

Queen Victoria empress of India. Liberals vehemently attacked his imperialism. It was hypocritical, immoral, and contrary to British values.

It is easy to misinterpret these liberal denunciations of imperialism without an understanding of the word games involved. As curious as it may seem to us today, it was entirely possible for British liberals to denounce imperialism while favoring "genuine colonialism." The terms did not mean the same thing.

The word "imperialism," like so many other isms, had been introduced into political discourse as a pejorative. It was used to vilify despots like Napoleon III and Bismarck and shared certain characteristics with Caesarism, which, as we know, was coined around the same time. Consider, for example, an article in the *Fortnightly Review* in 1878 carrying the telling title "What Does Imperialism Mean?" Its author explained that it meant the exertion of brute force over others. It was founded on selfishness and a complete disregard for moral duty.

Imperialists like Napoleon and Bismarck, it was frequently said, used the allure of empire to divert the attention of their poorer populations from the need for reform at home, while they increased their own power and allowed a small group of supporters to amass wealth at the expense of the public. In other words, imperialism was one of the ways in which dictators, in cahoots with aristocracy, plundered society and, by harnessing the support of the ignorant mob, tried to stop or even reverse liberal reforms. By accusing Disraeli of imperialism, British liberals were thus suggesting that he was deliberately misleading the public to further his own interests, those of the Crown and the English aristocracy. To make matters worse, he was appealing to the public's basest instincts in pursuit of his goals. His imperialism was called un-English; it was a pernicious form of Caesarism.

But such statements should not be taken to mean that liberals wished to disband their empire. To disapprove of one kind of empire did not necessarily mean disapproving of another. Gladstone spoke well of an empire that allowed for self-government and contrasted such an empire with what he called the selfish form of empire advocated by Disraeli. He could oppose *imperialism* but favor *colonies*.

Gladstone did not oppose the projection of British power and influence; he just professed to oppose the use of violence that often accompanied it. (His record as prime minister during the 1880s shows that he hardly lived up to these sentiments, however, as his armed intervention in Egypt in 1882 illustrates.) He believed that the British had a duty to spread their civilization and therefore the right to do so. About British rule over Indians, Gladstone said, "It is them and their interests that we are defending, even more, and far more, than our own."[8] Many liberals agreed. The *Manchester Guardian* stated that "liberalism stands, as it has always stood, for the humanitarian principles, for justice to the more backward people in India and Africa under our control, for fair dealing with foreign peoples, weak or strong, and for a helping hand for those who are struggling for a freedom which we have long since won for ourselves."[9]

American admirers of Gladstone concurred that countries like their own had a mission to colonize. They should not, however, follow what one writer called "the path of barbarism." In the 1890s, Charles Norton, editor of the *North American Review*, denounced the arrogance, militarism, and selfishness that underpinned imperialism. He admired Gladstone, whom he thought was the proponent of a truly "liberal foreign policy." American publications like the *Nation* and *Harper's* seconded such views. To them, Disraeli was seducing supporters with appeals to a wrong-minded form of national glory, all the while distracting the British people's attention away from pressing domestic issues. It seemed clear to Disraeli's critics that the main objective of his imperialism was to divert people from problems at home through aggrandizement abroad.[10]

Key liberal theorists like Hobson and Hobhouse also differentiated between good and bad forms of empire, between the positive "genuine colonialism" and base "imperialism." Imperialism, they said, benefited only a small group of "economic parasites," while it provided no long-term benefits for the lower classes. It diverted their attention from the need for reform at home.

Both men also argued that there was a better form of empire, namely one that furthered the "civilization of the world."[11] It did so by promoting the improvement and elevation of the character of the people under control. Like other liberals, they defended settler colonialism, which they both took to be a noncoercive and voluntary arrangement for mutual benefit. The goal, said Hobson, was "the elevation of humanity." Colonialism was genuine and benevolent if "it extend[ed] the bounds of civilisation, and lift[ed] the level of material and moral conduct in the world."[12] For James Fitzjames Stephen, the liberal judge, scholar, and member of the Colonial Council in India, who helped to frame and pass many legal reforms there, liberalism meant fulfilling an obligation to rule justly and to spread European civilization to the governed. This meant bringing peace, order, and law to India. Joseph Chamberlain explained that Britain's empire could be justified only if it made the people happy and improved their prospects.

Virtually all European advocates of empire—whether British, French, or German—believed that it would spread civilization and that Europeans had both a right and a duty to do just that. In France they spoke of a *mission civilisatrice*; in Germany the spreading of *Kultur*. Americans of course had their White Man's Burden. Last but not least, liberals frequently said that genuine colonialism would teach the lower races "the arts of government." The central principle of liberalism, wrote Hobhouse, was self-government,[13] and genuine colonialism should spread this principle around the world. Liberals frequently said that England was seeking to teach her native subjects to be self-dependent and to give them "in the fullness of time, and under the aegis of her own flag, a new and a better freedom."[14] This is also what it meant to spread civilization.

Somewhat paradoxically, Europeans also believed that the acquisition of empire would civilize and moralize *their own* populations. It would do so by turning unemployed and degenerate urban workers from Europe into productive farmers, thus making them more healthy, manly, and patriotic. Herbert Samuel believed that the empire fostered the "ennoblement of the [English] race."[15] In France, it was thought that colonies would encourage large families and thereby be a remedy for the country's declining birthrate, a pressing problem after its defeat in the Franco-Prussian War. Acquiring an empire would also go a long way toward restoring the country's honor.[16]

Such lofty words cannot mask the fact that liberals often whitewashed horrific violence. Even settler colonialism frequently involved the expropriation of property and cruelty. Many liberals were well aware of the atrocities being committed,[17] but seem to have chosen to denounce them and move on rather than seeking an end to empire. Samuel argued that despite the "occasional abuse of power," on balance empire was a force for good. One shouldn't take the missteps out of proportion.[18] In France, political economist Charles Gide suggested that European colonizers should confess their past sins and try to do better in the future. It was the duty of a great people like the French to colonize, but it should be done lovingly and peacefully.

## Racialization of the Anglo-Saxon Myth

Pro-colonial liberal discourse was saturated with overtly racist language. References to the "lower races," "subject races," and "barbarian races" abound. And although the purpose of genuine colonialism was ostensibly to promote their self-government, how long such lower races should expect to wait until they were permitted to govern themselves was often left vague. It depended on the level of their social development, how far they had been "civilized." "A barbarian race may prosper best if for a period, *even for a long period*, it surrenders the right of self-government in exchange for the teachings of civilization," wrote Samuel. It would happen "in the fullness of time."[19]

Since the very beginning, liberals had linked the right to vote to the possession of "capacity." Although women were often said to lack capacity for reasons of biology, when it came to men it was more often described as something that could, at least in principle, be gained. If you made enough money, acquired the requisite education and leisure time, you could acquire the vote.

During the last decades of the nineteenth century, this changed. Political capacity became progressively racialized and transformed into a matter of heredity. To a significant number of influential liberals, the capacity to vote now became the exclusive property of the "Anglo-Saxon race," sometimes also referred to as the "Teutonic race."

The Anglo-Saxon myth was, of course, centuries old. The legend held that England owed its notions of freedom and self-government to German tribes who had migrated from the forests of Germany to England in the early Middle Ages. It was widely disseminated in the nineteenth century, including by liberals such as Madame de Staël, in *On Germany*, and by writers of the *Staats-Lexikon*. In fact, many liberals continued to believe that the "Saxons" had brought to Britain their spirit of independence and knowledge of self-government. The Magna Carta and Bill of Rights, they said, were only a development of the "germs of liberty" brought to England by the German tribes.

In most of these instances, however, the term "Anglo-Saxon" referred mainly to a cultural inheritance. The tribes had brought their *ideas*, *values*, or a certain *spirit* to England. Now, during the closing years of the nineteenth century, the meaning of the word began to change. Under the impact of "race science," it came increasingly to designate a matter of biological heredity. John Burgess, founder of the *Political Science Quarterly* and one of the most influential political scientists of his period, wrote that the United States, Great Britain, and Germany—the "three great Teutonic powers"—shared not only an ethical and political bond, but a racial one. "If Great Britain is our motherland," he wrote, then "Germany is the motherland of our motherland."[20]

It is important, of course, not to oversimplify or generalize. The word "race" still had somewhat of a muddled meaning. Sometimes it appears to have been used as a simple synonym for "English-speaking," suggesting that, at least theoretically, once the colonized races learned English and were civilized, they would no longer be inferior. But sources also show that it was often assumed that white areas of the world would be more easy to civilize than others. In fact, nonwhite areas might *never* reach the level of civilization required for self-government.

Anglo-Saxons, on the other hand, were thought to have a special aptitude for democracy. Anglo-Saxon men, it was often said, were the possessors of superior political genius and therefore particularly well suited to teach the world good government. It is what entitled them to rule those parts of the world inhabited by the "unpolitical and barbaric races." It was their mission and manifest destiny to rule the world. World domination was "the birthright of the Anglo-Saxon race."[21]

If the Anglo-Saxon race occupied the top of the political capacity ladder, the black or "barbaric races" always occupied the bottom rung. Black skin, wrote Burgess, meant "membership in a race of men which has never of itself succeeded in subjecting passion to reason, has never, therefore, created any civilization of any kind."[22] Even more stunningly, in his *History of American Political Theories*, the progressive historian Charles Merriam wrote that "Barbaric races, if incapable, *may be swept away*," and that "such action violates no rights of these populations which are not petty and trifling in comparison with its transcendent right and duty to establish political and legal order everywhere."[23]

## From an Anglo-Saxon to an Anglo-American Liberal Empire

Some began to say that the superior political capacities of the Anglo-Saxons meant that they should cooperate in bringing their civilization and culture to other parts of the world. On this issue, a bond grew between Britain and the United States during the period leading up to World War I. Many Americans were moved by Gladstone's 1878 article in the *North American Review*, titled "Kin beyond the Sea," in which the British prime minister proposed a rapprochement between the two countries in the interest of world peace, prosperity, and "self-government." Gladstone called their Constitution "the most wonderful work ever struck off at a given time by the brain and purpose of man" and praised America's "splendid service to the general cause of popular government throughout the world." Soon, he predicted, the United States would surpass all other countries in wealth and power.

Stressing the resemblances between the two nations' forms of government, and their shared commitment to the principle of self-government, Gladstone noted that England and America would shortly be the two most powerful nations in the world. They should use their combined strength for the "highest purposes." They were the "two greater branches of a race born to command." Together, they would combat savagery and inhumanity while bringing peace, progress, and prosperity to the world. Having acquired great power, they had also acquired great responsibility to help advance the cause of civilization.[24]

Some went further, suggesting not only cooperation but the actual *merging* of Britain and America into "one confederacy . . . governed by a race speaking the same language, of superior intellect and energy."[25] Andrew Carnegie, in an essay published in the *North American Review*, spoke of a "Re-United States," a "race confederacy" that would dominate the world through its moral ascendency.[26] Another author in the same journal suggested that Britain should create "a new United States of the World."[27]

With a considerable amount of trepidation, the idea of an Anglo-Saxon imperial superiority was recognized abroad. The sensationalist work by the French pedagogue Edmond Demolins, titled *Where Does the Superiority of the Anglo-Saxons Come From?* (1897), triggered heated debate—and even a sense of panic—in France. Demolins produced statistics with which he predicted a world in which American, Canadian, South African, Australian, and English products would swamp all markets unless France reformed itself along Anglo-Saxon lines. Prominent writers responded to the book with equally polemical articles and books.[28] Those who believed in the superiority of Anglo-Saxon mores were always in a minority, but they had a considerable impact on French political thinking at the time, intensifying the perceived need for positive eugenics.

As World War I approached, American and British liberals increasingly felt the need to distinguish themselves and their political traditions from Germany. In a series of articles for the *New Republic* in 1915, philosopher and essayist George Santayana expounded on the differences between the British and German notions of freedom. England, he explained, had parliamentary government, whereas in Germany government was bureaucratic and authoritarian. In Germany the government promulgated sets of rules regarding the conduct of individuals toward each other and then compelled individuals to observe them. In Britain individuals were free to make their own decisions. The future would decide whether German or English notions of freedom would win.[29]

This trend was only magnified as the First World War approached and the menace of authoritarianism became more palpable. During the war itself, anti-German hostility grew. As the California Board of Education argued when it banned the teaching of the German language in public schools, German culture was steeped in "the ideals of autocracy, brutality, and hatred." Wartime propaganda personified the enemy as the "Prussian cur" and "the German beast."[30] The terms "Anglo-American" and "English-Speaking" increasingly replaced "Anglo-Saxon."

After the war, there was considerable embarrassment over the idea that there could be racial bond between Germany and America, or that American political thought might owe something of importance to Germany. Irving Fisher made sure to distance American traditions from German ones in his presidential address to the American Economic Association in December 1918, a speech that was then published in the

*American Economic Review*. As we know, the American Economic Association had been founded by a group of Americans who had studied in Germany and came back full of ideas about how the state could help the poor.

In his speech, Fisher acknowledged the importance of German political economy to the formation of the association. He added, however, that its members had now come to the realization that German economics had served a "criminal" state. It would be better, he concluded, for Americans to borrow from English economics, which was more liberal, more democratic, and healthier for the world.[31]

World War I thus tightened the sense of an Anglo-American alliance, and Germany's contribution to the history of liberalism was progressively forgotten or pushed aside. Soon the French contribution would be minimalized too. Meanwhile liberalism, democracy, and Western civilization became virtually synonymous, and America, because of its rising strength, was cast as their principal defender.

The equation between liberalism and America was further solidified and disseminated through Western civilization courses that were invented after the war and taught on US college campuses. Their purpose was to teach students what America had fought for in the Great War and what the country stood for.

During the 1920s and 1930s, European fascists, Nazis, and their progenitors and supporters agreed that liberalism was closely intertwined with Western civilization, democracy, and America, and it was precisely because of this that they defined themselves *against* it. Prominent German intellectuals, like Oswald Spengler, Friedrich Junger, Carl Schmitt, and Moeller van den Bruck, denounced liberalism as a foreign philosophy and the very antithesis of German culture. Liberalism, they said, was Germany's archenemy, which is why the patron saint of

National Socialism Moeller van den Bruck so happily claimed, incorrectly of course, that "there are no liberals in Germany today."[32] It is also why the Italian dictator Benito Mussolini held up fascism as the very "negation of liberalism,"[33] while Adolf Hitler declared that the chief goal of Nazism was "to abolish the liberalistic concept of the individual."[34]

Of course the claim that liberalism was somehow un-German was completely false, as this book has shown. The contention was forcefully refuted by the antifascist Italian writer Guido de Ruggiero in his *History of European Liberalism* of 1925. Ruggiero wrote that the crisis of liberalism (also the title of the epilogue) should not be taken to mean that there was no European liberal tradition. His book devoted a chapter each to Italian, German, and French liberalism to make his point. He did however admit that the "Anglo-Saxon" version of liberalism was stronger.

It is a curious fact that it was only in the late 1930s that liberalism as a political philosophy began to appear in American textbooks. George Sabine's *A History of Political Theory*, published in the 1930s, and used in most American undergraduate and graduate programs at the time, was the first major US textbook to discuss it. He described it as a British 19th century tradition and worried that it was a diminishing force.

The Second World War only fortified and spread the view of America as the prime representative and defender of liberalism, democracy, and Western civilization, which by now in many people's minds were virtually the same thing. Henry Luce's famous editorial "The American Century," which appeared in the February 17, 1941 issue of *Life*, called for "the most powerful and vital nation in the world" to assume world leadership. "We are the inheritors of all the great principles of Western Civilization," Luce wrote. "It now becomes our time to be the powerhouse."

## The Question of Government Intervention

It would be wrong to conclude from the growing association of liberalism with America that there was a consensus over what the word actually meant: how, for example, liberalism differed from democracy, or what it meant in terms of a government's role in the economy. While the progressives around the *New Republic* called themselves liberal, so did Herbert Hoover, but he meant something different. Sounding quite like Herbert Spencer, Hoover, who served as president of the United States from 1929 to 1933, insisted that liberalism's main concern was the protection of individual freedom. It stood for the idea that government should involve itself as little as possible in the economy. As president, Hoover oversaw the stock market crash of 1929 and the onset of the Great Depression. Despite the economic catastrophe, he continued to defend the laissez-faire version of liberalism well into the 1940s.

In continental Europe, powerful voices continued to spread the idea that liberalism meant laissez-faire. Those who meant something else had to add a qualifier such as "progressive" or "constructive" or speak of "liberal socialism." In his book *Liberalism*, published in 1927, the influential Austrian economist Ludwig von Mises lamented the disputes over the meaning of the word. True liberalism, he insisted, was not about any humanitarian objectives, however noble they might be. Liberalism had nothing else in mind than the advancement of a people's material welfare. Its central concepts were private property, freedom and peace. Anything beyond that was "socialism," for which Mises had only disdain. Those who thought that liberalism had something to do with spreading humanity and magnanimity were "pseudo liberals."[35]

Soon, however, the American philosopher John Dewey entered the fray, and put in a herculean effort to seal the progressive meaning of the term once and for all. Dewey received his doctorate in 1884 at Johns Hopkins University, where he studied under Richard Ely. In 1914, he became a regular contributor to the *New Republic*. Over the course of his long career, he taught mainly at the University of Chicago and Columbia and published over forty books and several hundred articles.

In the 1930s Dewey published numerous articles carrying titles such as "The Meaning of Liberalism," "The Meaning of the Term: Liberalism," "A Liberal Speaks Out for Liberalism," and "Liberalism and Civil Liberties"; there was also his book, *Liberalism and Social Action*, published in 1935.

According to Dewey, there were "two streams" of liberalism. One was more humanitarian and therefore open to government intervention and social legislation. The other was beholden to big industry, banking, and commerce and was therefore committed to laissez-faire. But American liberalism, he wrote, had nothing whatsoever to do with laissez-faire, and never had.[36] Nor did it have anything to do with the "gospel of individualism." American liberalism stood for "liberality and generosity, especially of mind and character."[37] Its aim was to promote greater equality and to combat plutocracy with the aid of government.

The person most responsible for making this meaning of liberalism dominant in America was Franklin Delano Roosevelt, president from 1933 to 1945. Like so many liberals before him, Roosevelt claimed the moral high ground for liberalism. Liberals, he said, believed in generosity and social mindedness. They were willing to sacrifice for the public good. Over the course of his years in office, President Roosevelt spoke often of the importance of human cooperation. The faith of a liberal, he said, was a belief in the effectiveness of people helping each other.

Roosevelt also solidified a link between Liberalism and the Democratic Party. He distinguished between this "liberal party," which favored government intervention, and a "conservative party," which did not. The liberal party, he said, believes that "as new conditions and problems arise beyond the power of men and women to meet as individuals, it becomes the duty of the Government itself to find new remedies with which to meet them." "The conservative party," by contrast, believes that "there is no necessity for the Government to step in."[38] The Democratic Party, he said, was the liberal party while the Republican Party was conservative.[39]

To emphasize the point, in his speech nominating Roosevelt as the Democratic candidate for the presidency in 1944, Henry Agard Wallace, who served as vice president from 1941 to 1945, secretary of commerce from 1945 to 1946, and editor of the *New Republic* from 1946 to 1947, used the word "liberal" no fewer than fifteen times, in one instance calling the president the "greatest liberal in the history of the United States."[40]

Roosevelt's meaning of the word was close to that of the British economist, social reformer, and member of the Liberal Party William Beveridge. Beveridge authored the so-called Beveridge Report of 1942, which served as the basis for the post–World War II British welfare state. In a 1945 pamphlet titled *Why I Am a Liberal*, he declared, "Liberty means more than freedom from the arbitrary power of Governments. It means freedom from economic servitude to Want and Squalor and other social evils; it means freedom from arbitrary power in any form. A starving man is not free."[41]

As it turns out, however, the battle over liberalism was not yet over, especially not in Europe. The Austrian-born economist Friedrich Hayek, a disciple of Mises, vehemently contested Beveridge's and Roosevelt's use of the word. Hayek joined the London School of Economics in 1931, where he became a virulent critic of FDR-style liberalism and the New Deal. Horrified by political developments on the European continent,

Hayek warned that embarking on "collectivist experiments" would put countries on a slippery slope to fascism. It was necessary, therefore, to return to "the old liberalism,"[42] by which Hayek of course meant government nonintervention. He grew more insistent and radical about this over time.

In 1944, Hayek published the best-selling *Road to Serfdom*. "It is necessary," Hayek wrote in his impassioned introduction, "to state the unpalatable truth that it is Germany whose fate we are in some danger of repeating." Liberal socialism was a contradiction in terms. It was not the role of government to be kind or generous. Rather, the government's role was to protect the freedom of the individual. Western civilization was "an individualist civilisation," and true liberal principles derived from the ideas of English individualism. Liberal socialism, on the other hand, was a German import, stemming from the ideas of Bismarck's advisors, and was a danger to Western civilization. It would invariably lead to "serfdom" and "totalitarianism," a relatively new word at the time.

Despite such efforts, only two years later Hoover acknowledged defeat. With discernible bitterness, he conceded: "We do not use the word 'liberal.' The word has been polluted and raped of all its real meanings. . . . Liberalism was founded to further more liberty for men, not less freedom."[43]

Similarly, in a 1948 speech titled "What Is a Liberal?," Republican senator Robert Taft complained that a word "which used to be a sound Anglo-Saxon word with a clear meaning, has lost all significance." Contrary to the administration's use, "the word 'liberal' in the political sense certainly does not connote 'generous.'" The basic meaning of the word remained pure and simple: "someone in favor of freedom."[44]

It seems that Hayek eventually gave up on the word too. In 1950, he moved to the University of Chicago, where he accepted a position as professor in the Committee on Social Thought.

There he inspired, among others, the American economist Milton Friedman and eventually became a favorite of those we now call "libertarians."[45] Many of his followers to this day claim that they are the true, that is "classical" or "orthodox," liberals.[46] Meanwhile Hayek called himself at various points a "consistent liberal," a "neoliberal," or a "radical" because liberalism no longer meant what it once had.[47]

Remarkably, these battles over the meaning of the word "liberal"—as pitched as they were—did not involve liberalism's origins. Both streams of liberalism claimed that their version lay in *English history*. To Hayek liberalism owed its origins to English individualism, while to Dewey it owed them to English humanitarianism. Neither man mentioned France or Germany.

This was only the beginning of the ejection of France and Germany from the history of liberalism. Over time, any French contribution receded to the background and Germany was seen as a source of *illiberalism*. By 1947, both versions, Dewey's as well as Hayek's, had, for better or worse, become "the American creed."[48] Liberalism was, as Lionel Trilling remarked in 1950, not only America's *dominant* tradition, but even its *sole* intellectual tradition.

# Epilogue

*Constant often sounds as if he were speaking of Hitler's Germany.*

—JOHN PLAMENATZ, 1963

TODAY, THE POLEMICS over liberalism continue. A word that began as an insult is still used that way by its right-wing critics. We have only to recall Ronald Reagan's famous reference to the "dreaded L-word" to recognize the word's polemical force. American Democrats avoid using it to describe themselves for fear that it will render them unelectable. Right-wing pundits call it a disease and a poison; it's a danger, they say, to moral values.

We've heard this all before. Since its genesis, liberalism has been subject to a barrage of similar attacks. The fact that liberals today disagree among themselves is also nothing new. Liberalism has never been a fixed or unified creed. Since the very beginning, it has encompassed lively debates. What *is* new is the way liberals today describe themselves and what they stand for. They overwhelmingly stress a commitment to individual rights and choices; they rarely mention duties, patriotism, self-sacrifice, or generosity to others. These terms are conspicuous by their absence in the contemporary liberal lexicon. Liberals have conceded the high ground to their adversaries.

The scholarship on liberalism reinforces and confirms this liberal self-definition. Countless works repeat the same message: liberalism is a doctrine whose core principle is the protection of the individual, his and her rights, interests, and choices. Any book, article, or essay, whether it is scholarly or polemical, and whether it approves or disapproves of liberalism, claims that its core principle is that governments exist to protect these rights, interests and choices. One renowned scholar of liberalism even asserts that it is founded on the "animal needs" of human beings.[1] From such self-descriptions it is only a short way to conclude, as one critic has, that liberals "explicitly rejected any notion of a common good. They wished to privatize and diminish, although not eliminate, the contents of human life."[2]

While they argued over many things, the great majority of liberals discussed in this book certainly did not defend animal needs or reject the common good. That is what their enemies said about them, not what they said about themselves. Over the course of the centuries, liberals consistently described their values as patriotic, selfless, and meant to promote the public good. When liberals fought for individual rights, it was because they thought that such rights enabled individuals to better perform their duties. Liberals constantly looked for ways to promote civic values. Morality was central to their goals.

All the liberals we have encountered in this book also believed that the purpose of governments was to serve the public good. At first this meant dismantling aristocratic impediments that kept wealth, power, and opportunity in the hands of a hereditary elite. Later it entailed intervening to fight plutocracy and the exploitation that accompanied it. At every point their underlying object was to promote the material and moral well-being of all.

From Benjamin Constant and his concern about fostering self-sacrifice to Alexis de Tocqueville, who worried about selfishness, and Leonard Hobhouse and Herbert Croly, who agonized about plutocracy, liberals were virtually obsessed with morality and the building of character. Early liberals, as we have seen, even shunned the word "individualism" because of its negative connotations. Constant, and many others after him, endorsed "individuality" instead; still others spoke of "personhood." "Personhood" and "character" were words that suggested the ability and need of individuals to cultivate their moral and intellectual potential, to understand their interconnectedness with others, and to understand their civic duty.

Liberals were far from perfect. Although they saw themselves as disinterested agents of reform, this was, at best, wishful thinking. Often it was a result of blindness. They were capable of excluding entire groups of people from their liberal vision: women, blacks, the colonized, and those they referred to as the "unfit." When they did this, however, there were always other liberals who accused them of betraying their liberal principles. They were urged to be true to the core meaning of being "liberal," which meant being not only freedom-loving and civic-minded, but also generous and compassionate. Being liberal was an aspirational ideal—something to live up to.

Why has this history been lost? Where did our focus on rights and interests come from? How and why were duties, self-sacrifice, and the common good downplayed or even written out of our histories of liberalism?

In this epilogue I venture some answers to these questions. I propose that an "Anglo-American liberal tradition" based so centrally on individual rights was a construction of the middle of the twentieth century, if not even later. Borrowing from the work of others, I argue that the "turn to rights" happened as the consequence of the two world wars and the Cold War. Two interrelated processes were involved. First, as we have seen, liberalism was Americanized. Second, it was reconfigured into a doctrine that prioritized individual rights. As the US historian Alan Brinkley has shown, liberals lowered their sights and adjusted their goals.[3]

## Liberalism and the Totalitarian Threat

Originally published in 1944, Friedrich Hayek's *Road to Serfdom* both profited from and helped amplify a growing fear of totalitarianism. Liberalism's association with a strong state and government intervention began to be seen as a liability. It was important to be aware, Hayek wrote in his surprise best seller, that "it is Germany whose fate we are in some danger of repeating."[4] The "social liberalism" toward which Britain and America were heading would invariably lead to totalitarianism.

In America, supporters of New Deal liberalism were labeled socialist or even communist, words which took on increasingly ominous meanings. Robert Taft, Republican senator from Ohio, in 1948 accused New Deal liberalism of having "acquired Russian overtones." Liberals who accepted John Dewey's or FDR's conceptions of liberalism were not really liberal; they were "totalitarian."

In this anxious and pessimistic climate, people became receptive to the ideas of several religious thinkers, both Catholic and Protestant, who blamed liberalism itself for the ethical crisis in which the West found itself. Among the most important of the Catholic theorists were Waldemar Gurian, a Russian-born German-American political scientist, and Jacques Maritain, a French philosopher. The most prominent Protestant theorist was Reinhold Niebuhr. Gurian, Maritain,

and Niebuhr all spread the idea that liberal societies themselves had a tendency to become illiberal. "Antiliberalism,"
wrote Gurian, was nothing but the "completion of liberalism."
The "totalitarian state" was not the rejection of liberalism, but
"its last and most radical consequence."[5]

Catholic and Protestant arguments overlapped in significant
ways. When you banish God from the world, these Christian
theorists said, every foundation of morality is undermined. The
loss of faith in God leads to a moral relativism that makes people
vulnerable to demagogues and dictators. Totalitarianism, which
these theorists were among the first to analyze, was the result of
liberal disenchantment with the world.

Niebuhr was one of the most influential American intellectuals of his generation. In articles carrying titles like "The
Pathos of Liberalism" or "The Blindness of Liberalism," he
weighed in on the dangers lurking within. Totalitarianism was
the logical outcome of human arrogance, a danger that threatened any place where the reality of original sin was denied and
Christian principles rejected.[6] Niebuhr cautioned Americans
about their liberal culture's failure to understand the depth of
evil to which they may sink when they tried "to play the role
of God in history." Given what had occurred in Germany, he
recommended that American liberals temper their plans for
social reform and view all collectivist answers to social problems with trepidation. Almost every experiment in social en-
gineering, he warned, contained "some peril of compounding
economic and political power." Hence "a wise community will
walk warily and test the effect of each new adventure before
further adventures."[7]

Knowingly or unknowingly, these Christian theorists repeated an old accusation: liberal secularism was to blame.
By attacking religion, liberals had brought this calamity on
themselves. We have heard this argument over and over again.

But we have also heard that throughout history, Christian liberals disputed such allegations. They insisted that liberalism had nothing to do with rejecting God or attacking religion. A liberal form of Christianity, that is, one more focused on morals rather than sinfulness, would help improve the world and is what God intended.

Niebuhr was very critical of liberal Christianity. He thought it projected a dangerously naïve and utopian idea of human goodness and educability. In an article titled "Let the Liberal Churches Stop Fooling Themselves!," he chastised their optimism and idealism, which he claimed had helped cause the European crisis.[8] Men were not naturally good, but sinful, irrational, violent, and selfish. Without recognizing that fact, no moral society was possible.

By 1945, the position of Pope Pius XII on the question was more than clear. In his Christmas Message that year, he repeated, in an updated form, the long-established and standard Catholic condemnation of liberalism. Simply stated, liberals had banished God from the world and had thus given rise to totalitarianism. Liberalism's destructive force, Pius declared, had brought only brutality, barbarity, and ruin.

Catholic propagandists spread this message. Jonathan Hallowell's book, *The Decline of Liberalism* of 1946, warned that the spiritual crisis out of which totalitarianism emerged was a crisis peculiar not only to Germany, but to all of Western civilization. Liberalism, with its rejection of transcendent truth, was to blame. In *The Rise and Decline of Liberalism* of 1953, Thomas Neill underlined the point. Since it destroyed all spiritual values, "the logic of liberalism" was to lead straight to totalitarianism.[9] Some years later, in 1964, yet another anticommunist Catholic crusader, James Burnham, called liberalism the "ideology of Western suicide," since it was infected with communism.[10]

Influential émigrés to the United States from Nazi Germany concurred with this damning appraisal of liberalism. Hannah Arendt, the German Jewish political philosopher and friend of Gurian who would later pen the now-famous *Origins of Totalitarianism* (1951), wrote that liberalism was the "spawn of hell" that gave rise to Nazism.[11] For the German Catholic émigré Eric Voegelin, communism was only the radical expression of liberalism. By supplanting the "truth of the soul" and promoting the disenchantment of the word, liberalism was in large part responsible for the self-destructive politics of the West.[12] Leo Strauss, another German Jewish émigré, accused what he took to be liberal relativism of opening the door to nihilism and totalitarianism. Liberals and totalitarians, he thought, had much in common.

## The Turn to Rights

Such prominent and powerful attacks on liberalism in the intellectual climate of the Cold War bred a defensiveness in American liberals, many of whom felt the need to clarify and accentuate what made their liberalism *not* totalitarianism. It was in so doing that they toned down their plans for social reconstruction and emphasized, rather, their commitment to defending the rights of individuals. Liberalism was reconfigured as the ideological "other" of totalitarianism, whether of the left or right. In the process, liberalism lost much of its moral core and its centuries-long dedication to the public good. Individualism replaced it as liberals lowered their sights and moderated their goals. Liberalism was once again reconfigured, and in the process its goals were downgraded.

The American historian and public intellectual Arthur Schlesinger was a key figure in this development. His widely read and much admired book *The Vital Center* (1949) illustrates well the change in the intellectual climate and shift in liberal sensibilities. A man deeply influenced by Niebuhr, Schlesinger regretted that so many liberals had been so slow to recognize the danger of totalitarianism and the threat it posed to the individual. It was imperative for them to reaffirm and reassert their fundamental commitment to each individual's rights. Liberalism, he said, could not afford to compromise with totalitarianism.

Another key figure in the Cold War transformation of liberalism was the Russian-British Jewish social and political philosopher Isaiah Berlin. In a seminal essay titled "Two Concepts of Liberty," which he originally delivered at Oxford University in 1958, Berlin addressed what he saw as the clash of ideologies that dominated the world. It was, he claimed, a conflict between two kinds of liberty, one that was totalitarian and the other liberal. The liberal kind of liberty was essentially negative. It was centrally concerned with shielding personal freedom, that is, with protecting the individual from government coercion. The totalitarian kind of liberty was associated with utopian projects promising "collective self-direction" and "self-realization."[13]

One after another, self-identified American liberals now showed their antitotalitarianism by emphasizing their support of individual rights. Genealogies based on a canon of great thinkers were constructed and anthologies published. Founding fathers of liberalism were discovered and many of the liberal theorists, politicians, and writers discussed in this book were passed over or their influence played down.

"Great thinkers" were read in ways that buttressed the liberal turn to rights and aspects of their thought that complicated such a reading were minimized. John Locke became a founding father of liberalism and his defense of property stressed. Occasionally, non-Anglophone thinkers were made to fit the canon. John Plamenatz's *Readings from Liberal Writers*,

*English and French* (1965) contained excerpts from Benjamin Constant. He noted with approval that "Constant often sounds as if he were speaking of Hitler's Germany."[14] Constant's defense of individual rights was emphasized above all his other concerns. His efforts at state building and constant worries about morals, religion, and "perfectibility" were downplayed or completely ignored.

Over time, then, liberalism's staunchest defenders rallied around the notion that liberalism was primarily about individual rights and interests. The history of liberalism recounted in this book was lost. In a sense, the twentieth-century liberals willingly adopted the argument traditionally used to malign them, in other words, that liberalism was, at its core, an individualist, if not selfish, philosophy.

In 1971, John Rawls's book *A Theory of Justice* appeared. Praised for revitalizing and enriching current debates about liberalism, it showed how a liberalism based on individualism and self-interest would, in fact, logically entail the welfare state. For the sake of argument, Rawls posited a group of self-interested but also rational individuals and showed that such persons—endeavoring to maximize their advantages in conditions of uncertainty—would choose not a laissez-faire society but the welfare state. In so arguing, he was, in a sense, turning a conservative and rights-based argument around against itself. In the process, however, he suggested that there was little need for any deliberate promotion of the common good for a liberal society to work. There was no need to worry about overcoming man's selfish impulses. It had become okay to be selfish.

What came to be known as the communitarian critique now accused liberalism of being too individualistic and too concerned with private rights at the expense of the common good. Liberalism, it was said, operated with a defective notion of the self, one that ignored the social constitution of individuals and the importance of communal bonds. It was blamed for undermining notions of citizenship and community, and for contributing to America's moral decline. Forgotten was the fact that liberals had championed community and morals for centuries.

Many liberals themselves began to lament the stress on rights and bemoan the chastened liberalism or "liberalism of fear" that was so impoverished that it seemed like a philosophy of mere damage control.[15] But they mostly accepted the idea that liberalism was about rights.

Given liberalism's concern with individual rights, feminists wondered how it could work for women. By being so individualistic, they said, liberalism was negligent toward the needs of women as women. It ignored the fact that all human beings have a core of moral "personhood." Here again, the debate about liberalism was sorely lacking in historical perspective.[16] As we have seen, liberals were almost obsessively concerned with women "as women" and they rarely spoke of women's individual "rights."

The liberal turn to rights also helped fuel a long debate about whether the founding values of America were liberal or republican, as if these two were contradictory. The question became another way of asking whether the United States was founded to protect rights ("liberalism") or to cultivate virtue ("republicanism"). Scholars interested in the purported differences between liberalism and republicanism were soon describing liberalism as "[a] modern, self-interested, competitive, individualistic ideology emphasizing private rights."[17]

## The (Supposed) Illiberalism of France and Germany

The use of this individualistic and rights-based Anglo-American liberalism as a yardstick made it possible for many to conclude that France and Germany had defective, or even nonexistent, liberal traditions. The many ways in which both countries in fact contributed to the history of liberalism receded to the background or disappeared altogether.

The experience of Nazism cast a long shadow on German history and caused historians to focus on what they concluded was the failure of German liberalism. In 1953, the German historian Friedrich Sell published *The Tragedy of German Liberalism*, which set the course for future studies. The problem with German liberalism, he said, was that the country had been inhospitable to the "Anglo-Saxon tradition." German liberalism was defective because it had never properly understood that the government's role was to protect individual rights.[18]

A great number of books followed Sell's, most of which spoke of the weakness, deficiency, or failure of liberalism in Germany.[19] People asked whether Germany even *had* a liberal tradition.[20] According to Columbia professor Fritz Stern's influential treatment, Germany had an *"illiberal,* namely an authoritarian rather than a liberal tradition."[21]

Those who believed that a liberal tradition did exist in Germany, declared it faulty because it was a "state liberalism"; it was a liberalism "that regarded the state as the essential instrument to realize the liberal program." The market model remained marginal in Germany, and its general pro-state orientation was said to be "the greatest weakness of early German liberalism."[22]

This focus on its supposed deficiencies sometimes turned into a search for the reasons why Germany was not England. Some said it had to do with Germany's flawed view of freedom, others that it lacked a bourgeoisie. It became interesting to discuss when and where German liberalism "deviated" from the "normative" process of development.[23] Apparently, German liberals lacked political ambitions.

Something similar happened in France, although a bit later. What has since been called an "antitotalitarian moment" occurred in the 1970s. Reacting against the post–World War II politics of many French intellectuals who had developed an attraction to communism, scholars began to look for the causes of this embarrassing truth. A number of them, among whom François Furet was an influential pioneer, attributed it to the supposed proto-totalitarianism of the French Revolution, and the related "fact" that France lacked a healthy liberal tradition.

French liberalism, it was concluded, was not a true liberalism because it lacked a strong emphasis on individual rights. Fundamentally an alien import, "genuine" liberalism had had trouble taking root in France.[24] And like the German variety, French liberalism was flawed because of its statism. Somewhat contradictorily, French liberalism was also said to "refuse the political," because of its purported confidence in free markets.[25] No wonder, then, that historians found it so very confused.[26] We hear of "the apparent inability of [French] liberals to recognize the central elements of their own doctrine." The problem is that they "did not have the philosophic resource to think through liberalism," because they didn't have a Locke.[27]

The French did, however, have a Benjamin Constant, who was now rediscovered and reread as one of the rare liberals in the true, individualist, Anglo-American sense. Constant's deep concern with building a viable state and *combating* individualism was ignored; and his lifelong interest in religion and interest in "self-sacrifice" was left out. Instead, prominent scholars determined that Constant's "master concept" was "individual independence,"[28] and that he espoused a "radical individualism."[29] Some noted that France also had a number of political economists who understood the liberal value of self-interest, the minimal state, and deregulated markets.

In France, as in America, this supposedly true and individualistic liberalism came under criticism. Compared to republicanism, with its emphasis on citizenship and virtue, critics described French liberalism as all too hedonistic.[30] The Catholic philosopher Pierre Manent accused liberalism's founders of rejecting any notion of a common good and, in a succinct summary of his view of liberalism, posited Machiavelli and Hobbes as its founders. Sounding much like the long line of Catholic critics of liberalism whom we have considered in this book, Manent reasoned that liberalism originated in an attack on the Christian Church. This, in Manent's estimation, is why liberalism has an ominous tendency to self-destruction and can lead ineluctably to totalitarianism.[31] Manent's is the now two-hundred-year-old Catholic critique repackaged.

Although liberalism today is widely regarded as the dominant political doctrine of the West, a kind of triumphalism coexists with pessimism. We often hear that liberalism is suffering from a crisis of confidence, a crisis made more intense by the recent rise of "illiberal democracy" around the world.[32] It is suggested that the problem could be solved if only liberals would agree about what they stood for and have courage in their convictions. Liberalism, there are those who say, contains within itself the resources it needs to articulate a conception of the good and a liberal theory of virtue.[33] Liberals should reconnect with the resources of their liberal tradition to recover, understand, and embrace its core values. This book is meant to relaunch that process. If it manages to reset and stimulate the debate on the history of liberalism, it will have served its purpose.

# NOTES

## Introduction

Unless otherwise indicated, all translations are my own.

1. On the meaning of "basic concepts" and the practice of conceptual history, a rapidly growing field, see the works listed in the method section of the selected bibliography.

2. For a recent example, see Larry Siedentop, *Inventing the Individual: The Origins of Western Liberalism* (Cambridge, MA: Harvard University Press, 2014).

3. Pierre Manent, *An Intellectual History of Liberalism*, trans. Rebecca Balinski (Princeton: Princeton University Press, 1996).

4. Duncan Bell, "What Is Liberalism?," *Political Theory* 42, no. 6 (2014): 682–715.

5. See, for example, Jörn Leonhard's pathbreaking *Liberalismus. Zur historischen Semantik eines europäischen Deutungsmusters* (Munich: R. Oldernbourg Verlag, 2001).

## Chapter One: What It Meant to Be Liberal from Cicero to Lafayette

1. Cicero, *On Duties*, bk. 1.

2. *Plutarch's Lives, Translated from the Original Greek: With Notes, Critical and Historical by John Langhorne and William Langhorne*, 6 vols. (London, 1770), 2:156–57.

3. Not of course without a great deal of distortion. See Hans Baron, "Cicero and the Roman Civic Spirit in the Middle Ages and Early Renaissance," *Journal of the John Rylands Library* 22 (1938): 73–97.

4. See St. Ambrose, *On the Duties of the Clergy*, chap. 28, para. 130. The text contains several sections on liberality.

5. The medieval rediscovery of Aristotle (384–322 BC) also helped disseminate the ancient notion of liberality.

6. Quoted by Guido Guerzoni, "Liberalitas, Magnificentia, Splendor: The Classic Origins of Italian Renaissance Lifestyles." *History of Political Economy* 31, suppl. (1999): 332–78.

7. Pietro Paolo Vergerio quoted in Kenneth Bartlett, ed., *The Civilization of the Italian Renaissance: A Sourcebook*, 2nd ed. (Toronto: University of Toronto Press, 2011), 184.

8. Juan Luis Vives, *The Education of a Christian Woman* (1524), bk. 1, para. 29.

9. An impressive list is provided by J. K. Sowards, "Erasmus and the Education of Women," *Sixteenth Century Journal* 13, no. 4 (1982): 77–89.

10. "Liberal" in *Oxford English Dictionary* (online), 3a.

11. *Christiani matrimonii institutio*, quoted by Sowards, "Erasmus," 87.

12. The Latin title of the book was *De pueris statim ac liberaliter instituendis* (1529).

13. Erasmus, *The Education of a Christian Prince*, ed. Lisa Jardine (Cambridge: Cambridge University Press, 2016), 77. When it came to the education of girls, Erasmus focused on the need to safeguard their chastity (Sowards, "Erasmus").

14. Leon Battista Alberti, "On Painting and on Sculpture," in *The Civilization of the Italian Renaissance: A Sourcebook*, ed. Kenneth Bartlett (Toronto: University of Toronto Press, 2011), 171.

15. Edgar Wind, *Pagan Mysteries in the Renaissance* (New York: Norton, 1968).

16. Antoniano ([1584] 1821), 2:39–40, in Guerzoni, "Liberalitas."

17. Piccolomini (1552), quoted in Guerzoni, "Liberalitas."

18. Fabrini (1547), quoted in Guerzoni, "Liberalitas."

19. A sixteenth-century translation found on ECCO has this as "freeharted princes," while the Italian and French versions employ the words "libérale" and "liberal." The 1724 English translation has it as "liberal princes."

20. Erasmus, *Education*, 78.

21. On the differences between Cicero and Machiavelli in this regard, see Marcia L. Colish, "Cicero's *De Officiis* and Machiavelli's *Prince*," *Sixteenth Century Journal* 9, no. 4 (1978): 80–93.

22. *The Essays of Michael Seigneur de Montaigne Translated into English* (London, 1759), 3:153.

23. Nicolas Faret, *L'Honeste-homme, ou l'art de plaire à la cour* (Paris: Du Bray, 1630).

24. Isaiah 32:5–8; Proverbs 11:25; 2 Corinthians 9:13.

25. Sermon 75 preached to the king at Whitehall, April 15, 1628.

26. Richard Allestree, *The Gentleman's Calling* (London, 1705), 58, 86.

27. Winthrop's famous sermon can be found in countless resources.

28. Roger L'Estrange, *Seneca's Morals by Way of Abstract* (Cork, 1797).

29. Thomas Hobbes, *Leviathan* (Cambridge: Cambridge University Press, 1996), 89; *On the Citizen* (Cambridge: Cambridge University Press, 1998), 21, 22, 25; *Leviathan*, "Of the Natural Condition of Mankind"; *Leviathan*, 102; *On the Citizen*, 149.

30. Jansenism was a seventeenth-century theological movement within Catholicism that emphasized original sin, human depravity, and the necessity of divine grace and predestination.

31. Blaise Pascal, *Pensées* (Paris, 1670), 89.

32. Pierre Nicole, "Of Charity and Self-Love," reprinted in Bernard Mandeville, *The Fable of the Bees and Other Writings*, ed. Mark Hulliung (Indianapolis: Hackett, 1997), 1.

33. Jacques Esprit, *La Fausseté des Vertus Humaines* (Paris, 1678), 487, emphasis added.

34. *Discourses: Translated from Nicole's Essays by John Locke with Important Variations from the Original French* (London, 1828), 172.

35. John Locke, *The Reasonableness of Christianity*, in *The Works*, vol. 6 (Liberty Fund Online Library of Liberty), 116, http://oll.libertyfund.org/titles/locke-the-works-vol-6-the-reasonableness-of-christianity.

36. John Locke, *Some Thoughts Concerning Education*, in *The Educational Writings of John Locke*, ed. James L. Axtell (Cambridge: Cambridge University Press, 1968).

37. Anthony Ashley Cooper Shaftesbury, *An Inquiry Concerning Virtue* (London, 1732), 293.

38. George Turnbull, *Observations on Liberal Education in All Its Branches* (London, 1742), 142, 136, 197, 141, 180, 321, 87.

39. *Dr. Johnson's Dictionary of the English Language* (London, 1755).

40. John Marshall, *John Locke: Resistance, Religion and Responsibility* (Cambridge: Cambridge University Press, 1996), 111.

41. Anthony Ashley Cooper Shaftesbury, *A Letter Concerning Enthusiasm*, in *Characteristicks*, vol. 1 (London, 1732), 333.

42. George Turnbull, *Observations upon Liberal Education, in All Its Branches*, ed. Terrence O. Moore Jr. (Indianapolis: Liberty Fund, 2003), chap. 4. See also Bruce Kimball, *Orators and Philosophers: A History of the Idea of Liberal Education* (New York: Teachers College Press, 1986), 14.

43. François de Salignac de La Mothe-Fénelon, *On the Education of Girls*, trans. Kate Lupton (Boston, 1891), 96, 65, 96, 13, 12.

44. Adam Smith, *An Inquiry into the Nature and Causes of the Wealth of Nations* (London, 1776), bk. 5, chap. 1, 302.

45. See, for example, Lieselotte Steinbrügge, *The Moral Sex: Woman's Nature in the French Enlightenment* (Oxford: Oxford University Press, 1995); Ludmilla Jordanova, "Sex and Gender," in *Inventing Human Science: Eighteenth-Century Domains*, ed. Christopher Fox, Roy Porter, and Robert Wokler (Berkeley: University of California Press, 1995), 152–83; and Anne Vila, "'Ambiguous Beings': Marginality, Melancholy, and the *Femme Savante*," in *Women, Gender and Enlightenment*, ed. Sarah Knott and Barbara Taylor (New York: Palgrave Macmillan, 2005), 53–69.

46. Francis Hutcheson, *A Short Introduction to Moral Philosophy* (Glasgow, 1747), 94.

47. Ibid., 87.

48. Jean-Baptiste Massillon, *Œuvres de Massillon* (Paris, 1803), 1:304.

49. John Locke, *Essay Concerning Understanding*, bk. 4, chap. 20.

50. David Armitage, "John Locke, Carolina, and the 'Two Treatises of Government,'" *Political Theory* 32, no. 5 (2004): 602–27.

51. Nathan Bailey, *An Universal Etymological English Dictionary*, 7th ed. (London, 1735).

52. As quoted by Gordon Wood, *The Radicalism of the American Revolution* (New York: Vintage, 1993), 27.

53. Peter Clark, *British Clubs and Societies 1580–1800* (Oxford: Clarendon, 2000); Davis McElroy, *Scotland's Age of Improvement: A Survey of Eighteenth-Century Literary Clubs and Societies* (Pullman: Washington State University Press, 1969).

54. Nicholas Phillipson, *Adam Smith: An Enlightened Life* (New Haven, CT: Yale University Press, 2010).

55. *The Works of William Robertson: History of the Reign of the Emperor Charles V*, 12 vols. (London, 1812), 4:82, 178, 78.

56. F. A. Brockhaus, *Allgemeine deutsche Real-Encyclopädie für die gebildeten Stände. Conversations-Lexicon*, vol. 5, 4th ed. (Leipzig, 1817), 674–75.

57. George Washington, "Circular to the States" (September 2, 1783), quoted in *The Encyclopedia of Libertariansim*, ed. Ronald Hamowy (Thousand Oaks, CA: Sage, 2008), 536.

58. Benigne de Bossuet, *Œuvres*, 23:625, quoted in Henrietta Louisa Farrer Lear, *Bossuet and His Contemporaries* (London: Rivingtons, 1874), 178.

59. John Locke, *A Letter Concerning Toleration and Other Writings*, ed. Mark Goldie (Indianapolis: Liberty Fund, 2010), emphasis added.

60. On the belief that Locke's ideas were not as anti-Catholic as has been claimed, see Emile Perreau-Saussine, "French Catholic Political Thought from the Deconfessionalisation of the State to the Recognition of Religious Freedom," in *Religion and the Political Imagination*, ed. Ira Katznelson and Gareth Stedman Jones (Cambridge: Cambridge University Press, 2010), 150–70.

61. Samuel Wright, quoted by Jörn Leonhard, *Liberalismus. Zur historischen Semantik eines europäischen Deutungsmusters* (Munich: R. Oldenbourg Verlag, 2001), 118.

62. Richard Price, "Sermons on the Christian Doctrine," in *Sermons on the Security and Happiness of a Virtuous Course, on the Goodness of God, and the Resurrection of Lazarus, to Which Are Added, Sermons on the Christian Doctrine* (Boston: E. W. Weld and W. Greenough, 1794), 175.

63. William Paley, *Principles of Moral and Political Philosophy* (1785).

64. "From George Washington to Roman Catholics in America, c.15 March 1790," *Founders Online*, https://founders.archives.gov/documents/Washington/05-05-02-0193.

65. "From George Washington to the Hebrew Congregation in Newport, Rhode Island, 18 August 1790," *Founders Online*, https://founders.archives.gov/documents/Washington/05-06-02-0135.

66. Eric Carlsson, personal communication, 2015.

67. This did not stop him from also embracing hermeticism. On this, see Peter Reill, "Between Theosophy and Orthodox Christianity: Johann Salomo Semler's Hermetic Religion," in *Polemical Encounters: Esoteric Discourse and Its Others*, ed. Olav Hammer and Kocku von Stuckrad (Leiden: Brill, 2007), 157–80.

68. *General Repository and Review* (1812).

69. John A. Buehrens, *Universalists and Unitarians in America: A People's History* (Boston: Skinner House, 2011).

70. Mr. Pratt, *Liberal Opinions; or, The History of Benignus*, vol. 1 (London, 1783), 2.

71. Alan Heimert, *Religion and the American Mind* (Cambridge, MA: Harvard University Press, 1968), 50, 169, 211.

72. Charles Chauncy, *Enthusiasm Described and Caution'd Against* (Boston, 1742).

73. Benjamin Whichcote, *The Works of the Learned Benjamin Whichcote*, vol. 2 (Aberdeen, 1751), 128.

74. Jean-Jacques Rousseau, *First* and *Second Discourses*; quotation is from the *Second Discourse*.

75. Adam Ferguson, *An Essay on the History of Civil Society*, ed. Duncan Forbes (Edinburgh: Edinburgh University Press, 1966), 217–20.

76. Ibid., 217–20.

77. See, for example, Karl Koppman, ed., *Die Recesse und andere Akten der Hansetage*, 8 vols. (Leipzig, 1870–97), where the English king has "liberaliter donatam et concessam."

78. See, for example, Joseph Lathrop, "A Sermon on a Day Appointed for Publick Thanksgiving," in *Political Sermons of the American Founding Era, 1730–1805*, ed. Ellis Sandoz (Indianapolis: Liberty Fund, 1998), 870: "The royal charters first granted to the American colonies, particularly to those of New-England, were of the most liberal kind, and fully agreeable to their views and wishes."

79. Letter to his editor, quoted by Dennis Carl Rasmussen, *The Problems and Promise of Commercial Society: Adam Smith's Response to Rousseau* (University Park: Pennsylvania State University Press, 2008), 99.

80. Adam Smith, *An Inquiry into the Nature and Causes of the Wealth of Nations*, vol. 1 (1776; Chicago: University of Chicago Press, 1977), iv, v, 47, 388, 75, 76, 77, 208, 250, emphasis added.

81. Adam Smith, *The Theory of Moral Sentiments* (1759), vi, ii. 3.3.

82. Ibid. (2016 version), 288.

83. Smith, *Wealth of Nations*, 519.

84. Ibid., 161. See Dennis C. Rasmussen, "Adam Smith on What Is Wrong with Economic Inequality," *American Political Science Review* 110, no. 2 (2016): 342–52.

85. Samuel Cooper, "A Sermon on the Day of the Commencement of the Constitution" (1780), in Sandoz, *Political Sermons of the American Founding Era*, 1:644, 655.

86. Ezra Stiles, "The United States Elevated to Glory and Honor," https://digitalcommons.unl.edu/etas/41/.

87. Joseph Lathrop, "Sermon on a Day Appointed for Public Thanksgiving," in *Political Sermons of the Founding Era*, vol. 1, ed. Ellis Sandoz (Indianapolis: Liberty Fund, 1998), 871.

88. David Ramsay, *The History of the American Revolution*, vol. 1 (1789), 357.

89. David Armitage, *Age of Revolutions in Global Context, c. 1760–1840* (New York: Palgrave Macmillan, 2010), 5n15.

90. In Germany, the debate about constitutions happened a bit later than elsewhere. See also Joyce Appleby, "America as a Model for the Radical French Reformers of 1789," *William and Mary Quarterly* 28, no. 2 (1971): 267–86.

91. Levi Hart of Preston, Connecticut, quoted by Jonathan Sassi, *A Republic of Righteousness: The Public Christianity of the Post-revolutionary New England Clergy* (New York: Oxford University Press, 2001), 58.

92. John Millar, *The Origin of the Distinction of Ranks* (Aalen: Scientia, 1986), 294, quoted by Domenico Losurdo, *Liberalism: A Counter-history* (New York: Verso, 2011), 11.

93. Christopher L. Brown, *Moral Capital: Foundations of British Abolitionism* (Chapel Hill: University of North Carolina Press, 2012).

94. Arthur Zilversmit, *First Emancipation: The Abolition of Slavery in the North* (Chicago: University of Chicago Press, 1967), 132; Robin Blackburn, *The Overthrow of Colonial Slavery: 1776–1848* (New York: Verso, 2011), 118; Losurdo, *Liberalism*, 59.

95. *Pennsylvania Journal*, April 4, 1781.

96. Edmund Burke, *The Works: A New Edition*, 16 vols. (London: Rivington, 1826), 3:54, quoted by Losurdo, *Liberalism*, 37.

97. Abigail Adams to John Adams, March 31, 1776, *Founders Online*, https://founders.archives.gov/documents/Adams/04-01-02-0241.

98. Abigail Adams to Mercy Otis Warren, April 27, 1776, *Founders Online*, https://founders.archives.gov/documents/Adams/04-01-02-0257.

99. Noah Webster, *On the Education of Youth in America*, cited in *Readings in American Educational Thought: From Puritanism to Progressivism*, ed. Andrew Milson, Chara Bohan, Perry Glanzer, and J. Wesley Null (Charlotte: Information Age, 2004), 106, emphasis added.

*Chapter Two: The French Revolution and
the Origins of Liberalism, 1789–1830*

1. Marquis de Lafayette, *Memoirs, Correspondence and Manuscripts of General Lafayette Published by His Family* (London, 1837), 2:192.

2. *Dictionnaire universel françois et latin, vulgairement appelé Dictionnaire de Trévoux...*, nouvelle ed. (Paris, 1771), 508.

3. For example, letter quoted above and letter to the president of Congress, Marquis de Lafayette, *Memoirs*, 1:286.

4. Germaine de Staël, *On Germany* (1810).

5. Richard Price, "A Discourse on the Love of Our Country" (London, 1790), 20.

6. *The Correspondence of the Revolution Society in London, with the National Assembly* (London, 1792), 157.

7. Edmund Burke, *Reflections on the Revolution in France*, ed. J.G.A. Pocock (Indianapolis: Hackett, 1987), 70, 163, 70, 69, emphasis added.

8. Ibid., 70, 33, 34, 66, 70.

9. See, for example, *A New Catechism for the Use of the Swinish Multitude* (1792).

10. Catherine Macaulay, *Observations on the Reflections of the Right Hon Edmund Burke on the Revolution in France* (London, 1791), 38–39.

11. Mary Wollstonecraft, *A Vindication of the Rights of Men*, ed. Sylvana Tomaselli (1790; Cambridge: Cambridge University Press, 2003), 16.

12. Thomas Paine, *Rights of Man, Being an Answer to Mr. Burke's Attack* (1791).

13. Germaine de Staël, *Considerations on the Principal Events of the French Revolution*, ed. Aurelian Craiutu (Indianapolis: Liberty Fund, 2008), 493, 190.

14. Joseph de Maistre, *Considerations on France*, ed. Richard Lebrun (Cambridge: Cambridge University Press, 2003), 41.

15. *Des réactions politiques*, in *De la force du gouvernement actuel de la France et de la nécessité de s'y rallier*, ed. Philippe Raynaud (Paris: Flammarion, 1988), 111, 115, 118. See K. Stephen Vincent, *Benjamin Constant and the Birth of French Liberalism* (New York: Palgrave Macmillan, 2011), 76–77, and "Benjamin Constant, the French Revolution, and the Origins of French Romantic Liberalism," *French Historical Studies* 23, no. 4 (2000): 607–37.

16. Quoted by Aurelian Craiutu, *A Virtue for Courageous Minds: Moderation in French Political Thought, 1748–1830* (Princeton: Princeton University Press, 2012), 178.

17. Mona Ozouf, "La Révolution française et la formation de l'homme nouveau," in *L'homme régénéré. Essais sur la Révolution française*, ed. Mona Oouf (Paris: Gallimard, 1989), 116–45.

18. Madame de Staël, *Des Circonstances actuelles qui peuvent terminer la révolution et des principes qui doivent fondre la république en France* (Paris: Libraire Fischbacher, 1906), 10, 146, 279.

19. Quoted by John C. Isbell, *The Birth of European Romanticism: Truth and Propaganda in Staël's* De l'Allemagne, *1810–1813* (Cambridge: Cambridge University Press, 1994), 131.

20. Benjamin Constant, *De Madame de Staël et de ses ouvrages*, in *Portraits, mémoires, souvenirs* (Paris, 1992), 222.

21. Kurt Klooke, *Benjamin Constant: une biographie intellectuelle* (Geneva: Droz, 1984); J. Lee, "The Moralization of Modern Liberty" (PhD diss., University of Wisconsin–Madison, 2003); and Helena Rosenblatt, *Liberal Values: Benjamin Constant and the Politics of Religion* (Cambridge: Cambridge University Press, 2008).

22. Benjamin Constant, "De la force du gouvernement actuel de la France et de la nécessité de s'y rallier," in *Œuvres complètes de Benjamin Constant*, vol. 1 (Tübingen: Max Niemeyer Verlag, 1998), 380.

23. As quoted in Rosenblatt, *Liberal Values*, 72.

24. Howard Brown, "From Organic Society to Security State: The War on Brigandage in France, 1797–1802," *Journal of Modern History* 69, no. 4 (1997): 661–65.

25. Another was Adrien Lamourette. See David Sorkin, *The Religious Enlightenment* (Princeton: Princeton University Press, 2011). There were many in Spain, the Spanish Americas, Italy, and other countries. On Grégoire, see Alyssa Goldstein Sepinwall, *The Abbé Grégoire and the French Revolution: The Making of Modern Universalism* (Berkeley: University of California Press, 2005).

26. *Annales de la religion*, vol. 1 (1795), 15, and vol. 15 (1802), 359.

27. Napoléon Bonaparte, *Correspondances de Napoléon 1er*, vol. 6 (Paris: Plon, 1862), 5–6.

28. Quoted by Guillaume de Bertier de Sauvigny, "Liberalism, Nationalism, Socialism: The Birth of Three Words," *Review of Politics* 32 (1970): 151–52.

29. In a letter of July 24, 1797, quoted by Julia von Leyden Blennerhassett in *Madame de Staël, Her Friends, and Her Influence in Politics and Literature*, vol. 3, trans. Jane Eliza Gordon Cumming (1889; Cambridge: Cambridge University Press, 2013), 429.

30. Marquis de Lafayette to Thomas Jefferson, June 21, 1801, *Founders Online*, http://founders.archives.gov/documents/Jefferson/01-34-02-0318.

31. Madame de Staël, *Considerations*, 422.

32. Speech to the Priests of Milan, June 5, 1800, in *In the Words of Napoleon*, ed. R. M. Johnston (Barnsley: Frontline Books, 2015).

33. Quotations from Jörn Leonhard, *Liberalismus. Zur historischen Semantik eines europäischen Deutungsmusters* (Munich: R. Oldernbourg Verlag, 2001), 208–24.

34. Quoted by H. C. Barnard, *Education and the French Revolution* (Cambridge: Cambridge University Press, 2009), 218.

35. In his anti-Napoleon tract "The Spirit of Conquest and Usurpation" of 1814.

36. A word first used in 1816 according to Berke Vardar, *Structure fondamentale du vocabulaire social et politique en France de 1815 à 1830* (Istanbul, 1973).

37. Melvin Richter, "Tocqueville and the French Nineteenth Century Conceptualizations of the Two Bonapartes and Their Empires," in *Dictatorship in History and Theory: Bonapartism, Caesarism and Totalitarianism*, ed. P. R. Baehr and Melvin Richter (Cambridge: Cambridge University Press, 2004), 83–102, 84. More on this in chapter 5.

38. Jean-Baptiste Say, *Traité d'économie politique*, 4th ed., vol. 1 (Paris, 1819), 197.

39. Ibid., 298. See Philippe Steiner, "Jean-Baptiste Say et les colonies ou comment se débarrasser d'un héritage intempestif," *Cahiers d'économie politique* 27–28 (1996): 153–73; and Jennifer Sessions, *By Sword and Plow: France and the Conquest of Algeria* (Ithaca, NY: Cornell University Press, 2015).

40. François-Louis-Auguste Ferrier, *Du Gouvernement considéré dans ses rapports avec le commerce* (Paris: Perlet, 1805), 14–15, 37.

41. Ibid., 26.

42. Lettres de Ferrier à Fiévée, June 5 and 20, 1816, in *Correspondance de Joseph Fiévée et de François Ferrier (1803–1837)*, ed. Etienne Hofmann (Bern: Peter Lang, 1994), 138, 142.

43. Benjamin Constant, "The Spirit of Conquest and Usurpation," in *Political Writings*, ed. Biancamaria Fontana (Cambridge: Cambridge University Press, 1993), 118, 126, 122, 121.

44. Cited in E.E.Y. Hales, *Napoleon and the Pope* (London, 1962), 89–90.

45. Charles de Villers, *Essai sur l'esprit et l'influence de la Réformation de Luther. Ouvrage qui . . .* (Paris, 1804), quoted in Rosenblatt, *Liberal Values*, 102–4.

46. On Sweden, see the pioneering scholarship of Arthur Thomson, "'Liberal': Några anteckningar till ordets historia," in *Festskrift tillägnad Theodor Hjelmqvist på sextiårsdagen den 11 april 1926* (Lund: Carl Bloms Boktryckeri, 1926), 147–91. On Spain, see the many publications of Javier Fernández Sebastián.

47. Madame de Staël, *De l'Allemagne*, vol. 1, ed. Simone Balayé (Paris: Garner-Flammarion, 1968), 73.

48. Jaime Rodriguez, *The Independence of Spanish America* (Cambridge: Cambridge University Press, 1998).

49. Ignacio Fernández Sarasola, "La proyección europea e iberoamericana de la Constitución de 1812," in *La Constitución de Cádiz. Origen, contenido y proyección internacional* (Madrid: Centro de Estudios Politicos y Constitucionales, 2011), 271–336.

50. Jaime E. Rodríguez O., "Introducción," in *Revolución, independencia y las nuevas naciones de América*, ed. Jaime E. Rodríguez O. (Madrid: Fundación Mapfre Tavera, 2005), 16.

51. Rodriguez, *Independence*, 105.

52. Harro M. Höpfl, "Isms," *British Journal of Political Science* 13, no. 1 (1983): 1–17.

53. Quoted by Javier Fernández Sebastián, "'Friends of Freedom': First Liberalisms in the Iberian Atlantic," in *In Search of European Liberalisms*, ed. Javier Fernández Sebastián, Jörn Leonhard, and Michael Freeden (New York: Berghahn Books, 2018).

54. "Déclaration de Saint-Ouen," reprinted in *La monarchie impossible: Les Chartes de 1814 et de 1830* (Paris: Gallimard, 1994), 90.

55. Constant to Lafayette, May 1, 1815, in Lafayette, *Memoirs*, 5:423.

56. Benjamin Constant, *Principles of Politics Applicable to All Governments*, in Fontana, *Political Writings*, 175, 179.

57. L'abbé Rauzan, "Toute constitution est un régicide" (April 1814), in René Rémond, *La Droite en France de 1815 à nos jours: Continuité et diversité d'une tradition politique* (Paris: Aubier Editions Montaigne, 1954), 36.

58. "Des élections, du ministère, de l'esprit public et du parti libéral en France," *La Minerve* 4, no. 1 (December 1818): 379–84.

59. *La Minerve française* 14, no. 1 (November 4–5, 1818): 14–22. The article was reprinted in 1819 in the *Cours de politique constitutionelle*, 3:53–58, emphasis added.

60. Quoted in Maria Luisa Sànchez-Mejìa, "La Inquisición contra el liberalismo. El Expediente de Calificación de los *Principes de Politique* de Benjamin Constant," *Cuadernos dieciochistas* 14 (2013): 283–303, 286.

61. Louis de Bonald, "Sur les langues," in *Œuvres de M. de Bonald* (Brussels: La Société nationale, 1845), 7:455.

62. *La Quotidienne*, August 23, 1814, 3.

63. *Les Idées libérales*, in *Le Nouvelliste français ou Recueil Choisi de Mémoires*, no. 12 (Pesth, 1815), 277.

64. Reforms are well described in Brendan Simms, *The Struggle for Mastery in Germany, 1779–1850* (Basingstoke: Palgrave Macmillan, 1988).

65. An 1814 text quoted by Rudolf Vierhaus, "Liberalismus," in *Geschichtliche Grundbegriffe. Historisches Lexikon zur politisch-sozialen Sprache in Deutschland*, vol. 3, ed. Reinhart Koselleck, Otto Bruner, and Werner Conze (Stuttgart, 1972–93).

66. "What does liberal mean?" in the first issue of the *Neue Alemannia* of 1816.

67. According to the *Revolutions-Almanach*, reforms were introducing new words into circulation that made them "holy" and gave them a "magical meaning." Vierhaus, "Liberalismus," 741.

68. Castlereagh speech, February 15, 1816, in *Hansard First Series: 1803–1820*, vol. 37, 602, quoted in Leonhard, *Liberalismus*, 236.

69. Andrew Robertson, *The Language of Democracy: Political Rhetoric in the United States and Britain, 1790–1900* (Charlottesville: University of Virginia Press, 2005), 62.

70. *Edinburgh Review* 24, no. 48 (November 1814–February 1815): 529.

71. Ibid.; subsequent articles use the word "liberal" repeatedly to refer to French politics, sometimes putting the term in italics.

72. A quick search of the America's Historical Newspapers database yielded the following references to "liberal parties" or politicians in France. *Columbian Centinel*, November 1, 1817, 2; *Centinel of Freedom*, May 26, 1818, 2; *Weekly Aurora*, September 14, 1818, 240; *Columbian Centinel*, December 26, 1818, 2; *National Gazette*, April 29, 1820, 2; *Baltimore Patriot*, October 10, 1822, 2; *Daily National Intelligencer*, October 12, 1822, 2; *National Gazette*, November 25, 1824, 1.

73. Metternich to Gentz, April 23, 1819, quoted by Vierhaus, "Liberalismus."

74. Quoted in Guillaume de Bertier de Sauvigny, *La Restauration* (Paris: Hachette, 1997), 168.

75. André Vissieux, *Essay on Liberalism; Being an Examination of the Nature and Tendency of the Liberal Opinions; with a View of the State of Parties on the Continent of Europe* (London: Pewtress, Low, and Pewtress, 1823), 103.

76. Christopher Bayly, "Rammohan Roy and the Advent of Constitutional Liberalism in India, 1800–1830," *Modern Intellectual History* 4 (2007): 25–41; and *Recovering Liberties: Indian Thought in the Age of Liberalism and Empire* (Cambridge: Cambridge University Press, 2011), 50–60.

77. Ignacio Fernandez Sarasola, "European Impression of the Spanish Constitution of Cadiz," *Forum historiae iuris*, http://fhi.rg.mpg.de/es/2016-09-sarasola/.

78. The first edition was called *Collection complète des ouvrages publiés sur le Gouvernement représentatif et la Constitution actuelle de la France formant une espèce de Cours de Politique constitutionnelle, par M. Benjamin de Constant.*

79. Maurizio Isabella, *Risorgimento in Exile: Italian Emigres and the Liberal International in the Post-Napoleonic Era* (Oxford: Oxford University Press 2009).

80. Rodriguez, *Independence*, 193.

81. C. J. Gilliard, *Réflexions sur les sociétés secrètes et les usurpations. Première partie: Ecueils et dangers des sociétés secrètes*, tome 2 (Arbois, 1823), 444–45.

82. Lafayette to Jefferson, July 20, 1820, in Gilbert Chinard, ed., *The Letters of Lafayette and Jefferson* (Baltimore, 1929), 398–99.

83. Achille de Vaulabelle, *Histoire des Deux Restorations*, 10 vols. (Paris, 1952), 6:283–324; see also Lafayette, *Memoirs*, 6:153.

84. *Morning Chronicle*, November 7, 1822.

85. Vissieux, *Essay on Liberalism*, viii, 6, 5.

86. *Monthly Censor* 2 (1823): 487. See Guillaume de Bertier de Sauvigny, "Libéralisme. Aux origines d'un mot," *Commentaire*, no. 7 (1979): 420–24; D. M. Craig, "The Origins of 'Liberalism' in Britain: The Case of *The Liberal*," *Historical Research* 85, no. 229 (2012): 469–87; Daisy Hay, "Liberals, Liberales and *the Liberal*," *European Romantic Review* 19 (2008): 307–20.

87. *Blackwood's Magazine* 13 (1823): 110.

88. See G.I.T. Machin, "Resistance to Repeal of the Test and Corporation Acts, 1828," *Historical Journal* 22, no. 1 (1979): 115–39; see also Craig, "Origins of 'Liberalism.'"

89. *La Macédoine libérale* (Paris, 1819).

90. For Mill's comments, see his *Essays on French History and Historians*, in *The Collected Works of John Stuart Mill*, vol. 20, ed. John M. Robson (Toronto: University of Toronto Press, 1985), 109, http://oll.libertyfund.org/titles/235.

91. Charles Hale, *Mexican Liberalism in the Age of Mora, 1821–1853* (New Haven, CT: Yale University Press, 1968).

92. Robert Alexander, *Re-writing the French Revolutionary Tradition* (Cambridge: Cambridge University Press, 2003).

93. Louis de Bonald, "De l'Esprit de corps et de l'esprit de parti," in *Œuvres de M. de Bonald* (Brussels: La Société nationale, 1845), 8:309.

94. Auguste Levasseur, *Lafayette en Amérique en 1824 et 1825 ou Journal d'un voyage aux Etats-Unis* (Paris, 1829), 1:440.

95. Quoted in Robert Bigler, *The Politics of German Protestantism: The Rise of the Protestant Church Elite in Prussia, 1815–1848* (Berkeley: University of California Press, 1972), 96, 101.

96. Wilhelm Traugott Krug, *Geschichtliche Darstellung des Liberalismus alter und neuer Zeit* (Leipzig, 1823), 65, 103, ix, 83, vii, 148.

97. Yun Kyoung Kwon, "When Parisian Liberals Spoke for Haiti: French Antislavery Discourses on Haiti under the Restoration, 1814 –30," *Atlantic Studies: Global Currents* 8, no. 3 (2011): 317–41.

98. "De M. Dunoyer et de quelques-uns de ses ouvrages," in Benjamin Constant, *Mélanges de littérature et de politique* (Paris, 1829), 128–62.

99. Quoted by Kwon, "When Parisian Liberals Spoke," 326.

100. Adam Smith, *An Inquiry into the Nature and Causes of the Wealth of Nations* (1776; Chicago: University of Chicago Press, 1977), bk. 1, chap. 11, 278.

101. David Todd, *L'Identité économique de la France. Libre-échange et protectionnisme, 1814–1851* (Paris: Grasset, 2008), 75.

102. Cited by Philippe Steiner, "Jean-Baptiste Say, la société industrielle et le libéralisme," in *La Pensée libérale. Histoire et controverses*, ed. Gilles Kévorkian (Paris: Ellipses, 2010), 105–32.

103. *Monthly Magazine* 6 (July 1796): 469–70.

104. Mary Wollstonecraft, *A Vindication of the Rights of Woman* (1792; Oxford: Oxford University Press, 2009), 134.

105. Madame de Staël, *De la littérature*, ed. Gérard Gengembre and Jean Goldzink (Paris: Flammarion, 1991), 336.

106. Louis de Bonald, *Du Divorce considéré au XIXe siècle relativement à l'état public de la société* (Paris: Le Clere, 1801), 5, 193, quoted by Joan De Joan, *Tender Geographies: Women and the Origins of the Novel in France* (New York: Columbia University Press, 1991), 262.

107. Claire Goldberg Moses, *French Feminism in the 19th Century* (Albany: State University of New York Press, 1985), 6.

108. *Preuves frappantes de l'imminence d'une seconde révolution* (Paris, 1827).

109. *Avis à tous les bons français. Catéchisme antilibéral. Projets impies, immoraux et anarchiques du libéralisme* (Marseilles: M. Olive, n.d.), iij.

*Chapter Three: Liberalism, Democracy, and the*
*Emergence of the Social Question, 1830–48*

1. C. A. Bayly, "Liberalism at Large: Mazzini and Nineteenth-Century Indian Thought," in *Giuseppe Mazzini and the Globalisation of Democratic Nationalism, 1830–1920*, edited by C. A. Bayly and Eugenio F. Biagini (Oxford: Oxford University Press, 2008), 355–74.

2. Quoted by F. B. Smith, "Great Britain and the Revolutions of 1848," *Labour History*, no. 33 (November 1977): 846.

3. A. Thiers, *La Monarchie de 1830* (Berlin, 1832), 150, 118.

4. François Guizot, *Histoire parlementaire de France, Recueil complet de discours prononcés dans les chambres de 1819 à 1848*, vol. 4 (Paris, 1863), 381.

5. Speech of March 13, 1834, cited by Pierre Rosanvallon, *La Démocratie inachevée* (Paris: Gallimard, 2000), 115.

6. Etienne Cabet, *Révolution de 1830, et situation présente* (Paris: Gallica, 1833).

7. John Stuart Mill, *Autobiography*, in *The Collected Works of John Stuart Mill*, vol. 1: *Autobiography and Literary Essays*, ed. John M. Robson and Jack

Stillinger (Toronto: University of Toronto Press, 1981), http://oll.libertyfund.org
/titles/242.

8. "Prospects of France, I," *Examiner*, September 19, 1830, 594–95, in *The Collected Works of John Stuart Mill*, vol. 22, ed. Ann P. Robson and John M. Robson (Toronto: University of Toronto Press, 1986), http://oll.libertyfund.org
/titles/256.

9. #85, "French News," *Examiner*, February 13, 1831, 106, and "The Prospects of France," *Examiner*, April 10, 1831, 225–26, in *The Collected Works of John Stuart Mill*, vol. 22, ed. Ann P. Robson and John M. Robson (Toronto: University of Toronto Press, 1986), http://oll.libertyfund.org/titles/256, emphasis added.

10. *Easton Gazette*, March 3, 1832, 3; *Charleston Courier*, April 14, 1831, 2; *Daily Picayune*, April 13, 1839, 2.

11. "Liberal, Liberalismus," in *Staats-Lexikon oder Encyclopädie der Staatswissenschaften*, vol. 9 (Altona: Verlag von Johann Friedrich Hammerich, 1840), 713–30.

12. Cited in Dieter Langewiesche, *Liberalism in Germany*, trans. Christiane Bannerji (Princeton: Princeton University Press, 2000), 12.

13. Quoted by Rosanvallon, *La Démocratie inachevée*, 123n1.

14. Thomas Jefferson to William Short, January 8, 1825, *Founders Online*, https://founders.archives.gov/documents/Jefferson/98-01-02-4848.

15. *Encyclopedia Americana. A Popular Dictionary of Arts, Sciences, Literature*, vol. 7 (Philadelphia, 1831), 533.

16. Alexis de Tocqueville, *Democracy in America*, vol. 2, bk. 2, chap. 2 and introduction.

17. Aurelian Craiutu and Jeremy Jennings, "The Third 'Democracy': Tocqueville's Views of America after 1840," *American Political Science Review* 98, no. 3 (2004): 391–404.

18. Nadia Urbinati, "Giuseppe Mazzini's International Political Thought," introduction to *A Cosmopolitanism of Nations: Giuseppe Mazzini's Writings on Democracy, Nation Building, and International Relations*, ed. Stefano Recchia and Nadia Urbinati, trans. Stefano Recchia (Princeton: Princeton University Press, 2009), 3.

19. Quoted by Denis Mack Smith, *Mazzini* (New Haven, CT: Yale University Press, 1994), 24.

20. John Morley, *The Life of William Ewart Gladstone* (London, 1903), bk. 10, 478; Morley, *The Works of John Morley*, vol. 1 (London, 1921), 223.

21. John Stuart Mill to Peter Alfred Taylor, August 22, 1870, in *The Collected Works of John Stuart Mill*, vol. 17, ed. Francis E. Mineka and Dwight N. Lindley (Toronto: University of Toronto Press, 1972), 1759, http://oll.libertyfund.org
/titles/254.

22. *Staats-Lexikon* (1834): 1:xxi.

23. Quoted by F. Gunther Eyck, "English and French Influence on German Liberalism before 1848," *Journal of the History of Ideas* 18, no. 3 (1957): 314.

24. Quoted by Thomas P. Neill, *The Rise and Decline of Liberalism* (Milwaukee: Bruce, 1953), 151.

25. Robert Owen's *Millennial Gazette*, no. 11 (1857): 58.

26. *New Moral World; or, Gazette of the Universal Community Society of Rational Religionists*, vol. 6 (Leeds, 1839), 673.

27. Cabet, *Révolution de 1830*, 362, 547.

28. "De la philosophie et du christianisme" (1832) and "La Carrosse de M. Aguado" (1847).

29. Victor Considérant, *Principes du socialisme suivie du procès de la démocratie pacifique* (Paris, 1847), 16.

30. Friedrich Engels, "Outlines of a Critique of Political Economy," in *The Young Hegelians*, ed. L. T. Stepelevich (New York: Cambridge University Press, 1983), 278–84.

31. Arthur Bestor, "The Evolution of the Socialist Vocabulary," *Journal of the History of Ideas* 9, 3 (1948): 259–302; and Gregory Claeys, "'Individualism,' 'Socialism' and 'Social Science': Further Notes on a Conceptual Formation 1800–1850," *Journal of the History of Ideas* 47, no. 1 (1986): 81–93.

32. See, for example, Frédéric Bastiat, *Sophismes économiques* (Paris: Guillaumin, 1846), 139, emphasis added.

33. *Journal des économistes* 8 (April–July 1844): 60; 4 (December 1842–March 1843): 260.

34. Cobden, as quoted by Anthony Howe, *Free Trade and Liberal England, 1846–1946* (Oxford: Clarendon, 1997), 119.

35. *Discours parlementaires de M. Thiers*, 16 vols., ed. M. Calmon (Paris, 1879–89), 9:139–43, emphasis added.

36. Quoted by Dennis Sherman, "The Meaning of Economic Liberalism in Mid-Nineteenth Century France," *History of Political Economy* 6, no. 2 (1974): 185.

37. Frédéric Bastiat, "À Messieurs les électeurs de l'arrondissement de Saint-Séver," in *Œuvres complètes de Frédéric Bastiat* (Paris: Guillaumin et Cie, 1855), 1:464.

38. Louis Blanc, *Louis Blanc on the Working Classes: With Corrected Notes, and a Refutation of His Destructive Plan*, trans. James Ward (London, 1848), 223.

39. See, for example, Louis Blanc, *The History of Ten Years; or, France under Louis Philippe*, trans. Walter Kelly (Philadelphia: Lea & Blanchard, 1848), 83, 19.

40. Tocqueville, *Democracy in America*, vol. 2, bk. 3, chap. 7; bk. 4, chap. 7; and *Memoir on Pauperism*, ed. and trans. Seymour Drescher (London: IEA, 1917), 36, 16.

41. Jonathan Riley, introduction to John Stuart Mill, *Principles of Political Economy and Chapters on Socialism*, ed. Jonathan Riley (Oxford: Oxford University Press, 2008).

42. Mill, *Principles of Political Economy*, bk. 5, chap. 11, 335; chap. 1, 161, 162, 165.

43. Mark Donoghue, "The Early Economic Writings of William Thomas Thornton," *History of Political Economy* 39, no. 2 (2007): 209–52.

44. J. R. McCulloch, *Principles of Political Economy*, 5th ed. (Edinburgh: Charles Black, 1864), 187–88.

45. David Roberts, *The Victorian Origins of the British Welfare State* (New Haven, CT: Yale University Press, 1960), 81.

46. William Leggett, "The Natural System," 179, and "The Legislation of Congress," 20, both in *Democratick Editorials: Essays in Jacksonian Political Economy* (1834), http://oll.libertyfund.org/titles/leggett-democratick-editorials-essays-in-jacksonian-political-economy.

47. Francis Lieber, quoted in *The Progressive Evolution in Politics and Political Science: Transforming the American Regime*, ed. John Marini and Ken Masugi (Lanham, MD: Rowman & Littlefield, 2005), 227–28.

48. Francis Lieber, *Manual of Political Ethics: Designed Chiefly for the Use of Colleges*, 2nd ed. (Boston, 1847), 347.

49. Rudolf Walther, "Economic Liberalism," trans. Keith Tribe, *Economy and Society* 13, no. 2 (1984): 178–207.

50. Steven Lukes, "The Meanings of 'Individualism,'" *Journal of the History of Ideas* 32, no. 1 (1971): 54.

51. Quoted by Donald Rohr, *The Origins of Social Liberalism in Germany* (Chicago: University of Chicago Press, 1963), 130.

52. A list of necessary government interventions is provided by Rohr, *Origins*, 127.

53. "Eigenthum," *Das Staatslexikon*, 2nd ed., ed. Karl von Rotteck and Karl Welcker (1846), 4:211–17. For other interventionist policies advocated by Rotteck, see Rohr, *Origins*, 110–11.

54. Marwan Buheiry, "Anti-colonial Sentiment in France during the July Monarchy: The Algerian Case" (PhD diss., Princeton University, 1973), 230.

55. T. P. Thompson, "East India Trade," *Westminster Review* 14 (January 1831): 101; see also "The British in India," *Westminster Review* 4 (October 1825): 265–66.

56. Bernard Semmel, *The Rise of Free Trade Imperialism: Classical Political Economy, the Empire of Free Trade and Imperialism 1750–1850* (Cambridge: Cambridge University Press, 1970), 154.

57. Anna Gambles, *Protection and Politics in Conservative Economic Discourse, 1815–1852* (Suffolk: Boydell Press, 1999), 241.

58. Tocqueville, quoted by Melvin Richter, "Tocqueville on Algeria," *Review of Politics* 25, no. 3 (1963): 379.

59. J.-J. O. Pellion, "Alger-Algérie," in *Dictionnaire politique; Encyclopédie du langage et de la science politiques* (Paris: Pagnerre, 1842), 48.

60. As quoted in Semmel, *Rise*, 148.

61. John Stuart Mill, *Principles of Politics*, ed. Jonathan Riley (Oxford: Oxford University Press, 2008), 119.

62. Jean-Baptiste Say, *De l'Angleterre et les Anglais* (Paris, 1815), 55.

63. Jennifer Sessions, *By Sword and Plow: France and the Conquest of Algeria* (Ithaca, NY: Cornell University Press, 2015), 179.

64. John Stuart Mill, *On Liberty* (1859), chap. 1.

65. Quoted in Helena Rosenblatt, *Liberal Values: Benjamin Constant and the Politics of Religion* (Cambridge: Cambridge University Press, 2008), 203.

66. *L'Avenir*, January 3, 1831.

67. J.-C.-L. Simonde de Sismondi, *Epistolario*, vol. 3, ed. Carlo Pelligrini (Florence: La nuova Italia, 1933–75), #437, 123.

68. "Kirschenverfassung, katholische," *Staats-Lexikon* (1840): 9:310–27; Friedrich Kolb, "Klöster," *Staats-Lexikon* (1840): 9:416–51; S. Jordan, "Jesuiten," *Staats-Lexikon* (1839): 8:437–538, 538; quoted by Bigler, *Politics of German Protestantism*, 194; Andreas Buchner, "Religion," *Staats-Lexikon* (1848): 11:475.

69. "Heilige Schriften des neuen Testaments," *Staats-Lexikon* (1847): 6:668; Gotllieb Christian Abt, "Atheismus," *Staats-Lexikon* (1845): 1:755, 752, 754.

70. Andrew Gould, *Origins of Liberal Dominance: State, Church and Party in Nineteenth-Century Europe* (Ann Arbor: University of Michigan Press, 1999), 75.

71. I am not sure whether they called themselves "liberal Jews" yet. The earliest use of the term I have found is in Moses Hess's eighth letter of Rome and Jerusalem of 1862, where he speaks of "liberal circles of German Jewry," "liberal Jew," and "liberal Christian." See http://www.zionism-israel.com/zionism_docu ments.htm.

72. Dagmar Herzog, https://www.ohio.edu/chastain/rz/strg.htm, and *Intimacy and Exclusion: Religious Politics in Baden 1803–1849* (Princeton: Princeton University Press, 1996), 117.

73. German liberal anti-Semitism is explored in Marcel Stoeltzer, *The State, the Nation and the Jews: Liberalism and the Anti-Semitism in Bismarck's Germany* (Lincoln: University of Nebraska Press, 2008).

74. Malcolm Chase, *Chartism: A New History* (Manchester: Manchester University Press, 2007).

75. Etienne Cabet, *Le vrai Christianisme suivant Jésus Christ* (Paris, 1846); Edward Berenson, *Populist Religion and Left-Wing Politics in France* (Princeton: Princeton University Press, 1984).

76. Giuseppe Mazzini, "On the Duties of Man" (London, 1862).

## Chapter Four: The Question of Character

1. William Fortescue, "Morality and Monarchy: Corruption and the Fall of the Regime of Louis-Philippe in 1848," *French History* 16, no. 1 (2002): 83–100.

2. Mill, quoted by Georgios Varouxakis, "French Radicalism through the Eyes of John Stuart Mill," *History of European Ideas* 30 (2004): 450.

3. John Stuart Mill, "Vindication of the French Revolution of February 1848," in *The Collected Works of John Stuart Mill*, vol. 20, ed. John M. Robson (Toronto: University of Toronto Press, 1985), 325, http://oll.libertyfund.org/titles/235.

4. Quoted in Eugene Curtis, *The French Assembly of 1848 and American Constitutional Doctrine* (New York: Columbia University, 1918), 83.

5. Quoted by David Barclay, *Frederick William IV and the Prussian Monarchy 1840–1862* (Oxford: Oxford University Press, 1995), 134.

6. Quoted by Tim Chapman, *The Risorgimento: Italy, 1815–1871* (Humanities e-books, 2010), 42.

7. *Journal des Débats*, quoted by John Merriman, *The Agony of the Left: Repression of the Left in Revolutionary France* (New Haven, CT: Yale University Press, 1978), 24.

8. Adolphe Thiers, *De la propriété* (Paris: Paulin, 1848), 179.

9. Quoted in Michael Burleigh, *Earthly Powers: The Clash of Religion and Politics in Europe from the French Revolution to the Great War* (New York: HarperCollins, 2005), 208.

10. Adolphe Thiers, *De la propriété*, 383.

11. Quoted by Pamela Pilbeam, *French Socialists before Marx: Workers, Women and the Social Question in France* (Montreal: McGill-Queen's University Press, 2000), 69.

12. Quoted by Roger D. Price, *Napoleon III and the Second Empire* (London: Routledge, 1997), 254.

13. Allan Mitchell, *The Divided Path: The German Influence on Social Reform in France after 1870* (Chapel Hill: University of North Carolina Press, 2010), 10.

14. Mill, "Vindication of the French Revolution," 354.

15. See Alexandre Laya, *France et Amérique ou des institutions républicaines* (1850) and Auguste Romieu, *L'ère des Césars* (1850), a book translated into German the following year.

16. *Histoire de Jules César*, t. 1, 280, quoted by Pierre Rosanvallon, *La Démocratie inachevée* (Paris: Gallimard, 2000), 194.

17. Melvin Richter, "Tocqueville, Napoleon and Bonapartism," in *Reconsidering Tocqueville's Democracy in America*, ed. S. E. Eisenstadt (New Brunswick, NJ: Rutgers University Press, 1988), 110–45.

18. Varouxakis, "French Radicalism."

19. Quoted by David Barclay, "Prussian Conservatives and the Problem of Bonapartism," in *Dictatorship in History and Theory: Bonapartism, Caesarism and Totalitarianism*, ed. P. R. Baehr and Melvin Richter (Cambridge: Cambridge University Press, 2004), 67.

20. Burleigh, *Earthly Powers*, 210.

21. Joseph Gaume, *Le ver rongeur des sociétés modernes ou le paganisme dans l'éducation* (Paris, 1851), 1–2.

22. Juan Donoso Cortés, quoted by Thomas Neill, "Juan Donos Cortés: History and 'Prophesy,'" *Catholic History Review* 40 (January 1955): 403.

23. Ibid., 401.

24. Quoted in Michael Gross, *The War against Catholicism: Liberalism and the Anti-Catholic Imagination in Nineteenth-Century Germany* (Ann Arbor: University of Michigan Press, 2004), 48, 93.

25. Vierhaus, "Liberalismus," 77.

26. Quoted by James Sheehan, "The German States and the European Revolution," in *Revolution and the Meanings of Freedom in the Nineteenth Century*, ed. Isser Woloch (Stanford: Stanford University Press, 1996), 275.

27. Alexis de Tocqueville, *Recollections: The French Revolution of 1848*, ed. J. P. Mayer and A. P. Kerr, trans. George Lawrence (New Brunswick, NJ: Transaction, 2003), 35, 74.

28. Richard Rohrs, "American Critics of the French Revolution of 1848," *Journal of the Early Republic* 14, no. 3 (Autumn 1994): 376.

29. W. R. Greg, "Difficulties of Republican France," *Edinburgh Review* 92 (1850): 523–24.

30. *Aberdeen Journal*, March 29, 1848.

31. *Bristol Gazette*, July 8, 1852, as quoted by Andrew Robertson, *The Language of Democracy: Political Rhetoric in the United States and Britain, 1790–1900* (Charlottesville: University of Virginia Press, 2005), 112.

32. Frédéric Bastiat, *The Law*, in *Œuvres complètes*, 1:97.

33. "Economie politique," in *Dictionnaire de l'économie politique*, vol. 1, ed. Ch. Coquelin et Guillaumin (Paris, 1873), 666.

34. Frédéric Bastiat, *Harmonies of Political Economy* (London, 1860).

35. John Stuart Mill, *Autobiography*, in *The Collected Works of John Stuart Mill*, vol. 1, ed. John M. Robson and Jack Stillinger (Toronto: University of Toronto Press, 1981), 241, http://oll.libertyfund.org/titles/242.

36. John Stuart Mill, preface to the third edition of *Principles of Political Economy*, in *The Collected Works of John Stuart Mill*, vol. 2, ed. John M. Robson (Toronto: University of Toronto Press, 1965), http://oll.libertyfund.org/titles/102.

37. See Alan Kahan, *Aristocratic Liberalism: The Social and Political Thought of Jacob Burckhardt, John Stuart Mill and Alexis de Tocqueville* (New Brunswick, NJ: Transaction, 2001), for a compelling explanation of Mill's view of socialism.

38. François Huet, *La Science de l'Esprit* (Paris, 1864), 306.

39. François Huet, *Le Règne social du christianisme* (Paris, 1853).

40. Charles Dupont-White, *L'Individu et l'état* (Paris: Guillaumin, 1856, 1865), 5.

41. Charles Dupont-White, *Essai sur les relations du travail* (Paris: Guillaumin, 1846), 358, 369, 346.

42. Tocqueville, *Democracy in America*, bk. 3, chap. 9.

43. As quoted by Timothy M. Roberts, *Distant Revolutions: 1848 and the Challenge to American Exceptionalism* (Charlottesville: University of Virginia Press, 2009), 91.

44. Giuseppe Mazzini, *An Essay on the Duties of Man Addressed to Working Men* (New York, 1892), 64–69, originally published in Italian in 1860.

45. John Stuart Mill, "On the Subjection of Women," in *On Liberty and Other Writings*, ed. Stefan Collini (Cambridge: Cambridge University Press, 1989).

46. Sarah Grimké, *Letters on the Equality of the Sexes and the Condition of Women* (Boston, 1838), 11.

47. Mill, "On the Subjection of Women," 138.

48. As quoted by Gross, *War against Catholicism*, 201.

49. John Stuart Mill, "Inaugural Address Delivered to the University of St. Andrews," in *The Collected Works of John Stuart Mill*, vol. 21, ed. John M. Robson, introduction by Stefan Collini (Toronto: University of Toronto Press, 1984), 244, http://oll.libertyfund.org/titles/255.

50. John Stuart Mill, "Utility of Religion," in *The Collected Works of John Stuart Mill*, vol. 10, ed. John M. Robson (London: Routledge and Kegan Paul, 1985), 422, http://oll.libertyfund.org/titles/241.

51. Quoted by Gregory Claeys, "Mazzini, Kossuth and British Radicalism, 1848–1854," *Journal of British Studies* 28, no. 3 (1989): 237.

52. Johann Bluntschli, *Staatswörterbuch in drei Bänden*, ed. Edgar Löning (Zürich, 1871–72), 2:479.

53. Jules Simon, *La religion naturelle* (Paris, 1857).

54. J. J. Clamageran, *De l'état actuel du protestantisme en France* (Paris, 1857).

55. As quoted by Gross, *War against Catholicism*, 93.

56. Quoted by Stefan-Ludwig Hoffmann, "Brothers and Strangers? Jews and Freemasons in Nineteenth Century Germany," *German History* 18, no. 2 (2000): 157.

57. Quoted in Robin Healy, *The Jesuit Specter in Imperial Germany* (Leiden: Brill, 2003), 48, emphasis added.

58. "Jews," in Bluntschli, *Staatswörterbuch*, 2:306–11.

59. "Freemasonry," in Bluntschli, *Staatswörterbuch*, 1:684–86.

60. Quoted by Stefan-Ludwig Hoffmann, "Civility, Male Friendship and Masonic Sociability in Nineteenth-Century Germany," *Gender and History* 13, no. 2 (2001): 231.

61. *Essays on Church and State*, ed. Douglas Woodruff (London, 1834), 82, 42, 37, 71.

## Chapter Five: Caesarism and Liberal Democracy

1. Karl Marx, *The Eighteenth Brumaire of Louis Bonaparte*, quoted by David Baguley, *Napoleon III and His Regime: An Extravaganza* (Baton Rouge: Louisiana State University Press, 2000), 277, and Richard Price, *Napoleon III and the Second Empire* (London: Routledge, 1997), 3.

2. Quoted by Timothy M. Roberts, *Distant Revolutions: 1848 and the Challenge to American Exceptionalism* (Charlottesville: University of Virginia Press, 2009), 140.

3. Ibid., 143.

4. Aurelian Craiutu and Jeremy Jennings, "The Third 'Democracy': Tocqueville's Views of America after 1840," *American Political Science Review* 98, no. 3 (2004): 391–404.

5. Tocqueville, *Democracy in America*, bk. 4, chap. 6.

6. Napoleon III, *History of Julius Caesar* (New York, 1865), 1:xi–xiv.

7. For example, V. Vidal, *L'opposition libérale en 1863* (Paris, 1863); *La Coalition libérale*, par. Ernest Duvergier de Hauranne (Paris, 1869); *L'Union libérale et les partis*, par. E. Wiart (Paris, 1870); *Programme libéral par Louis de Lavalette* (Paris, 1869); C. de Senneval, *Napoléon III et la France libérale* (Paris, 1861); Henri Galos, *Le Gouvernement libéral en France, Extrait de la Revue des deux mondes*, September 1, 1869.

8. Jules Simon, *La politique radicale* (Paris, 1868), quoted by Françoise Melonio, "Les libéraux français et leur histoire," in *Les libéralismes, la théorie politique et l'histoire*, ed. Siep Stuurman (Amsterdam: Amsterdam University Press, 1994), 36.

9. Edouard de Laboulaye, *Le parti libéral, son programme, son avenir*, 5th ed. (Paris, 1864), v.

10. Galos, *Le Gouvernement libéral en France*, 10.

11. This article was translated and published in English in *Cyclopaedia of Political Science, Political Economy, and of the Political History of the United States: By the Best American and European Writers*, vol. 2, ed. John J. Lalor (1881; New York: Merrill, 1889).

12. Montalembert, *L'Eglise libre dans l'Etat libre. Extrait du Journal de Bruxelles des 25 et 26 août 1863* (Brussels, 1863), 19, 132.

13. *L'Eglise Libre dans l'Etat Libre. Discours prononcés au congrès catholique de Malines par Le Comte de Montalembert* (Paris: Douniol, 1863), 17.

14. Walter Bagehot, "Caesarianism as It Now Exists," in *The Collected Works of Walter Bagehot*, vol. 4, ed. St. Johns-Stevas (London, 1868), 111–16.

15. As quoted by Peter Baehr, *Caesarism, Charisma and Fate: Historical Sources and Modern Resonances in the Work of Max Weber* (New Brunswick, NJ: Transaction, 2009), 40.

16. "Libéralisme," published as an appendix to Lucien Jaume, *L'individu effacé ou le paradoxe du libéralisme français* (Paris: Fayard, 1997), 557–67.

17. Louis Veuillot, *L'Illusion libérale*, 5th ed. (Paris, 1866), 99.

18. Albert Réville, *Théodore Parker. Sa vie et ses œuvres. Un chapitre de l'histoire de l'abolition de l'esclavage aux Etats-Unis* (Paris, 1865), 237.

19. Speech at Peoria, Illinois, October 16, 1854, in *Collected Works of Abraham Lincoln*, vol. 2 (Ann Arbor: University of Michigan Digital Library Production Services, 2001), 276.

20. Agénor de Gasparin, *Les Etats-Unis en 1861: Un grand peuple qui se relève* (Paris, 1861); *L'Amérique devant l'Europe, principes et intérêts* (Paris, 1862), 483.

21. *Collected Works of Abraham Lincoln*, vol. 5, ed. Roy P. Basler (New Brunswick, NJ: Rutgers University Press, 1953), 355–56, as quoted by Timothy

Verhoeven, *Transatlantic Anti-Catholicism: France and the United States in the Nineteenth Century* (New York: Palgrave Macmillan, 2010), 39.

22. Quoted in Leslie Butler, "The Mugwump Dilemma. Democracy and Cultural Authority in Victorian America" (PhD diss., Yale University, 1997), 165; Leslie Butler, *Critical Americans: Victorian Intellectuals and Transatlantic Liberal Reform* (Chapel Hill: University of North Carolina Press, 2007), 69, 83; "England and America," *Atlantic Monthly* 14, no. 86 (December 1864): 756; Butler, *Critical Americans*, 86; Adam I. P. Smith, " 'The Stuff Our Dreams Are Made Of': Lincoln in the English Imagination," in *The Global Lincoln*, ed. Richard Carwardine and Jay Sexton (Oxford: Oxford University Press, 2011), 125; Butler, *Critical Americans*, 89.

23. Luca Codignola, "The Civil War: The View from Italy," *Reviews in American History* 3, no. 4 (1975): 457–61.

24. Pope Pius IX to Jefferson Davis, in Varina Davis, *Jefferson Davis: Ex-president of the Confederate States of America: A Memoir by His Wife Varina Davis* (Baltimore: Nautical and Aviation Publishing Company, 1990), 2:448.

25. Quoted in John McGreevy, *Catholicism and American Freedom: A History* (New York: Norton, 2003), 85.

26. Charles de Montalembert, "La Victoire du Nord aux Etats-Unis," in *Œuvres polémiques et diverses de M. le comte de Montalembert t. 3* (Paris: Lecoffre Fils et Cie, Successeurs, 1868), 345.

27. Giuseppe Mazzini, "To Our Friends in the United States," in *A Cosmopolitanism of Nations: Giuseppe Mazzini's Writings on Democracy, Nation Building, and International Relations*, ed. Stefano Recchia and Nadia Urbinati, trans. Stefano Recchia (Princeton: Princeton University Press, 2009).

28. Charles Norton, "American Political Ideas," *North American Review* 101, no. 209 (1865): 550–66.

29. Stephen Sawyer, "An American Model for French Liberalism: The State of Exception in Edouard Laboulaye's Constitutional Thought," *Journal of Modern History* 85, no. 4 (2013): 739–71.

30. *Speeches, Correspondence and Political Papers of Carl Schurz*, vol. 2, ed. Frederic Bancroft (New York: Putnam, 1913), 356.

31. *Liberator*, March 11, 1864.

32. Quoted in Cedric Collyer, "Gladstone and the American Civil War," in *Proceedings of the Leeds Philosophical and Literary Society* (Leeds: Leeds Philosophical and Literary Society, 1944–52).

33. Stephen Peterson, "Gladstone, Religion, Politics and America: Perceptions in the Press" (PhD diss., University of Stirling, 2013).

34. Max Weber, *Politics as a Vocation*, in *Max Weber's Complete Writings on Academic and Political Vocations*, ed. John Dreijmans, trans. Gordon Wells (New York: Algora, 2008), 183.

35. *Speeches of the Right Honourable William Ewart Gladstone, M.A., in South-West Lancashire, October, 1868* (Liverpool, n.d.), 27.

36. Quoted by David W. Bebbington, *The Mind of Gladstone: Religion, Mind and Politics* (Oxford: Oxford University Press, 2004), 282.

37. Alan Kahan, *Liberalism in Nineteenth-Century Europe: The Political Culture of Limited Suffrage* (New York: Palgrave Macmillan, 2003), 135.

38. Quoted by Stefan Collini, *Public Moralists: Political Thought and Intellectual Life in Britain* (Oxford: Oxford University Press, 1991), 65.

39. Bebbington, *Mind of Gladstone*, 257.

40. Quoted by John Vincent, *The Foundations of the Liberal Party* (London: Constable, 1966), 160.

41. Baehr, *Caesarism, Charisma and Fate*; see also Peter Baehr, "Max Weber as a Critic of Bismarck," *European Journal of Sociology* 29, no. 1 (1988): 149–64.

42. Quoted by Jonathan Steinberg, *Bismarck: A Life* (Oxford: Oxford University Press, 2013), 247, 244.

43. Hermann Beck, *The Origins of the Authoritarian Welfare State in Prussia: Conservatives, Bureaucracy and the Social Question, 1815–70* (Ann Arbor: University of Michigan Press, 1997).

44. "Liberalismus," in Hermann Wagener, *Staatslexikon*, vol. 12 (Berlin, 1863), 279–80.

45. Quoted by James J. Sheehan, *German Liberalism in the Nineteenth Century* (New York: Humanity Books, 1995), 117.

46. Quoted in Peter Baehr, ed., *Caesarism, Charisma and Fate: Historical Sources and Modern Resonances in the Work of Max Weber* (New York: Transaction, 2008), 36, https://www.researchgate.net/publication/265729593_Caesarism_Charisma_and_Fate/overview.

47. Quoted by Verhoeven, *Transatlantic Anti-Catholicism*, 173.

48. Quoted by Michael Gross, *The War against Catholicism: Liberalism and the Anti-Catholic Imagination in Nineteenth-Century Germany* (Ann Arbor: University of Michigan Press, 2004), 207, 258, emphasis added.

49. Quoted in Francis Arlinghaus, "British Public Opinion and the Kulturkampf, 1871–1875," *Catholic Historical Review* 34, no. 4 (January 1949): 389.

50. *Fraser's Magazine* (1873), quoted in Arlinghaus, "British Public Opinion," 392.

51. Quoted by McGreevy, *Catholicism and American Freedom*, 100; Peterson, "Gladstone, Religion, Politics and America," 111; McGreevy, *Catholicism and American Freedom*, 99.

52. Quoted by McGreevy, *Catholicism and American Freedom*, 107.

53. Quoted in Richard Shannon, *Gladstone: God and Politics* (New York: Continuum, 2007), 263.

54. Quoted in Arlinghaus, "British Public Opinion," 395.

55. Oskar Klein-Hattingen, *Geschichte des Deutschen Liberalismus*, vol. 2 (Berlin, 1912), 649.

56. Quoted in Steinberg, *Bismarck*, 108, emphasis original.

## Chapter Six: The Battle to Secularize Education

1. *Beneficia Dei*, June 4, 1871.

2. *New York Times*, April 17, 1871.

3. Quoted in Nancy Cohen, *The Reconstruction of American Liberalism, 1865–1914* (Chapel Hill: University of North Carolina Press, 2002).

4. Alfred Fouillée, *La Réforme intellectuelle et morale* (Paris, 1871).

5. Georgios Varouxakis, "French Radicalism through the Eyes of John Stuart Mill," *History of European Ideas* 30 (2004): 457.

6. Quoted by John McGreevy, *Catholicism and American Freedom: A History* (New York: Norton, 2003), 114.

7. Quoted in *Dictionnaire de pédagogie et d'instruction primaire*, partie 1, tome 1, ed. Ferdinand Buisson (Paris: Hachette, 1887), 1090.

8. Eugène Spuller, "La République et l'enseignement" (1884), in *Education de la démocratie troisième série de conférences populaires* (Paris, 1892), 30–31.

9. Quoted in Patrick Cabanel, "Catholicisme, protestantisme et laïcité: réflexion sur la trace religieuse dans l'histoire contemporaine de la France," *Modern & Contemporary France* 10, no. 1 (2002): 92.

10. George Chase, "Ferdinand Buisson and Salvation by National Education," in *L'offre d'école: éléments pour une étude comparée des politiques éducatives au XIXe siècle: actes du troisième colloque international, Sèvres, 27–30 septembre 1981* (Paris: Publications de la Sorbonne, 1983), 263–75.

11. Quoted in Patrick Cabanel, *Le Dieu de la République. Aux sources protestantes de la laïcité (1860–1900)* (Rennes: Presses Universitaires de Rennes, 2003), 63.

12. Ferdinand Buisson, *L'Ecole et la nation en France. Extrait de l'Année Pédagogique* (1913), 15.

13. Pierre Ognier, *Une école sans Dieu? 1880–1895. L'invention d'une moral laïque sous la IIIème république* (Toulouse: Presses universitaires du Mirail, 2008), 33.

14. Mann's ideas were first introduced to the French by Laboulaye. The *Revue pédagogique* published extracts of his work, and in 1888 *Horace Mann, son œuvre et ses écrits* was published, with a second edition in 1897.

15. Ognier, *Une école sans Dieu?*, 34.

16. See Paul Bert, *L'instruction civique à l'école: notions fondamentales* (Paris, 1882).

17. Judith Surkis, *Sexing the Citizen: Morality and Masculinity in France, 1870–1920* (Ithaca, NY: Cornell University Press, 2011), 48.

18. Here I am following very closely Sanford Elwitt, *The Making of the Third Republic: Class and Politics in France, 1868–1884* (Baton Rouge: Louisiana State University Press, 1975).

19. Jules Simon, quoted in Sandra A. Horvath, "Victor Duruy and the Controversy over Secondary Education for Girls," *French Historical Studies* 9, no. 1 (1975): 83–104.

20. Ferdinand Buisson, "Filles," in *Dictionnaire de pédagogie et d'instruction primaire*, partie 1, tome 1 (Paris, 1887), 1011–25.

21. Henri Marion, *L'éducation des jeunes filles* (Paris, 1902).

22. See, for example, *L'homme, la famille et la société considérés dans leurs rapports avec le progrès moral de l'humanité*, vol. 2, *La famille* (Paris, 1857), 15–16.

23. Bishop McQuaid and Francis E. Abbot, *The Public School Question, as Understood by a Catholic American Citizen, and by a Liberal American Citizen. Two Lectures, before the Free Religious Association, in Horticultural Hall, Boston* (Boston: Free Religious Association, 1876).

24. Amy Hackett, "The Politics of Feminism in Wilhelmine Germany, 1890–1918" (PhD diss., Columbia University, 1976), 15.

25. Elizabeth Cady Stanton, Susan B. Anthony, and Matilda Joslyn Gage, eds., *History of Woman Suffrage*, 3 vols. (London, 1887).

26. *New York Daily Tribune*, March 18, 1895, 101.

27. Patrick Carey, *Catholics in America: A History* (Westport, CT: Praeger, 2004).

28. Quoted in Roderick Bradford, *D. M. Bennett: The Truth Seeker* (Amherst, NY: Prometheus Books, 2006), 356.

29. Linda Gordon, "Voluntary Motherhood: The Beginnings of Feminist Birth Control in the United States," *Feminist Studies* 1, nos. 3–4 (1973): 11.

30. Ibid., 11.

31. E. Lynn Lynton, "The Revolt against Matrimony," *Forum* 19 (January 1891): 585, 593.

32. Timothy Verhoeven, *Transatlantic Anti-Catholicism: France and the United States in the Nineteenth Century* (New York: Palgrave Macmillan, 2010).

33. Quoted by Sandra Horvath, "Victor Duruy and the Controversy over Secondary Education for Girls," *French Historical Studies* 9, no. 1 (1975): 94.

34. Ibid., 88.

35. It was translated and published in the United States by the National Catholic Welfare Conference in 1939. The English translation is titled less belligerently *What Is Liberalism?*

36. Robert Cross, *The Emergence of Liberal Catholicism in America* (Chicago: Quadrangle, 1968), 201–2.

37. Ibid., 201–2.

38. Quoted in Jay Dolan, *The American Catholic Experience: A History from Colonial Times to the Present* (Garden City, NY: Doubleday, 1987), 312.

39. *Histoire critique du catholicisme libéral jusqu'au pontificat de Léon XIII* (Saint-Dizier, 1897).

40. Pope Leo XIII, *Testem Benevolentiae Nostrae: Concerning New Opinions, Virtue, Nature and Grace, with Regard to Americanism* (1899), http://www.papalencyclicals.net/leo13/l13teste.htm.

41. Benjamin Martin Jr., "The Creation of the Action Libérale Populaire: An Example of Party Formation in Third Republic France," *French Historical Studies* 9, no. 4 (1976): 660–89.

## Chapter Seven: Two Liberalisms

1. *Jahrbücher für Nationalökonomie und Statistik* 21 (1873): 122.

2. Quoted in Robert Adcock, *Liberalism and the Emergence of American Political Science: A Transatlantic Tale* (Oxford: Oxford University Press, 2014), 83.

3. Paul Leroy-Beaulieu, *L'Etat Moderne et ses fonctions*, troisième ed., revue et augmenté (1889; Paris: Guillaumin, 1900).

4. Paul Cère, *Les populations dangereuses et les misères sociales* (Paris, 1872), 116, 306, quoted in John Weiss, "Origins of the French Welfare State: Poor Relief in the Third Republic, 1871–1914," *French Historical Studies* 13, no. 1 (1983): 47–78.

5. Charles Gide, "The Economic Schools and the Teaching of Political Economy in France," *Political Science Quarterly* 5, no. 4 (1890): 603–35.

6. Richard White, *The Republic for Which It Stands: The United States during Reconstruction and the Gilded Age, 1865–1896* (Oxford: Oxford University Press, 2017).

7. Quoted by Adcock, *Liberalism and the Emergence of American Political Science*, 47.

8. E. L. James, "History of Political Economy," in *Cyclopaedia of Political Science, Political Economy, and of the Political History of the United States: By the Best American and European Writers*, vol. 2, ed. John J. Lalor (1881; New York: Merrill, 1889).

9. Herbert Spencer, *The Man versus the State*, in *Political Writings*, ed. John Offer (Cambridge: Cambridge University Press, 1993), 77–78.

10. William Graham Sumner, *What Social Classes Owe Each Other* (New York, 1883).

11. Sidney Fine, *Laissez Faire and the General-Welfare State* (Ann Arbor: University of Michigan Press, 1969), 56.

12. *Daily Chronicle*, January 30, 1896, 4, quoted by Peter Weiler, *The New Liberalism: Liberal Social Theory in Great Britain, 1889–1914* (London: Routledge, 1982), 66.

13. John A. Hobson, *The Crisis of Liberalism: New Issues of Democracy* (London: P.S. King & Son, 1909), 3, xiii.

14. "Are We all Socialists Now?," *Speaker*, May 13, 1893, quoted in Michael Freeden, *The New Liberalism* (Oxford: Clarendon, 1978), 26.

15. Winston Spencer Churchill, *Liberalism and the Social Problem: A Collection of Early Speeches as a Member of Parliament* (London: Hodder & Stoughton, 1909), 43.

16. Francis A. Walker, "Socialism," in *Discussions in Economics and Statistics* (1887; New York, 1899), 2:250.

17. "Socialism and Communism," in Johann Bluntschli, *Staatswörterbuch in drei Bänden*, ed. Edgar Löning (Zürich, 1871–72), 3:476–97.

18. Serge Audier, *Le Socialisme libéral* (Paris: La Découverte, 2006).

19. Léon Bourgeois, *Essai d'une philosophie de la Solidarité* (Paris, 1907), 34.

20. Leonard T. Hobhouse, *Democracy and Reaction* (London: T. Fisher Unwin, 1904), 229.

21. Hobson, *Crisis of Liberalism*, 3, 92, 138.

22. *Journal des débats*, March 16, 1889, 1.

23. Quoted in Judith Surkis, *Sexing the Citizen: Morality and Masculinity in France, 1870–1920* (Ithaca, NY: Cornell University Press, 2011), 130.

24. Hobson, *Crisis of Liberalism*, 132.

25. Churchill, *Liberalism and the Social Problem* (1909), a speech delivered in 1908 under the title "Liberalism and Socialism."

26. One of the characters in Mrs. Humphrey Ward's popular but controversial *Robert Elsemere* (1888) was modeled on him.

27. Quoted in G.F.A. Best, "The Religious Difficulties of National Education in England, 1800–70," *Cambridge Historical Journal* 12, no. 2 (1956): 171, emphasis added.

28. Joseph Henry Allen, *Our Liberal Movement in Theology* (Boston: Roberts Brothers, 1892).

29. Quoted by William Shanahan, "Friedrich Naumann: A Mirror of Wilhelmian Germany," *Review of Politics* 13, no. 3 (1951): 272.

30. Richard Ely, "The Next Thing in Social Reform," *Methodist Magazine* 36 (December 1892): 151.

31. John A. Hobson, *The Social Problem: Life and Work* (London: James Nisbet, 1902), 214.

32. Quoted by Thomas Leonard, *Illiberal Reformers: Race, Eugenics and American Economics in the Progressive Era* (Princeton: Princeton University Press, 2016), 74.

33. Ibid., 110.

34. Ibid., 50.

35. Ibid., 170.

36. Karen Offen, "Depopulation, Nationalism, and Feminism in Fin-de-Siècle France," *American Historical Review* 89, no. 3 (1984): 648–76; Philip Nord, "The Welfare State in France 1870–1914," *French Historical Studies* 18, no. 3 (1994): 821–38.

37. Herbert Samuel, *Contemporary Liberalism in England* (London, 1902), 246, 249, 250.

38. Quoted by Millicent Fawcett, *Women's Suffrage: A Short History of a Great Movement* (CreateSpace, 2016).

39. David Morgan, *Suffragists and Liberals: The Politics of Woman Suffrage in England* (Lanham, MD: Rowman & Littlefield, 1975); Constance Rover, *Women's Suffrage and Party Politics in Britain 1866–1914* (London: Routledge, 1967); see also Brian H. Harrison, *Separate Spheres: The Opposition to Women's Suffrage in Britain* (London: Croom Helm, 1978); Allison L. Sneider, *Suffragists in an Imperial Age: U.S. Expansion and the Woman Question, 1870–1929* (Oxford: Oxford University Press, 2008).

40. Quoted by Amy Hackett, "The Politics of Feminism in Wilhelmine Germany, 1890–1918" (PhD diss., Columbia University, 1976), 397.

41. Ibid., 688.

42. Samuel, *Contemporary Liberalism*, 251.

43. Ibid., 251.

44. Quoted by Hackett, "Politics of Feminism," 715, 721, 718, 799.

45. Ibid., 324.

46. Ibid., 618, 621.

47. Ibid., 716–20.

48. Quoted in Fawcett, *Women's Suffrage*, 95.

49. Quoted by Hackett, "Politics of Feminism," 173, 715.

50. Ibid., 721.

51. Walker, "The Present Standing of Political Economy" (1879), reprinted in Walker, *Discussions in Economics and Statistics*, 1:318.

52. Alfred Fouillée, *La propriété sociale et la démocratie* (Paris: Hachette, 1884).

53. Beatrice Webb, July 30, 1886, quoted by Emma Rothschild, *Economic Sentiments: Adam Smith, Condorcet and the Enlightenment* (Cambridge, MA: Harvard University Press, 2001), 65.

### Chapter Eight: Liberalism Becomes the American Creed

1. "Liberalism in America," *New Republic* 21 (December 31, 1919).

2. David Green, *Shaping Political Consciousness: The Language of Politics in America from McKinley to Ronald Reagan* (Ithaca, NY: Cornell University Press, 1987), 76.

3. Quoted in Ronald J. Pestritto, *Woodrow Wilson and the Roots of Modern Liberalism* (Lanham, MD: Rowman & Littlefield, 2005), 57–58.

4. Quoted in *A Cosmopolitanism of Nations: Giuseppe Mazzini's Writings on Democracy, Nation Building, and International Relations,* ed. Stefano Recchia and Nadia Urbinati, trans. Stefano Recchia (Princeton: Princeton University Press, 2009), 3.

5. J. L. Hammond, cited in Peter Weiler, *The New Liberalism: Liberal Social Theory in Great Britain, 1889–1914* (New York: Routledge, 2017), 85.

6. Leonard T. Hobhouse, *Democracy and Reaction* (London: T. Fisher Unwin, 1904), 47.

7. Robert Lowe, "Imperialism," *Fortnightly Review* 24 (1878), reprinted in Peter Cain, ed., *Empire and Imperialism: The Debate of the 1870s* (South Bend, IN: Saint Augustine's Press, 1999), 268.

8. Gladstone, "England's Mission," quoted in Peter Cain, "Radicals, Gladstone, and the Liberal Critique of Disraelian 'Imperialism,'" in *Victorian Visions of Global Order*, ed. Duncan Bell (Cambridge: Cambridge University Press, 2007), 229.

9. Quoted by Peter Weiler, *The New Liberalism: Liberal Social Theory in Great Britain, 1889–1914* (London: Routledge, 1982), 98.

10. Leslie Butler, *Critical Americans: Victorian Intellectuals and Transatlantic Liberal Reform* (Chapel Hill: University of North Carolina Press, 2007), 255, 46, 231.

11. John Hobson, *Imperialism: A Study* (London: George Allen & Unwin, 1902). The phrase is repeated often.

12. Quoted in Gregory Claeys, *Imperial Sceptics: British Critics of Empire, 1850–1920* (Cambridge: Cambridge University Press, 2010), 238.

13. Leonard T. Hobhouse, *Democracy and Reaction* (London: T. Fisher Unwin, 1904), 47.

14. Herbert Samuel, *Contemporary Liberalism in England* (London, 1902), 332.

15. Ibid., 324.

16. Lucien Prévost-Paradol, *La France nouvelle* (Paris: Michel Levy Frères, 1868).

17. See, for example, "colonies," in *Nouveau dictionnaire d'économie politique* (Paris: Guillaumin, 1900), 1:432–48.

18. Samuel, *Contemporary Liberalism*, 325.

19. Ibid., 330, emphasis added.

20. John Burgess, "Germany, Great Britain and the US," *Political Science Quarterly* 19 (1904): 904.

21. Edward Dicey, "The New American Imperialism," *Nineteenth Century: A Monthly Review*, September 1898, 487–501, 489, 501.

22. John W. Burgess, *Reconstruction and the Constitution, 1866–1876* (New York: Charles Scribner's Sons, 1903), 133.

23. Charles Merriam, *A History of American Political Theories* (New York: Macmillan, 1920), 314, emphasis added.

24. William Gladstone, "Kin beyond the Sea," *North American Review* 264 (September–October 1878): 185, 212, 181, 182.

25. Quoted by Reginald Horsman, *Race and Manifest Destiny* (Cambridge, MA: Harvard University Press, 2009), 293.

26. Andrew Carnegie, "A Look Ahead," *North American Review* 156, no. 439 (June 1893).

27. Lymon Abbott, "The Basis for an Anglo-American Understanding," *North American Review* 166, no. 498 (1898): 521.

28. See, for example, G. Valbert, "La supériorité des Anglo-Saxons et le livre de M. Demolins," *Revue des deux Mondes* 67 (1897): 697–708; Gabriel Tarde, *Sur la prétendue décadence des peuples latins* (Bordeaux, 1901).

29. See also George Santayana, "Classic Liberty," *New Republic* 4 (August 21, 1915): 65–66; "German Freedom," *New Republic* 4 (August 28, 1915): 94–95; "Liberalism and Culture," *New Republic* 4 (September 4, 1915): 123–25.

30. Alan Brinkley, *Liberalism and Its Discontents* (Cambridge, MA: Harvard University Press, 1998), 85.

31. Irving Fisher, "Economists in Public Service: Annual Address of the President," *American Economic Review* 9, no. 1, suppl. (1991): 7.

32. Arthur Moeller van den Bruck, *Sozialismus und Aussenpolitik* (Breslau: W.G. Korn, 1933), 100.

33. Benito Mussolini, *The Political and Social Doctrine of Fascism*, trans. Jane Soames (London: Hogarth, 1934), 17–19.

34. Quoted in John Weiss, *The Fascist Tradition* (New York: Harper & Row, 1967), 9.

35. Ludwig von Mises, *Liberalism in the Classical Tradition*, trans. Ralph Raico (New York: Foundation for Economic Education, 1985), 199.

36. John Dewey, "Toward a New Individualism," in *The Later Works of John Dewey, 1925–1953*, vol. 5: *1929–1930. Essays: The Sources of a Science of Education, Individualism, Old and New, and Construction and Criticism*, ed. Jo Ann Boydston (Carbondale: Southern Illinois University Press, 1984), 85.

37. John Dewey, "The Meaning of the Term 'Liberalism,'" in *The Later Works of John Dewey, 1925–1953*, vol. 14: *1939–1941. Essays, Reviews and Miscellany*, ed. Jo Ann Boydston (Carbondale: Southern Illinois University Press, 2008), 253.

38. Quoted in Green, *Shaping Political Consciousness*, 119.

39. Franklin Delano Roosevelt, "Introduction to Franklin Delano Roosevelt's Public Papers and Addresses," cited by Samuel Eliot Morison, *Freedom in Contemporary Society* (Boston: Little, Brown, 1956), 69. In 1943, the Liberal Party of New York State, still in existence, was formed to help Roosevelt get elected.

40. Henry Agard Wallace, *American Dreamer: A Life of Henry Wallace* (New York: Norton, 2000).

41. William Beveridge, *Why I Am a Liberal* (London: Jenkins, 1945), 64.

42. As quoted by Alan Brinkley, *The End of Reform: New Deal Liberalism in Recession and War* (New York: Vintage, 2011), 158; Theodore Rosenof, "Freedom, Planning, and Totalitarianism: The Reception of F. A. Hayek's *Road to Serfdom*," *Canadian Review of American Studies* 5 (1974): 150–60.

43. Green, *Shaping Political Consciousness*, chaps. 4–5; and Ronald Rotunda, *The Politics of Language: Liberalism as Word and Symbol* (Iowa City: University of Iowa Press, 1986), chap. 4.

44. "Taft, in Defining Liberalism, Warns of a Gradual Loss of Privileges," *Omaha Evening World-Herald*, February 14, 1948, 5.

45. See chapter on him in Angus Burgin, *The Great Persuasion: Reinventing Free Markets since the Depression* (Cambridge, MA: Harvard University Press, 2015).

46. See Mario Rizzo, "Libertarianism and Classical Liberalism: Is There a Difference?," *ThinkMarkets*, February 5, 2014, https://thinkmarkets.wordpress.com/2014/02/05/libertarianism-and-classical-liberalism-is-there-a-difference.

47. Burgin, *Great Persuasion*, chap. 5.

48. Arthur Murphy, "Ideals and Ideologies, 1917–1947," *Philosophical Review* 56 (1947): 386.

## Epilogue

1. *Les Libéraux*, ed. Pierre Manent (Paris: Gallimard, 2001), 13.

2. Daniel J. Mahoney, introduction to Pierre Manent, *Modern Liberty and Its Discontents: Pierre Manent*, ed. and trans. Daniel J. Mahoney and Paul Senton (Lanham, MD: Rowman & Littlefield, 1998), 8.

3. Alan Brinkley, *The End of Reform: New Deal Liberalism in Recession and War* (New York: Vintage, 2011).

4. Friedrich A. Hayek, *The Road to Serfdom* (Chicago: University of Chicago Press, 2007), 58.

5. Quoted by James Chappel, "The Catholic Origins of Totalitarianism Theory in Interwar Europe," *Modern Intellectual History* 8, no. 3 (2011): 579.

6. "The Pathos of Liberalism," *Nation*, September 11, 1935; see also "The Blindness of Liberalism," *Radical Religion*, (Autumn 1936).

7. Quoted in Alan Brinkley, *Liberalism and Its Discontents* (Cambridge, MA: Harvard University Press, 2000), 106, 86.

8. Reinhold Niebuhr, "Let the Liberal Churches Stop Fooling Themselves!," *Christian Century* 48 (March 25, 1931).

9. Thomas P. Neill, *The Rise and Decline of Liberalism* (Milwaukee: Bruce, 1953). See Neill's self-description at http://www.catholicauthors.com/neill.html.

10. James Burnham, *Suicide of the West: An Essay on the Meaning and Destiny of Liberalism* (New York: Encounter, 1964).

11. As quoted by Chappel, "Catholic Origins of Totalitarianism Theory," 590.

12. Eric Voegelin, *The New Science of Politics: An Introduction* (Chicago: University of Chicago Press, 1987), 178.

13. Berlin's speech is readily available, online and elsewhere.

14. John Plamenatz, ed., *Readings from Liberal Writers, English and French* (New York: Barnes & Noble, 1965).

15. Judith Shklar, "The Liberalism of Fear," in *Liberalism and the Moral Life*, ed. Nancy Rosenblum (Cambridge, MA: Harvard University Press, 1989), 21–38.

16. An important exception is Karen Offen, "Defining Feminism: A Comparative Historical Approach," *Signs* 14, no. 1 (1988): 119–57; Amy Hackett, "The Politics of Feminism in Wilhelmine Germany, 1890–1918" (PhD diss., Columbia University, 1976), objects to the "American bias" in scholarship on feminism, by which she means an overemphasis on rights as a feminist goal.

17. Isaac Kramnick, *Republicanism and Bourgeois Radicalism: Political Ideology in Late Eighteenth Century England and America* (Ithaca, NY: Cornell University Press, 1990), 35.

18. Friedrich Sell, *Die Tragödie des deutschen Liberalismus* (Stuttgart: DVA, 1953).

19. For example, works by Ralf Dahrendorf, Hajo Holborn, Leonard Krieger, James Sheehan, and Theodore Hamerow.

20. Hans Vorländer, "Is There a Liberal Tradition in Germany?," in *The Liberal Political Tradition: Contemporary Reappraisals*, ed. James Meadowcroft (Cheltenham: Edward Elgar, 1996).

21. For a good survey and critique of the literature on German "illiberalism," see Konrad Jarausch, "Illiberalism and Beyond: German History in Search of a Paradigm," *Journal of Modern History* 55, no. 2 (1983): 268–84.

22. Geoff Eley, "James Sheehan and the German Liberals: A Critical Appreciation," *Central European History* 14, no. 3 (1981): 273–88.

23. David Blackbourn and Richard J. Evans, eds., *The German Bourgeoisie: Essays on the Social History of the German Middle Class from the Late Eighteenth to the Early Twentieth Century* (London: Routledge, 1991).

24. Jack Hayward, review *of L'individu effacé, History of European Ideas* 24, no. 3 (1998): 239–42.

25. Pierre Rosanvallon, *Le capitalisme utopique. Critique de l'idéologie économique* (Paris: Seuil, 1979).

26. Sudhir Hazareesingh, *From Subject to Citizen: The Second Empire and the Emergence of Modern French Democracy* (Princeton: Princeton University Press, 1998), 166, 163.

27. Lucien Jaume, *L'individu effacé ou le paradoxe du libéralisme français* (Paris: Fayard, 1997), 14.

28. Raymond Polin, *Le libéralisme, oui* (Paris: Editions de La Table Ronde, 1984), 186.

29. Philippe Raynaud, "Constant," in *New French Thought*, ed. Mark Lilla (Princeton: Princeton University Press, 2014), 85.

30. François Furet and Mona Ozouf, *Le siècle de l'avènement republican* (Paris: Gallimard, 1993), 20–21.

31. Manent, *Modern Liberty and Its Discontents*.

32. "The Rise of Illiberal Democracy" is the title of an influential article by Fareed Zaria in *Foreign Affairs* 76, no. 6 (November–December 1997): 22–43. See also William Galston, "The Growing Threat of Illiberal Democracy," *Wall Street Journal*, January 3, 2017.

33. See, for example, Peter Berkowitz, *Virtue and the Making of Modern Liberalism* (Princeton: Princeton University Press, 1999); William Galston, *Liberal Purposes* (New York: Cambridge University Press, 1991); and Rosenblum, *Liberalism and the Moral Life*.

# SELECTED BIBLIOGRAPHY

## Method

Ball, Terence, James Farr, and Russell L. Hanson. "Editors' Introduction." In Ball, Farr, and Hanson, *Political Innovation and Conceptual Change*, 1–5.

———, eds. *Political Innovation and Conceptual Change*. Cambridge: Cambridge University Press, 1989.

Ball, Terence. *Transforming Political Discourse: Political Theory and Conceptual History*. Oxford: Blackwell, 1988.

Burke, Martin, and Melvin Richter, eds. *Why Concepts Matter: Translating Social and Political Thought*. Leiden: Brill, 2012.

Farr, James. "Understanding Conceptual Change Politically." In Ball, Farr, and Hanson, *Political Innovation and Conceptual Change*, 24–49.

Freeden, Michael. *Ideologies and Political Theory: A Conceptual Approach*. Oxford: Clarendon, 1996.

Hampshire-Monk, Iain, Karin Tilmans, and Frank van Vree, eds. *History of Concepts: Comparative Perspectives*. Amsterdam: Amsterdam University Press, 1998.

Koselleck, Reinhart. *The Practice of Conceptual History: Timing History, Spacing Concepts*. Translated by T. S. Presener et al. Stanford: Stanford University Press, 2002.

Pocock, J.G.A. "Verbalizing a Political Act: Towards a Politics of Speech." In *Language and Politics*, edited by Michael Shapiro, 25–43. Oxford: Wiley Blackwell, 1984.

Richter, Melvin. "Begriffsgeschichte and the History of Ideas." *Journal of the History of Ideas* 48, no. 2 (1987): 247–63.

———. *The History of Political and Social Concepts: A Critical Introduction*. New York: Oxford University Press, 1995.

———. "Reconstructing the History of Political Languages: Pocock, Skinner and the Geschichtliche Grundbegriffe." *History and Theory* 29, no. 1 (1990): 38–70.

Sebastián, Javier Fernández, ed. *Political Concepts and Time: New Approaches to Conceptual History*. Santander: Cantabria University Press, 2011.

Skinner, Quentin. "Meaning and Understanding in the History of Ideas." *History and Theory* 8 (1969): 3–53. Reprinted in *Meaning and Context: Quentin Skinner and His Critics*, edited by James Tully. Princeton: Princeton University Press, 1988.

———. "Language and Social Change." In *The State of the Language*, edited by Christopher Ricks and Leonard Michaels, 562–78. Berkeley: University of California Press, 1980.

Steinmetz, Willibald, Michael Freeden, and Javier Fernández Sebastián, eds. *Conceptual History in the European Space*. New York: Berghahn, 2017.

## Scholarship on the Concepts *Liberal*, *Liberality*, and *Liberalism*

Bell, Duncan. "What Is Liberalism?" *Political Theory* 42, no. 6 (2014): 682–715.

Bertier de Sauvigny, Guillaume de. "Libéralisme. Aux origines d'un mot." *Commentaire*, no. 7 (1979): 420–24.

———. "Liberalism, Nationalism, Socialism: The Birth of Three Words." *Review of Politics* 32 (1970): 151–52.

Claeys, Gregory. "'Individualism,' 'Socialism' and 'Social Science': Further Notes on a Conceptual Formation 1800–1850." *Journal of the History of Ideas* 47, no. 1 (1986): 81–93.

Cox, Richard. "Aristotle and Machiavelli on Liberality." In *The Crisis of Liberal Democracy*, edited by Kenneth L. Deutsch and Walter Soffer, 125–47. Albany: State University of New York Press, 1987.

Guerzoni, Guido. "Liberalitas, Magnificentia, Splendor: The Classic Origins of Italian Renaissance Lifestyles." *History of Political Economy* 31, suppl. (1999): 332–78.

Gunnell, John G. "The Archeology of American Liberalism." *Journal of Political Ideologies* 6, no. 2 (2001): 125–45.

Hamburger, Philip. "Liberality." *Texas Law Review* 78, no. 6 (2000): 1215–85.

Leonhard, Jörn. "From European Liberalism to the Languages of Liberalisms: The Semantics of *Liberalism* in European Comparison." *Redescriptions* 8 (2004): 17–51.

———. *Liberalismus. Zur historischen Semantik eines europäischen Deutungsmusters*. Munich: R. Oldernbourg Verlag, 2001.

Manning, C. E. "'Liberalitas'—The Decline and Rehabilitation of a Virtue." *Greece & Rome* 32, no. 1 (April 1985): 73–83.

Opal, Jason M. "The Labors of Liberality: Christian Benevolence and National Prejudice in the American Founding." *Journal of American History* 94 (2008): 1082–1107.

Rotunda, Ronald. *The Politics of Language: Liberalism as Word and Symbol*. Iowa City: University of Iowa Press, 1986.

Sahagun, Alberto. "The Birth of Liberalism: The Making of Liberal Political Thought in Spain, France and England 1808–1823." PhD diss., Washington University in St. Louis, 2009.

Sebastián, Javier Fernández. "Liberales y Liberalismo en Espana, 1810–1850. La Forja de un Concepto y la Creacion de una Identidad Politica." In *La aurora de la libertad. Los primeros liberalism en el mundo iberomaricano*, edited by Javier Fernández Sebastián, 265–306. Madrid: Marcial Pons Historia, 2012.

————. "Liberalismos nacientes en el Atlántico iberoamericano. 'Liberal' como concepto y como identitad política, 1750–1850." In *Iberconceptos*, edited by Javier Fernández Sebastián. Vol. 1, *Diccionario político y social del mundo iberoamericano: La era de las revoluciones, 1750–1850*, edited by C. Aljovìn de Losada et al. Madrid: Fundación Carolina-SECC-CEPC, 2009.

————. "The Rise of the Concept of 'Liberalism': A Challenge to the Centre/ Periphery Model?" In *Transnational Concepts, Transfers and the Challenge of the Peripheries*, edited by Gürcan Koçan, 182–200. Istanbul: Istanbul Technical University Press, 2008.

Thomson, Arthur. "'Liberal': Några anteckningar till ordets historia." In *Festskrift tillägnad Theodor Hjelmqvist på sextiårsdagen den 11 april 1926*, 147–91. Lund: Carl Bloms Boktryckeri, 1926.

Vierhaus, Rudolf. "Liberalismus." In *Geschichtliche Grundbegriffe. Historisches Lexikon zur politisisch-sozialen Sprache in Deutschland*, vol. 3, edited by Reinhart Koselleck, Otto Bruner, and Werner Conze, 744–85. Stuttgart: E. Klett, 1972–93.

Walther, Rudolf. "Economic Liberalism." Translated by Keith Tribe. *Economy and Society* 13, no. 2 (1984): 178–207.

## Liberal Religion and Its Critics

Aner, Karl. *Die Theologie der Lessingzeit*. Halle: Niemeyer, 1929.

Arlinghaus, Francis A. "British Public Opinion and the *Kulturkampf* in Germany, 1871–75." *Catholic Historical Review* 34, no. 4 (1949): 385–413.

Best, G.F.A. "The Religious Difficulties of National Education in England, 1800–70." *Cambridge Historical Journal* 12, no. 2 (1956): 155–73.

Biagini, Eugenio F. "Mazzini and Anticlericalism: The English Exile." In *Giuseppe Mazzini and the Globalisation of Democratic Nationalism, 1830–1920*, edited by C. A. Bayly and Eugenio F. Biagini, 145–66. Oxford: Oxford University Press, 2008.

Bigler, Robert. *The Politics of German Protestantism: The Rise of the Protestant Church Elite in Prussia, 1815–1848*. Berkeley: University of California Press, 1972.

Blackbourn, David. "Progress and Piety: Liberalism, Catholicism and the State in Imperial Germany." *History Workshop Journal* 26 (1988): 57–78.

Bokenkotter, Thomas. *Church and Revolution: Catholics and the Struggle for Democracy and Social Justice*. New York: Random House, 2011.

Buehrens, John. *Universalists and Unitarianism in America: A People's History*. Boston: Skinner House Books, 2011.

Burleigh, Michael. *Earthly Powers: The Clash of Religion and Politics in Europe from the French Revolution to the Great War*. New York: HarperCollins, 2005.

Cabanel, Patrick. *Le Dieu de la République. Aux sources protestantes de la laïcité (1860–1900)*. Rennes: Presses universitaires de Rennes, 2003.

————. *Les Protestants et la République*. Paris: Editions Complexe, 2000.

Carey, Patrick. *Catholics in America: A History*. Westport, CT: Praeger, 2004.

Carlsson, Eric. "Johann Salomo Semler, the German Enlightenment and Protestant Theology's Historical Turn." PhD diss., University of Wisconsin–Madison, 2006.

Clark, Christopher, and Wolfram Kaiser, eds. *Culture Wars: Secular-Catholic Conflict in Nineteenth-Century Europe*. Cambridge: Cambridge University Press, 2003.

Cross, Robert. *The Emergence of Liberal Catholicism in America*. Chicago: Quadrangle, 1968.

Dolan, Jay. *The American Catholic Experience: A History from Colonial Times to the Present*. Garden City, NY: Doubleday, 1987.

Dorrien, Gary. *The Making of American Liberal Theology: Imagining Progressive Religion, 1805–1900*. Louisville: Westminster John Knox, 2001.

Douglass, R. Bruce, and David Hollenbach, eds. *Catholicism and Liberalism*. Cambridge: Cambridge University Press, 1994.

Grodzins, Dean. *American Heretic: Theodore Parker and Transcendentalism*. Chapel Hill: University of North Carolina Press, 2002.

Gross, Michael. "The Catholics' Missionary Crusade and the Protestant Revival in Nineteenth-Century Germany." In *Protestants, Catholics and Jews in Germany, 1800–1914*, edited by H. Walser Smith, 245–66. New York: Berg.

———. *The War against Catholicism: Liberalism and the Anti-Catholic Imagination in Nineteenth-Century Germany*. Ann Arbor: University of Michigan Press, 2005.

Hamburger, Philip. *Separation of Church and State*. Cambridge, MA: Harvard University Press, 2002.

Heimert, Alan. *Religion and the American Mind*. Cambridge, MA: Harvard University Press, 1968.

Herzog, Dagmar. "Anti-Judaism in Intra-Christian Conflicts: Catholics and Liberals in Baden in the 1840s." *Central European History* 27 (1994): 267–81.

———. *Intimacy and Exclusion: Religious Politics in Pre-revolutionary Baden*. Princeton: Princeton University Press, 1996.

Hill, Ronald. *Lord Acton*. New Haven, CT: Yale University Press, 2000.

Hollinger, David. *After Cloven Tongues of Fire: Protestant Liberalism in Modern American History*. Princeton: Princeton University Press, 2013.

Hopkins, Charles Howard. *The Rise of the Social Gospel in American Protestantism, 1865–1915*. New Haven, CT: Yale University Press, 1940.

Hurth, Elisabeth. "Sowing the Seeds of 'Subversion': Harvard's Early Göttingen Students." In *Studies in the American Renaissance*, edited by Joel Myerson, 91–106. Charlottesville: University of Virginia Press, 1992.

Isabella, Maurizio. "Citizens or Faithful? Religion and the Liberal Revolutions of the 1820s in Southern Europe." *Modern Intellectual History* 12, no. 3 (2015): 555–78.

Jacoby, Susan. *Freethinkers: A History of American Secularism*. New York: Metropolitan Books, 2005.

Joskowicz, Ari. *The Modernity of Others: Jewish Anti-Catholicism in Germany and France*. Stanford: Stanford University Press, 2014.

Kittelstrom, Amy. *The Religion of Democracy: Seven Liberals and the American Moral Tradition*. New York: Penguin, 2015.

Kroen, Sheryl. *Politics and Theater: The Crisis of Legitimacy in Restoration France*. Berkeley: University of California Press, 2000.

———. "Revolutionizing Religious Politics during the Restoration." *Historical Studies* 21, no. 1 (1998): 27–53.

Kuklick, Bruce. *Churchmen and Philosophers: From Jonathan Edwards to John Dewey*. New Haven, CT: Yale University Press, 1985.

Lee, James Mitchell. "Charles Villers and German Thought in France, 1797–1804." *Proceedings of the Annual Meeting of the Western Society for French History* 25 (1998): 55–66.

Lyons, Martyn. "Fires of Expiation: Book-Burnings and Catholic Missions in Restoration France." *French History* 10, no. 2 (1996): 240–66.

MacKillop, I. D. *The British Ethical Societies*. Cambridge: Cambridge University Press.

Martin, Benjamin, Jr. "The Creation of the Action Libérale Populaire: An Example of Party Formation in Third Republic France." *French Historical Studies* 9, no. 4 (1976): 660–89.

McGreevy, John. *Catholicism and American Freedom. A History*. New York: Norton, 2003.

Meyer, Michael. *Response to Modernity: A History of the Reform Movement in Judaism*. Detroit: Wayne State University Press, 1995.

Moyn, Samuel. "Did Christianity Create Liberalism?" *Boston Review* 40, no. 1 (2015): 50–55.

Murphy, Howard R. "The Ethical Revolt against Christian Orthodoxy in Early Victorian England." *American Historical Review* 60 (1955): 800–817.

Nord, Philip. "Liberal Protestants." In *The Republican Moment: Struggles for Democracy in Nineteenth-Century France*, edited by Philip Nord, 90–114. Cambridge, MA: Harvard University Press, 1998.

Perreau-Saussine, Emile. *Catholicism and Democracy: An Essay in the History of Political Thought*. Translated by Richard Rex. Princeton: Princeton University Press, 2012.

Phayer, J. Michael. "Politics and Popular Religion: The Cult of the Cross in France, 1815–1840." *Journal of Social History* 2, no. 3 (1978): 346–65.

Printy, Michael. "Protestantism and Progress in the Year XII: Charles Villers' *Essay on Spirit and Influence of Luther's Reformation* (1804)." *Modern Intellectual History* 9, no. 2 (2012): 303–29.

Rader, Benjamin. "Richard T. Ely: Lay Spokesman for the Social Gospel." *Journal of American History* 53, no. 1 (1966): 61–74.

Riasanovsky, Maria. "Trumpets of Jericho: Domestic Missions and Religious Revival in France." PhD diss., Princeton University, 2001.

Richter, Melvin. *The Politics of Conscience: T.H. Green and His Age*. Cambridge, MA: Harvard University Press, 1974.

———. "T. H. Green and His Audience: Liberalism as a Surrogate Faith." *Review of Politics* 18, no. 4 (1956): 444–72.

Rosenblatt, Helena. *Liberal Values: Benjamin Constant and the Politics of Religion.* Cambridge: Cambridge University Press, 2008.

———. "Sismondi, from Republicanism to Liberal Protestantism." In *Sismondi: Républicanisme moderne et libéralisme critique / Modern Republicanism and Critical Liberalism,* edited by Béla Kapossy and Pascal Bridel, 123–43. Geneva: Slatkine, 2013.

Ross, Ronald J. *The Failure of Bismarck's Kulturkampf: Catholicism and State Power in Imperial Germany, 1871–1887.* Washington, DC: Catholic University of America Press, 1998.

Rurup, Reinhard. "German Liberalism and the Emancipation of the Jews." *Leo Baeck Institute Yearbook* 20 (1975): 59–68.

Sevrin, Ernst. *Les missions religieuses en France sous la Restauration, 1815–1830.* Saint-Mandé: Procure des prêtres de la Miséricorde, 1948.

Sperber, Jonathan. "Competing Counterrevolutions: The Prussian State and the Catholic Church." *Central European History* 19 (1986): 45–62.

Stoetzler, Marcel. *The State, the Nation, and the Jews: Liberalism and the Antisemitism Dispute in Bismarck's Germany.* Lincoln: University of Nebraska Press, 2008.

Vance, Norman. *The Sinews of the Spirit: The Ideal of Christian Manliness in Victorian Literature and Religious Thought.* Cambridge: Cambridge University Press, 1985.

Verhoeven, Timothy. *Transatlantic Anti-Catholicism: France and the United States in the Nineteenth Century.* New York: Palgrave Macmillan, 2010.

Weill, Georges. *Histoire du Catholicisme libéral en France 1828–1908.* Paris: F. Alcan, 1909.

Wright, Conrad. *The Beginnings of Unitarianism in America.* Boston: Beacon, 1960.

———. *The Liberal Christians.* Boston: Beacon, 1970.

### Economic Liberalism, Socialism, and the Origins of the Welfare State

Adcock, Robert. *Liberalism and the Emergence of American Political Science: A Transatlantic Tale.* Oxford: Oxford University Press, 2014.

Audier, Serge. *Le Socialisme libéral.* Paris: La Découverte, 2006.

Beck, Hermann. *The Origins of the Authoritarian Welfare State in Prussia: Conservatives, Bureaucracy and the Social Question, 1815–70.* Ann Arbor: University of Michigan Press, 1997.

Chase, Malcom. *Chartism: A New History.* Manchester: Manchester University Press, 2007.

Claeys, Gregory. *Citizens and Saints: Politics and Anti-politics in Early British Socialists.* Cambridge: Cambridge University Press, 1989.

———. " 'Individualism,' 'Socialism' and 'Social Science': Further Notes on a Conceptual Formation 1800–1850." *Journal of the History of Ideas* 47, no. 1 (1986): 81–93.

——. *Machinery, Money and the Millennium: From Moral Economy to Socialism 1815–1860*. Princeton: Princeton University Press, 1987.

Cohen, Nancy. *The Reconstruction of American Liberalism, 1865–1914*. Chapel Hill: University of North Carolina Press, 2002.

Collini, Stefan. *Liberalism and Sociology: L.T. Hobhouse and Political Argument in England, 1880–1914*. Cambridge: Cambridge University Press, 1983.

Digeon, Claude. *La Crise Allemande de la pensée française (1870–1914)*. Paris: PUF, 1959.

Dorfman, Joseph. "Role of the German Historical School in American Economic Thought." *American Economic Review* 45, no. 2 (1955): 17–28.

Fine, Sidney. *Laissez Faire and the General-Welfare State*. Ann Arbor: University of Michigan Press, 1969.

——. "Richard T. Ely, Forerunner of Progressivism, 1880–1901." *Mississippi Valley Historical Review* 37 (1951): 599–624.

Forcey, Charles. *The Crossroads of Liberalism. Croly, Weyl, Lippmann and the Progressive Era 1900–1925*. Oxford: Oxford University Press, 1961.

Forget, Evelyn. "Jean-Baptiste Say and Spontaneous Order." *History of Political Economy* 33, no. 2 (2001): 193–218.

Freeden, Michael. *Liberal Languages: Ideological Imaginations and Twentieth-Century Progressive Thought*. Princeton: Princeton University Press, 2005.

——. *Liberalism Divided: A Study in British Political Thought, 1914–1939*. Oxford: Oxford University Press, 1986.

——. *The New Liberalism*. Oxford: Clarendon, 1978.

Fried, Barbara. *The Progressive Assault on Laissez Faire: Robert Hale and the First Law and Economics Movement*. Cambridge, MA: Harvard University Press, 1998.

Fries, Sylvia. "*Staatstheorie* and the New American Science of Politics." *Journal of the History of Ideas* 34, no. 3 (1973): 391–404.

Gambles, Anna. *Protection and Politics in Conservative Economic Discourse, 1815–1852*. Suffolk: Boydell Press, 1999.

Goldman, Eric. *Rendezvous with Destiny: A History of Modern American Reform*. New York: Ivan R. Dee, 2001.

Green, David. *Shaping Political Consciousness: The Language of Politics from McKinley to Reagan*. Ithaca, NY: Cornell University Press, 1987.

Hart, David M. "Class Analysis, Slavery and the Industrialist Theory of History in French Liberal Thought, 1814–1830: The Radical Liberalism of Charles Comte and Charles Dunoyer." http://davidmhart.com/liberty/Papers/Comte Dunoyer/CCCD-PhD/CCCD-longthesis1990.pdf.

Hayward, J.E.S. "The Official Social Philosophy of the French Third Rep: Léon Bourgeois and Solidarism." *International Review of Social History* 6 (1961): 19–48.

——. "Solidarity: The Social History of an Idea in Nineteenth-Century France." *International Review of Social History* 4 (1959): 261–84.

Herbst, Jurgen. *The German Historical School in American Scholarship: A Study in the Transfer of Culture*. Ithaca, NY: Cornell University Press, 1965.

Hirsch, Jean-Pierre. "Revolutionary France, Cradle of Free Enterprise." *American Historical Review* 94 (1989): 1281–89.

Hirsch, Jean-Pierre, and Philippe Minard. "'Libérez-nous, Sire, protégez-nous beaucoup': Pour une histoire des pratiques institutionnelles dans l'industrie française, XVIIIème–XIXème siècles." In *La France n'est-elle pas douée pour l'industrie?*, edited by Louis Bergeron and Patrice Bourdelais, 135–58. Paris: Belin, 1998.

Horn, Jeff. *The Path Not Taken: French Industrialization in the Age of Revolution, 1750–1830*. Cambridge, MA: MIT Press, 2006.

Horne, Janet. *A Social Laboratory for Modern France: The Musée Social and the Rise of the Welfare State*. Durham, NC: Duke University Press, 2002.

Kloppenberg, James. *Uncertain Victory: Social Democracy and Progressivism in European and American Thought, 1870–1920*. New York: Oxford University Pres, 1986.

Koven, Seth, and Sonya Michel, eds. *Mothers of a New World: Maternalist Politics and the Origins of Welfare States*. New York: Routledge, 1993.

Leroux, Robert. *Political Economy and Liberalism in France: The Contributions of Frédéric Bastiat*. New York: Routledge, 2011.

Levy, David. *Herbert Croly of the New Republic: The Life and Thought of an American Progressive*. Princeton: Princeton University Press, 1985.

Lutfalla, Michel. "Aux Origines du libéralisme économique en France: Le *Journal des Economistes*. Analyse du contenu de la première série 1841–1853." *Revue d'histoire économique et sociale* 50 (1972): 495–516.

Mandler, Peter. *Liberty and Authority in Victorian Britain*. Oxford: Oxford University Press, 2006.

Minart, Gérard. *Frédéric Bastiat (1801–1850): La croisé du libre-échange*. Paris: Editions Harmattan, 2004.

Mitchell, Allan. *The Divided Path: The German Influence on Social Reform in France after 1870*. Chapel Hill: University of North Carolina Press, 2010.

Moon, Parker Thomas. *The Labor Problem and the Social Catholic Movement in France: A Study in the History of Social Politics*. New York: Macmillan, 1921.

Myles, Jack. "German Historicism and American Economics: A Study of the Influence of the German Historical School on American Economic Thought." PhD diss., Princeton University, 1956.

Nord, Philip. "Republicanism and Utopian Vision: French Freemasonry in the 1860s and 1870s." *Journal of Modern History* 63, no. 2 (1991): 213–29.

———. "The Welfare State in France 1870–1914." *French Historical Studies* 18, no. 3 (1994): 821–38.

Palen, Marc-William. *The "Conspiracy" of Free Trade. The Anglo-American Struggle over Empire and Economic Globalisation, 1846–1896*. Cambridge: Cambridge University Press, 2016.

Pilbeam, Pamela. *French Socialists before Marx: Workers, Women and the Social Question in France*. Montreal: McGill-Queen's University Press, 2000.

Roberts, David. *The Victorian Origins of the British Welfare State*. New Haven, CT: Yale University Press, 1960.

Rodgers, Daniel. *Atlantic Crossings: Social Politics in a Progressive Age*. Cambridge, MA: Harvard University Press, 2000.

Rohr, Donald. *The Origins of Social Liberalism in Germany*. Chicago: University of Chicago Press, 1963.

Ross, Dorothy. *The Origins of American Social Science*. Cambridge: Cambridge University Press, 1992.

Russell, Dean. "Frederic Bastiat and the Free Trade Movement in France and England, 1840–1850." PhD thesis, University of Geneva, 1959.

Ryan, Alan. *John Dewey and the High Tie of American Liberalism*. New York: Norton, 1997.

Schäfer, Axel R. *American Progressives and German Social Reform, 1875–1920: Social Ethics, Moral Control and the Regulatory State in a Transatlantic Context*. Stuttgart: Franz Steiner Verlag, 2000.

Seidman, Steven. *Liberalism and the Origins of European Social Theory*. Berkeley: University of California Press, 1984.

Sherman, Dennis. "The Meaning of Economic Liberalism in Mid-Nineteenth Century France." *History of Political Economy* 6, no. 2 (1974): 171–99.

Sorenson, Lloyd R. "Some Classical Economists, *Laissez Faire*, and the Factory Acts." *Journal of Economic History* 12, no. 3 (1952): 247–62.

Steiner, Philippe. "Competition and Knowledge: French Political Economy as a Science of Government." In *French Liberalism from Montesquieu to the Present Day*, edited by Raf Geenens and Helena Rosenblatt, 192–207. Cambridge: Cambridge University Press, 2012.

———. "Jean-Baptiste Say, la société industrielle et le libéralisme." In *La Pensée libérale. Histoire et controverses*, edited by Gilles Kévorkian, 105–32. Paris: Ellipses, 2010.

Stettner, Edward. *Shaping Modern Liberalism: Herbert Croly and Progressive Thought*. Lawrence: University Press of Kansas, 1993.

Stone, Judith. *The Search for Social Peace: Reform Legislation in France, 1890–1914*. Albany: State University of New York Press, 1985.

Todd, David. *L'Identité économique de la France. Libre-échange et protectionnisme, 1814–1851*. Paris: Grasset, 2008.

Tyrell, Ian. *Reforming the World: The Creation of America's Moral Empire*. Princeton: Princeton University Press, 2010.

Walker, Kenneth O. "The Classical Economists and the Factory Acts." *Journal of Economic History* 1, no. 2 (1941): 168–77.

Walther, Rudolf. "Economic Liberalism." Translated by Keith Tribe. *Economy and Society* 13, no. 2 (1984): 178–207.

Warshaw, Dan. *Paul Leroy-Beaulieu and Established Liberalism in France*. DeKalb: Northern Illinois University Press, 1991.

Weiler, Peter. *The New Liberalism: Liberal Social Theory in Great Britain, 1889–1914*. London: Routledge, 1982.

Weiss, John. "Origins of the French Welfare State: Poor Relief in the Third Republic, 1871–1914." *French Historical Studies* 13, no. 1 (1983): 47–78.

White, Lawrence H. "William Leggett: Jacksonian Editorialist as Classical Liberal Political Economist." *History of Political Economy* 18, no. 2 (1986): 307–24.

## Colonies, Anglo-Saxonism, and Race

Anderson, Stuart. *Race and Rapprochement: Anglo-Saxonism and Anglo-American Relations, 1895–1904*. Madison, NJ: Fairleigh Dickinson University Press, 1981.

Ballantyne, Tony. "The Theory and Practice of Empire-Building. Edward Gibbon Wakefield and "Systematic Colonisation." In *The Routledge History of Western Empires*, edited by Robert Aldrich and Kirsten McKenzie, 89–101. London: Routledge, 2014.

Belich, James. *Replenishing the Earth: The Settler Revolution and the Rise of the Anglo-World, 1783–1939*. Oxford: Oxford University Press, 2009.

Bell, Duncan. *The Idea of Greater Britain: Empire and the Future of World Order 1860–1900*. Princeton: Princeton University Press, 2007.

———. *Reordering the World: Essays on Liberalism and Empire*. Princeton: Princeton University Press, 2016.

Buheiry, Marwan. "Anti-colonial Sentiment in France during the July Monarchy: The Algerian Case." PhD diss., Princeton University, 1973.

Burrows, Mathew. "'Mission Civilisatrice': French Cultural Policy in the Middle East, 1860–1914." *Historical Journal* 29, no. 1 (1986): 109–35.

Cain, Peter. "Character, 'Ordered Liberty' and the Mission to Civilize: British Moral Justification of Empire, 1870–1914." *Journal of Imperial and Commonwealth History* 40, no. 4 (2012): 557–78.

———, ed. *Empire and Imperialism: The Debate of the 1870s*. South Bend, IN: Saint Augustine's Press, 1999.

———. *Hobson and Imperialism*. Oxford: Oxford University Press, 2002.

———. "Radicals, Gladstone, and the Liberal Critique of Disraelian 'Imperialism.'" In *Victorian Visions of Global Order*, edited by Duncan Bell, 215–39. Cambridge: Cambridge University Press, 2007.

Claeys, Gregory. *Imperial Sceptics: British Critics of Empire, 1850–1920*. Cambridge: Cambridge University Press, 2010.

Conklin, Alice. *A Mission to Civilize: The Republican Idea of Empire in France and West Africa, 1895–1930*. Stanford: Stanford University Press, 1997.

Conrad, Sebastian. *German Colonialism: A Short History*. Cambridge: Cambridge University Press, 2012.

Cullinane, Michael Patrick. *Liberty and American Anti-Imperialism, 1898–1909*. New York: Palgrave Macmillan, 2012.

Davis, David Brion. *The Problem of Slavery in the Age of Revolution 1770–1823*. New York: Vintage, 2014.

Démier, Francis. "Adam Smith et la reconstruction de l'empire français au lendemain de l'épisode révolutionnaire." *Cahiers d'économie politique* 27, no. 1 (1996): 241–76.

Freeden, Michael. "Eugenics and Progressive Thought: A Study in Ideological Affinity." *Historical Journal* 22, no. 3 (1979): 645–71.

———. "Eugenics and Progressive Thought: A Study in Ideological Affinity." In *Liberal Languages, Ideological Imaginations and Twentieth-Century Progressive Thought*, 144–72. Princeton: Princeton University Press, 2005.

Gallagher, John, and Ronald Robinson. "The Imperialism of Free Trade." *Economic History Review*, 2nd ser., 6 (1953): 1–15.

Gavronsky, Serge. "Slavery and the French Liberals an Interpretation of the Role of Slavery in French Politics during the Second Empire." *Journal of Negro History* 51, no. 1 (1966): 36–52.

Gerstle, Gary. *American Crucible: Race and Nation in the Twentieth Century.* Princeton: Princeton University Press, 2017.

Hall, Ian, ed. *British International Thinkers from Hobbes to Namier.* New York: Palgrave Macmillan, 2009.

Haller, Mark H. *Eugenics: Hereditarian Attitudes in American Thought.* New Brunswick, NJ: Rutgers University Press.

Hart, David M. "Class Analysis, Slavery and the Industrialist Theory of History in French Liberal Thought, 1814–1830: The Radical Liberalism of Charles Comte and Charles Dunoyer." http://davidmhart.com/liberty/Papers/Comte Dunoyer/CCCD-PhD/CCCD-longthesis1990.pdf.

Hofstadter, Richard. *Social Darwinism in American Thought.* Boston: Beacon, 1944.

Horsman, Reginald. "The Origins of Racial Anglo-Saxonism in Great Britain before 1850." *Journal of the History of Ideas* 37, no. 3 (1976): 387–410.

———. *Race and Manifest Destiny.* Cambridge, MA: Harvard University Press, 2009.

Kahan, Alan. "Tocqueville: Liberalism and Imperialism." In *French Liberalism from Montesquieu to the Present Day*, edited by Raf Geenens and Helena Rosenblatt, 152–68. Cambridge: Cambridge University Press, 2012.

Kevles, Daniel J. *In the Name of Eugenics: Genetics and the Uses of Human Heredity.* Cambridge, MA: Harvard University Press, 1998.

Klaus, Alisa. "Depopulation and Race Suicide: Maternalism and Pronatalist Ideologies in France and the United States." In *Mothers of a New World: Maternalist Politics and the Origins of Welfare States*, edited by Seth Koven and Sonya Michel, 188–212. New York: Routledge, 1993.

Koebner, Richard, and Helmut Dan Schmidt. *Imperialism: The Story and Significance of a Political Word.* Cambridge: Cambridge University Press, 1964.

Kramer, Paul. "Empires, Exceptions, and Anglo-Saxons: Race and Rule between the British and United States Empire, 1880–1910." *Journal of American History* 88, no. 4 (2002): 1315–53.

Kwon, Yun Kyoung. "When Parisian Liberals Spoke for Haiti: French Anti-slavery Discourses on Haiti under the Restoration, 1814–30." *Atlantic Studies: Global Currents* 8, no. 3 (2011): 317–41.

Leonard, Thomas. *Illiberal Reformers: Race, Eugenics and American Economics in the Progressive Era.* Princeton: Princeton University Press, 2016.

Losurdo, Domenico. *Liberalism: A Counter-History.* Translated by Gregory Elliott. London: Verso, 2011.

Matthew, H.C.G. *The Liberal Imperialists: The Ideas and Politics of a Post-Gladstonian Élite.* Oxford: Oxford University Press, 1973.

Mehta, Uday. *Liberalism and Empire: A Study in Nineteenth-Century British Social Thought.* Chicago: University of Chicago Press, 1999.

Moses, Dirk, ed. *Genocide and Settler Society.* Oxford: Oxford University Press, 2004.

Pitt, Alan. "A Changing Anglo-Saxon Myth: Its Development and Function in French Political Thought, 1860–1914." *French History* 14, no. 2 (2000): 150–73.

Pitts, Jennifer. "Political Theory of Empire and Imperialism." *Annual Review of Political Science* 13 (2010): 211–35.

———. "Republicanism, Liberalism and Empire in Post-revolutionary France." In *Empire and Modern Political Thought*, edited by Sankar Muthu, 261–91. Cambridge: Cambridge University Press, 2012.

———. *A Turn to Empire: The Rise of Imperial Liberalism in Britain and France.* Princeton: Princeton University Press, 2009.

Plassart, Anna. "'Un impérialiste libéral?' Jean-Baptiste Say on Colonies and the Extra-European World." *French Historical Studies* 32, no. 2 (2009): 223–50.

Richter, Melvin. "Tocqueville on Algeria." *Review of Politics* 25, no. 3 (1963): 362–98.

Ryan, A. "Introduction." In *J. S. Mill's Encounter with India*, edited by Martin I. Moir, Douglas M. Peers, and Lynn Zastoupil, 3–17. Toronto: University of Toronto Press, 1999.

Schneider, William. "Toward the Improvement of the Human Race: The History of Eugenics in France." *Journal of Modern History* 54, no. 2 (1982): 268–91.

Searle, G. R. *The Quest for National Efficiency. A Study in British Politics and Political Thought, 1899–1914.* Berkeley: University of California Press, 1971.

Semmel, Bernard. *The Liberal Ideal and the Demons of Empire: Theories of Imperialism from Adam Smith to Lenin.* Baltimore: Johns Hopkins University Press, 1993.

———. *The Rise of Free Trade Imperialism: Classical Political Economy, the Empire of Free Trade and Imperialism 1750–1850.* Cambridge: Cambridge University Press, 1970.

Sessions, Jennifer. *By Sword and Plow: France and the Conquest of Algeria.* Ithaca, NY: Cornell University Press, 2015.

Steiner, Philippe. "Jean-Baptiste Say et les colonies ou comment se débarrasser d'un héritage intempestif." *Cahiers d'économie politique* 27–28 (1996): 153–73.

Sullivan, E. P. "Liberalism and Imperialism: J. S. Mill's Defense of the British Empire." *Journal of the History of Ideas* 44, no. 4 (1983): 599–617.

Taylor, Miles. "Imperium et Libertas?" *Journal of Imperial and Commonwealth History* 19, no. 1 (1991): 1–23.

Todd, David. "Transnational Projects of Empire in France, c.1815–c.1870." *Modern Intellectual History* 12, no. 2 (2015): 265–93.

Welch, Cheryl. "Colonial Violence and the Rhetoric of Evasion: Tocqueville on Algeria." *Political Theory* 31, no. 2 (2003): 235–64.

Winks, Robin. "Imperialism." In *The Comparative Approach to American History*, edited by C. Vann Woodward, 253–70. Oxford: Oxford University Press, 1998.

Wolfe, Patrick. "Settler Colonialism and the Elimination of the Native." *Journal of Genocide Research* 8, no. 4 (2006): 387–409.


## Liberal Internationalism

Adams, Iestyn. *Brothers across the Ocean: British Foreign Policy and the Origins of the Anglo-American Special Relationship 1900–1905.* London: I.B. Tauris, 2005.

Bayly, C. A. "Rammohan Roy and the Advent of Constitutional Liberalism in India, 1800–1830." *Modern Intellectual History* 4 (2007): 25–41.

———. *Recovering Liberties: Indian Thought in the Age of Liberalism and Empire.* Cambridge: Cambridge University Press, 2011.

Bell, Duncan. "Beyond the Sovereign State: Isopolitan Citizenship, Race and Anglo-American Union." *Political Studies* 62, no. 2 (2014): 418–34.

Hall, Ian, ed. *British International Thinkers from Hobbes to Namier.* New York: Palgrave Macmillan, 2009.

Isabella, Maurizio. *Risorgimento in Exile: Italian Emigres and the Liberal International in the Post-Napoleonic Era.* Oxford: Oxford University Press 2009.

Neely, Sylvia. "The Politics of Liberty in the Old World and the New: Lafayette's Return to America." *Journal of the Early Republic* 6 (1986): 151–71.

Recchia, Stefano, and Nadia Urbinati, eds. *A Cosmopolitanism of Nations: Giuseppe Mazzini's Writings on Democracy, Nation Building, and International Relations.* Translated by Stefano Recchia. Princeton: Princeton University Press, 2009.

Rodriguez, Jaime, ed. *The Divine Charter: Constitutionalism and Liberalism in Nineteenth-Century Mexico.* Lanham, MD: Rowman & Littlefield, 2007.

Smith, Denis Mack. *Mazzini.* New Haven, CT: Yale University Press, 1994.


## Liberal Education

Acomb, Evelyn. *The French Laic Laws (1879–1889): The First Anti-clerical Campaign of the Third French Republic.* New York: Columbia University Press, 1941.

Beisel, Neisel. *Imperiled Innocents: Anthony Comstock and Family Reproduction in Victorian America.* Princeton: Princeton University Press, 1997.

Bradford, Roderick. *D.M. Bennett: The Truth Seeker.* Amherst, NY: Prometheus Books, 2006.

Burnham, John C. "The Progressive Era Revolution in American Attitudes toward Sex." *Journal of American History* 59, no. 4 (1973): 885–908.

Cabanel, Patrick. *Le Dieu de la République. Aux sources protestantes de la laïcité (1860–1900)*. Rennes: Presses Universitaires de Rennes, 2003.

Chase, George. "Ferdinand Buisson and Salvation by National Education." In *L'offre d'école: éléments pour une étude comparée des politiques éducatives au XIXe siècle: actes du troisième colloque international, Sèvres, 27–30 septembre 1981*, 263–75. Paris: Publications de la Sorbonne, 1983.

Clark, Linda L. *Schooling the Daughters of Marianne*. Albany: State University of New York Press, 1984.

Frisken, Amanda. "Obscenity, Free Speech, and 'Sporting News' in 1870s America." *Journal of American Studies* 42, no. 3 (2008): 537–77.

Gordon, Linda. "Voluntary Motherhood: The Beginnings of Feminist Birth Control in the United States." *Feminist Studies* 1, nos. 3–4 (1973): 5–22.

Harrigan, Patrick J. "Church, State, and Education in France from the Falloux to the Ferry Laws: A Reassessment." *Canadian Journal of History* 36, no. 1 (2001): 51–83.

Horvath, Sandra A. "Victor Duruy and the Controversy over Secondary Education for Girls." *French Historical Studies* 9, no. 1 (1975): 83–104.

Katznelson, Ira, and Margaret Weir. *Schooling for All: Class, Race, and the Decline of the Democratic Ideal*. New York: Basic Books, 1985.

Kimball, Bruce. *Orators and Philosophers: A History of the Idea of Liberal Education*. New York: Teachers College Press, 1986.

Lefkowitz Horowitz, Helen. *Rereading Sex: Battles over Sexual Knowledge and Suppression in Nineteenth-Century America*. New York: Knopf, 2002.

Ligou, Daniel. *Frédéric Desmons et la franc-maçonnerie sous la 3e république*. Paris: Gedlage, 1966.

Loeffel, Laurence. *La Morale à l'école selon Ferdinand Buisson*. Paris: Tallandier, 2013.

Margadant, Jo Burr. *Madame le Professeur: Women Educators in the Third Republic*. Princeton: Princeton University Press, 1990.

Nash, Margaret. *Women's Education in the United States, 1780–1840*. New York: Palgrave Macmillan, 2005.

Ognier, Pierre. *Une école sans Dieu? 1880–1895. L'invention d'une moral laïque sous la IIIème république*. Toulouse: Presses universitaires du Mirail, 2008.

Ozouf, Mona. *L'Ecole, l'Eglise et la République*. Paris: PTS, 2007.

Ponteil, Felix. *Histoire de l'enseignement, 1789–1965*. Paris: Sirey, 1966.

Prost, Antoine, *L'enseignement en France, 1800–1967*. Paris: Armand Colin, 1968.

Rabban, David. *Free Speech in the Forgotten Years, 1870–1920*. Cambridge: Cambridge University Press, 1999.

Sears, Hal D. *The Sex Radicals: Free Love in High Victorian America*. Lawrence: University Press of Kansas, 1977.

Stock-Morton, Phyllis. *Moral Education for a Secular Society: The Development of Morale Laïque in Nineteenth-Century France*. Albany: State University of New York Press, 1988.

Warren, Sidney. *American Freethought, 1860–1914*. New York: Columbia University Press, 1943.


## *Feminism*

Allen, Ann Taylor. "Spiritual Motherhood: German Feminists and the Kindergarten Movement, 1848–1911." *History of Education Quarterly* 22, no. 3 (1982): 319–39.

Barry, David. *Women and Political Insurgency: France in the Mid-Nineteenth Century*. Basingstoke: Macmillan, 1996.

Clawson, Ann. *Constructing Brotherhood: Class, Gender, and Fraternalism*. Princeton: Princeton University Press, 1989.

Falchi, Federica. "Democracy and the Rights of Women in the Thinking of Giuseppe Mazzini." *Modern Italy* 17 (2012): 15–30.

Frazer, Elizabeth. "Feminism and Liberalism." In *The Liberal Political Tradition: Contemporary Reappraisals*, edited by James Meadowcroft, 115–37. Cheltenham: Edward Elgar, 1996.

Gleadle, Kathryn. *The Early Feminists: Radical Unitarians and the Emergence of the Women's Rights Movement, 1831–51*. New York: Palgrave Macmillan, 1995.

Hackett, Amy. "The Politics of Feminism in Wilhelmine Germany, 1890–1918." PhD diss., Columbia University, 1976.

Hartley, Christie, and Lori Watson. "Is a Feminist Political Liberalism Possible?" *Journal of Ethics and Social Philosophy* 5, no. 1 (2010): 1–21.

Hause, Steven. *Women's Suffrage and Social Politics in the French Third Republic*. Princeton: Princeton University Press, 1984.

Hirsch, Pamela. "Mary Wollstonecraft: A Problematic Legacy." In *Wollstonecraft's Daughters: Womanhood in England and France, 1780–1920*, edited by Clarissa Campbell-Orr, 43–60. Manchester: Manchester University Press, 1996.

MacKinnon, Catherine. *Toward a Feminist Theory of the State*. Cambridge, MA: Harvard University Press, 1989.

Morgan, David. *Suffragists and Liberals: The Politics of Woman Suffrage in England*. Lanham, MD: Rowman & Littlefield, 1975.

Moses, Claire Goldberg. *French Feminism in the 19th Century*. Albany: State University of New York Press, 1985.

Nussbaum, Martha C. "The Feminist Critique of Liberalism." Lindley Lecture, University of Kansas, 1997.

Offen, Karen. "Defining Feminism: A Comparative Historical Approach." *Signs* 14, no. 1 (1988): 119–57.

———. "Depopulation, Nationalism, and Feminism in Fin-de-Siècle France." *American Historical Review* 89, no. 3 (1984): 648–76.

Ozouf, Mona. *Les mots des femmes: essai sur la singularité francaise*. Paris: Fayard, 1995.

Pugh, Martin. "Liberals and Women's Suffrage, 1867–1914." In *Citizenship and Community: Liberals, Radicals and Collective Identities in the British Isles,*

*1865–1931*, edited by Eugenio F. Biagini, 45–65. Cambridge: Cambridge University Press, 1996.

Riot-Sarcey, Michèle. *La démocratie à l'épreuve des femmes: trois figures critiques du pouvoir, 1830–1848*. Paris: A. Michel, 1994.

Schaeffer, Denise. "Feminism and Liberalism Reconsidered: The Case of Catharine MacKinnon." *American Political Science Review* 95, no. 3 (2001): 699–708.

Scott, Joan. *Only Paradoxes to Offer: French Feminists and the Rights of Man*. Cambridge, MA: Harvard University Press, 1997.

Zirelli, Linda. "Feminist Critiques of Liberalism." In *Cambridge Companion to Liberalism*, edited by Steven Wall, 355–80. Cambridge: Cambridge University Press, 2015.

## Liberal Leadership, Character, and Caesarism

Baehr, Peter. *Caesarism, Charisma and Fate: Historical Sources and Modern Resonances in the Work of Max Weber*. New Brunswick, NJ: Transaction, 2009.

———. "Max Weber as a Critic of Bismarck." *European Journal of Sociology* 29, no. 1 (1988): 149–64.

Beaven, Brad, and John Griffiths. "Creating the Exemplary Citizen: The Changing Notion of Citizenship in Britain 1870–1939." *Contemporary British History* 22, no. 2 (2008): 203–25.

Bebbington, David W. *The Mind of Gladstone: Religion, Mind and Politics*. Oxford: Oxford University Press, 2004.

Biagini, Eugenio. *Liberty, Retrenchment and Reform: Popular Liberalism in the Age of Gladstone, 1860–1880*. Cambridge: Cambridge University Press, 2004.

Carrington, Tyler. "Instilling the 'Manly' Faith: Protestant Masculinity and the German Jünglingsvereine at the fin de siècle." *Journal of Men, Masculinities and Spirituality* 3, no. 2 (2009): 142–54.

Carwardine, Richard, and Jay Sexton, eds. *The Global Lincoln*. Oxford: Oxford University Press, 2011.

Chevallier, Pierre. *Histoire de la franc-maçonnerie française 1725–1945*. Paris: Fayard, 1974.

———. *La Séparation de l'église et l'école. Jules Ferry et Léon XIII*. Paris: Fayard, 1981.

Collini, Stefan. "The Idea of 'Character' in Victorian Political Thought." *Transactions of the Royal Historical Society* 35 (1985): 29–50.

———. *Public Moralists: Political Thought and Intellectual Life in Britain*. Oxford: Oxford University Press, 1991.

Davis, Michael. *The Image of Lincoln in the South*. Knoxville: University of Tennessee Press, 1971.

Gollwitzer, Heinz. "The Caesarism of Napoleon III as Seen by Public Opinion in Germany." *Economy and Society* 16 (1987): 357–404.

Gray, Walter D. *Interpreting American Democracy in France: The Career of Edouard Laboulaye, 1811–1883.* Newark: University of Delaware Press, 1994.

Hamer, D. A. "Gladstone: The Making of a Political Myth." *Victorian Studies* 22 (1978): 29–50.

———. *Liberal Politics in the Age of Gladstone and Rosebery.* Oxford: Oxford University Press, 1972.

Hoffmann, Stefan-Ludwig. "Civility, Male Friendship and Masonic Sociability in Nineteenth-Century Germany." *Gender and History* 13, no. 2 (2001): 224–48.

———. *The Politics of Sociability: Freemasonry and German Civil Society, 1840–1918.* Translated by Tom Lampert. Ann Arbor: University of Michigan Press, 2007.

Kahan, Alan. "The Victory of German Liberalism? Rudolf Haym, Liberalism, and Bismarck." *Central European History* 22, no. 1 (1989): 57–88.

Mandler, Peter. *The English National Character: The History of an Idea from Edmund Burke to Tony Blair.* New Haven, CT: Yale University Press, 2006.

Mork, Gordon R. "Bismarck and the 'Capitulation' of German Liberalism." *Journal of Modern History* 43, no. 1 (1971): 59–75.

Mosse, George L. "Caesarism, Circuses, and Monuments." *Journal of Contemporary History* 6, no. 2 (1971): 167–82.

Nord, Philip. "Republicanism and Utopian Vision: French Freemasonry in the 1860s and 1870s." *Journal of Modern History* 63 (1991): 213–29.

Parry, Jonathan P. *Democracy and Religion: Gladstone and the Liberal Party 1867–1875.* Cambridge: Cambridge University Press, 1989.

———. "The Impact of Napoleon III on British Politics, 1851–1880." *Transactions of the Royal Historical Society* 11 (2001): 147–75.

Peterson, Merril D. *Lincoln in American Memory.* New York: Oxford University Press, 1995.

Peterson, Stephen. "Gladstone, Religion, Politics and America: Perceptions in the Press." PhD diss., University of Stirling, 2013.

Richter, Melvin. "Tocqueville and the French Nineteenth Century Conceptualizations of the Two Bonapartes and Their Empires." In *Dictatorship in History and Theory: Bonapartism, Caesarism and Totalitarianism,* edited by P. R. Baehr and Melvin Richter, 83–102. Cambridge: Cambridge University Press, 2004.

Scott, John. *Republican Ideas and the Liberal Tradition in France.* New York: Columbia University Press, 1951.

Shannon, Richard. *Gladstone: God and Politics.* New York: Continuum, 2007.

Sproat, John G. *"The Best Men": Liberal Reformers in the Gilded Age.* Oxford: Oxford University Press, 1968.

Steinberg, Jonathan. *Bismarck: A Life.* Oxford: Oxford University Press, 2013.

Testritto, Ronald J. *Woodrow Wilson and the Roots of Modern Liberalism.* Lanham, MD: Rowman & Littlefield, 2005.

Thomas, Daniel H. "The Reaction of the Great Powers to Louis Napoleon's Rise to Power in 1851." *Historical Journal* 13, no. 2 (1970): 237–50.

Tudesq, André-Jean. "La légende napoléonienne en France en 1848." *Revue historique* 218 (1957): 64–85.

Wyke, Maria. *Caesar in the USA.* Berkeley: University of California Press, 2012.

## Early French Liberals

Alexander, Robert. *Re-writing the French Revolutionary Tradition.* Cambridge: Cambridge University Press, 2003.

Berlin, Isaiah. "Two Concepts of Liberty." In *Four Essays on Liberty,* 118–72. Oxford: Oxford University Press, 1969.

Craiutu, Aurelian. "Faces of Moderation: Mme de Staël's Politics during the Directory." *Jus Politicum,* no. 6 (2008). http://juspoliticum.com/article/Faces -of-Moderation-Mme-de-Stael-s-Politics-during-the-Directory-380.html.

———. *Liberalism under Siege: The Political Thought of the French Doctrinaires.* Lanham, MD: Lexington Books, 2003.

———. *A Virtue for Courageous Minds: Moderation in French Political Thought, 1748–1830.* Princeton: Princeton University Press, 2012.

Fontana, Bianca-Maria. *Benjamin Constant and the Post-revolutionary Mind.* New Haven, CT: Yale University Press, 1991.

———. *Germaine de Staël: A Political Portrait.* Princeton: Princeton University Press, 2016.

———. *The Invention of the Modern Republic.* Cambridge: Cambridge University Press, 1994.

Girard, Louis. *Les libéraux français: 1814–1875.* Paris: Aubier, 1985.

Gunn, J.A.W. *When the French Tried to Be British: Party, Opposition, and the Quest for Civil Disagreement, 1814–1848.* Montreal: McGill-Queen's University Press, 2009.

Hazareesingh, Sudhir. *From Subject to Citizen: The Second Empire and the Emergence of Modern French Democracy.* Princeton: Princeton University Press, 1998.

Holmes, Stephen. *Benjamin Constant and the Making of Modern Liberalism.* New Haven, CT: Yale University Press, 1984.

Jainchill, Andrew. *Reimagining Politics after the Terror: The Republican Origins of French Liberalism.* Ithaca, NY: Cornell University Press, 2008.

Jardin, André. *Histoire du libéralisme politique: de la crise de l'absolutisme à la Constitution de 1875.* Paris: Hachette Littérature, 1985.

Jaume, Lucien. *L'individu effacé ou le paradoxe du libéralisme français.* Paris: Fayard, 1997.

Jennings, Jeremy. *Revolution and the Republic: A History of Political Thought in France since the Eighteenth Century.* Oxford: Oxford University Press, 2011.

Kalyvas, Andreas, and Ira Katznelson. *Liberal Beginnings: Making a Republic for the Moderns.* Cambridge: Cambridge University Press, 2008.

Kelly, George. *The Humane Comedy: Constant, Tocqueville and French Liberalism.* Cambridge: Cambridge University Press, 1992.

————. "Liberalism and Aristocracy in the French Restoration." *Journal of the History of Ideas* 26, no. 4 (1965): 509–30.

Manent, Pierre. *An Intellectual History of Liberalism.* Translated by Rebecca Balinski. Princeton: Princeton University Press, 1995.

Paulet-Grandguillot, Emmanuelle. *Libéralisme et démocratie: De Sismondi à Constant, à partir du Contrat social (1801–1806).* Geneva: Slatkine, 2010.

Rosanvallon, Pierre. *Le moment Guizot.* Paris: Galimard, 1985.

Rosenblatt, Helena. *Liberal Values: Benjamin Constant and the Politics of Religion.* Cambridge: Cambridge University Press, 2008.

Rosenblatt, Helena, ed. *Cambridge Companion to Constant.* Cambridge: Cambridge University Press, 2009.

Spitz, Jean-Fabien. *Le Moment républicain en France.* Paris: Gallimard, 2005.

Spitzer, Alan B. *Old Hatreds and Young Hopes: The French Carbonari against the Bourbon Restoration.* Cambridge, MA: Harvard University Press, 1971.

Tenenbaum, Susan. "Staël: Liberal Political Thinker." In *Germaine de Staël: Crossing the Borders,* edited by Madelyn Gutwirth, Avriel Goldberger, and Karyna Szmurlo, 159–63. New Brunswick, NJ: Rutgers University Press, 1991.

Vincent, Steven K. *Benjamin Constant and the Birth of French Liberalism.* New York: Palgrave Macmillan, 2011.

Whatmore, Richard. *Republicanism and the French Revolution: An Intellectual History of Jean-Baptiste Say's Political Economy.* Oxford: Oxford University Press, 2000.

## Epilogue

Bellamy, Richard. *Liberalism and Modern Society: An Historical Argument.* University Park: Pennsylvania State University Press, 1992.

Berkowitz, Peter. *Virtue and the Making of Modern Liberalism.* Princeton: Princeton University Press, 1999.

Brinkley, Alan. *The End to Reform: New Deal Liberalism in Recession and War.* New York: Vintage, 1995.

————. *Liberalism and Its Discontents.* Cambridge, MA: Harvard University Press, 2000.

Burgin, Angus. *The Great Persuasion: Reinventing Free Markets since the Depression.* Cambridge, MA: Harvard University Press, 2015.

Canto-Sperber, Monique. *Le libéralisme et la gauche.* Paris: Pluriel, 2008.

————. "Pourquoi les démocrates ne veulent-ils pas être libéraux?" *Le Débat* 131 (2004): 109–26.

Chappel, James. "The Catholic Origins of Totalitarianism Theory in Interwar Europe." *Modern Intellectual History* 8, no. 3 (2011): 561–90.

Christofferson, Michael Scott. "An Antitotalitarian History of the French Revolution: François Furet's Penser la Révolution française in the Intellectual Politics of the Late 1970s." *French Historical Studies* 22, no. 4 (1999): 557–611.

———. "François Furet between History and Journalism, 1958–1965." *French History* 15, no. 4 (2001): 421–47.

Diggins, John Patrick. *The Lost Soul of American Politics: Virtue, Self-Interest, and the Foundations of Liberalism.* Chicago: University of Chicago Press, 1984.

Eley, Geoff. "James Sheehan and the German Liberals: A Critical Appreciation." *Central European History* 14, no. 3 (1981): 273–88.

Galston, William. "The Growing Threat of Illiberal Democracy." *Wall Street Journal,* January 3, 2017.

———. *Liberal Purposes.* New York: Cambridge University Press, 1991.

Gauchet, Marchel. *L'Avènement de la démocratie II: La crise du libéralisme.* Paris: Gallimard, 2007.

Gerstle, Gary. "The Protean Character of American Liberalism." *American Historical Review* 99, no. 4 (1994): 1043–73.

Glendon, Mary Ann. *Rights Talk: The Impoverishment of Political Discourse.* New York: Free Press, 1993.

Hartz, Louis. *The Liberal Tradition in America: An Interpretation of American Political Thought since the Revolution.* New York: Harcourt Brace, 1955.

Hulliung, Mark, ed. *The American Liberal Tradition Reconsidered: The Contested Legacy of Louis Hartz.* Lawrence: University Press of Kansas, 2010.

Jarausch, Konrad. "Illiberalism and Beyond: German History in Search of a Paradigm." *Journal of Modern History* 55, no. 2 (1983): 268–84.

Jarausch, Konrad, and Larry Eugene Jones, eds. *In Search of a Liberal Germany: Studies in the History of German Liberalism from 1789 to the Present.* Oxford: Berg, 1990.

Jaume, Lucien. *L'individu effacé ou le paradoxe du libéralisme français.* Paris: Fayard, 1997.

Jones, Gareth Stedman. *Masters of the Universe: Hayek, Friedman, and the Birth of Neoliberal Politics.* Princeton: Princeton University Press, 2012.

Jones, Larry Eugene. *German Liberalism and the Dissolution of the Weimar Party System, 1918–1933.* Chapel Hill: University of North Carolina Press, 1988.

Krieger, Leonard. *The German Idea of Freedom: History of a Political Tradition.* Chicago: University of Chicago Press, 1957.

Langewiesche, Dieter. *Liberalism in Germany.* Translated by Christiane Bannerji. Princeton: Princeton University Press, 2000.

Laski, Harold. *The Rise of European Liberalism.* London: Unwin Books, 1962.

Macpherson, C. B. *The Political Theory of Possessive Individualism: From Hobbes to Locke.* Oxford: Oxford University Press, 1962.

Mosse, George L. *The Crisis of German Ideology: Intellectual Origins of the Third Reich.* New York: Schocken, 1981.

Moyn, Samuel. "The Politics of Individual Rights: Marcel Gauchet and Claude Lefort." *French Liberalism from Montesquieu to the Present Day,* edited by Raf Geenens and Helena Rosenblatt, 291–310. Cambridge: Cambridge University Press, 2012.

Neill, Thomas P. *The Rise and Decline of Liberalism*. Milwaukee: Bruce, 1953.

Nemo, Philippe, and Jean Petitot, eds. *Histoire du libéralisme en Europe*. Paris: PUF, 2006.

Rosanvallon, Pierre. "Fondement et problèmes de l'illibéralisme français." In *La France du nouveau siècle*, edited by Thierry de Montbrial, 85–95. Paris: PUF, 2000.

Rosenblum, Nancy L. *Another Liberalism: Romanticism and the Reconstruction of Liberal Thought*. Cambridge, MA: Harvard University Press, 1987.

———, ed. *Liberalism and the Moral Life*. Cambridge: Harvard University Press, 1987.

Ruggiero, Guido de. *The History of European Liberalism*. Translated by G. Collingwood. Boston: Beacon, 1927.

Sawyer, Stephen, and Iain Stewart, eds. *In Search of the Liberal Moment: Democracy, Anti-totalitarianism, and Intellectual Politics in France since 1950*. New York: Palgrave Macmillan, 2016.

Sell, Friedrich C. *Die Tragödie des deutschen Liberalismus*. Stuttgart: Deustche Verlags-Anstalt, 1953.

Sheehan, James J. *German Liberalism in the Nineteenth Century*. New York: Humanity Books, 1995.

Shklar, Judith. "The Liberalism of Fear." In *Political Thought and Political Thinkers*, 3–20. Chicago: University of Chicago Press, 1998.

Siedentop, Larry. *Inventing the Individual: The Origins of Western Liberalism*. Cambridge, MA: Harvard University Press, 2014.

Stern, Fritz. *The Politics of Cultural Despair: A Study in the Rise of Germanic Ideology*. Berkeley: University of California Press, 1961.

Strauss, Leo. *Liberalism: Ancient and Modern*. Chicago: University of Chicago Press, 1968.

Zakaria, Fareed. *The Future of Freedom: Illiberal Democracy at Home and Abroad*. New York: Norton, 2007.

———. "The Rise of Illiberal Democracy." *Foreign Affairs* (November–December 1997): 22–43.

# A NOTE ON THE TYPE

THIS BOOK has been composed in Miller, a Scotch Roman typeface designed by Matthew Carter and first released by Font Bureau in 1997. It resembles Monticello, the typeface developed for The Papers of Thomas Jefferson in the 1940s by C. H. Griffith and P. J. Conkwright and reinterpreted in digital form by Carter in 2003.

Pleasant Jefferson ("P. J.") Conkwright (1905–1986) was Typographer at Princeton University Press from 1939 to 1970. He was an acclaimed book designer and AIGA Medalist.

The ornament used throughout this book was designed by Pierre Simon Fournier (1712–1768) and was a favorite of Conkwright's, used in his design of the *Princeton University Library Chronicle*.